Microsoft®

ACCESS/VISUAL BASIC®

Step by Step

Other titles in the *Step by Step* series:

Microsoft® ACCESS/VISUAL BASIC®

Step by Step

Evan Callahan

Microsoft Press

PUBLISHED BY
Microsoft Press
A Division of Microsoft Corporation
One Microsoft Way
Redmond, Washington 98052-6399

Library of Congress Cataloging-in-Publication Data
Callahan, Evan, 1966-
    Microsoft Access/Visual Basic step by step / Evan Callahan.
        p.   cm.
    Includes index.
    ISBN 1-55615-890-4
    1. Database management.   2. Microsoft Access.   3. Microsoft Visual
BASIC   I. Title.
    QA76.9.D3C33   1995
    005.75'65--dc20   95-38998
                                                                      CIP

Printed and bound in the United States of America.

1 2 3 4 5 6 7 8 9   QMQM   9 8 7 6 5

Distributed to the book trade in Canada by Macmillan of Canada, a division of Canada
Publishing Corporation.

A CIP catalogue record for this book is available from the British Library.

Microsoft Press books are available through booksellers and distributors worldwide. For further
information about international editions, contact your local Microsoft Corporation office. Or
contact Microsoft Press International directly at fax (206) 936-7329.

Acquisitions Editor: Casey D. Doyle
Project Editor: Laura Sackerman
Editing and Production: WASSER, Inc.

Acknowledgments

This book began over a year ago during a casual chat with Casey Doyle, who was looking for someone to write the book but had no idea I might be interested. I'm very grateful to Casey for his help throughout this project. I also want to thank Margaret Delp for her support during the development of this book. Additionally, I should mention the many talented and generous people on the Access team I had the good fortune to work alongside during my years at Microsoft. Although there are too many to name here, I'm especially grateful to Margaret McGee and Bryce Holmes for their important insights on my work.

More importantly, I dedicate this book to my family—Mom, Dad, and Melissa—who don't use Microsoft Access but are very wonderful people.

Contents at a Glance

Table of Contents

Table of Contents

Table of Contents

Table of Contents

Customizing a database you create with a wizard, see "Using Wizards for Application Development," page 4 (Lesson 1)

Working with drop-down combo boxes, see "Creating a Combo Box to Find Records," page 48 (Lesson 3)

Setting values automatically in a data-entry form, see "Performing Actions as the User Changes Data," page 77 (Lesson 4)

Allowing users to choose which records are displayed, see "Creating an Option Group to Filter Data," page 62 (Lesson 3)

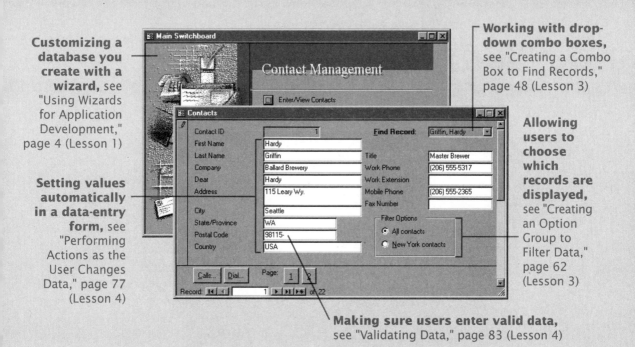

Making sure users enter valid data, see "Validating Data," page 83 (Lesson 4)

Viewing and editing code in the Module window, see "Customizing a Command Button," page 24 (Lesson 2)

Using variables and arguments to store and manipulate data, see "Adding Arguments to a Procedure," page 103 (Lesson 5)

Writing your own Visual Basic functions, see "Creating General Procedures in a Standard Module," page 99 (Lesson 5)

Communicating with users, see "Displaying a Message to the User," page 42 (Lesson 2)

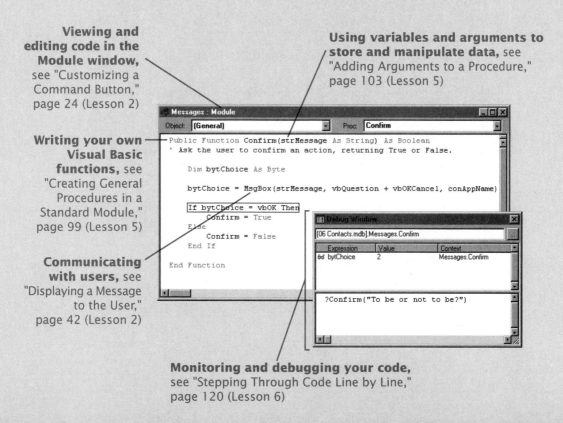

Monitoring and debugging your code, see "Stepping Through Code Line by Line," page 120 (Lesson 6)

Designing a dialog box form, see "Using Dialog Boxes in Your Applications," page 172 (Lesson 8)

Working with list boxes and other objects in code, see "Using a Multiple-Selection List Box," page 271 (Lesson 12)

Creating buttons that run Visual Basic code, see "Adding a Command Button to a Form," page 16 (Lesson 1)

Accessing databases directly in code, see "Working with Data Access Objects," page 273 (Lesson 12)

Responding to user actions in a form, see "Creating Event Procedures for Form Events," page 40 (Lesson 2)

Providing menus for your user interface, see "Creating a Custom Menu Bar," page 223 (Lesson 10)

Preparing your custom application for delivery to users, see "Controlling How Your Application Starts," page 242 (Lesson 11)

Creating toolbar buttons that open forms and reports, see "Customizing Toolbars," page 231 (Lesson 10)

Helping users navigate in an application, see "Making Forms Work Together," page 200 (Lesson 9)

Synchronizing data between forms, see "Displaying Related Records in a Pop-Up Form," page 201 (Lesson 9)

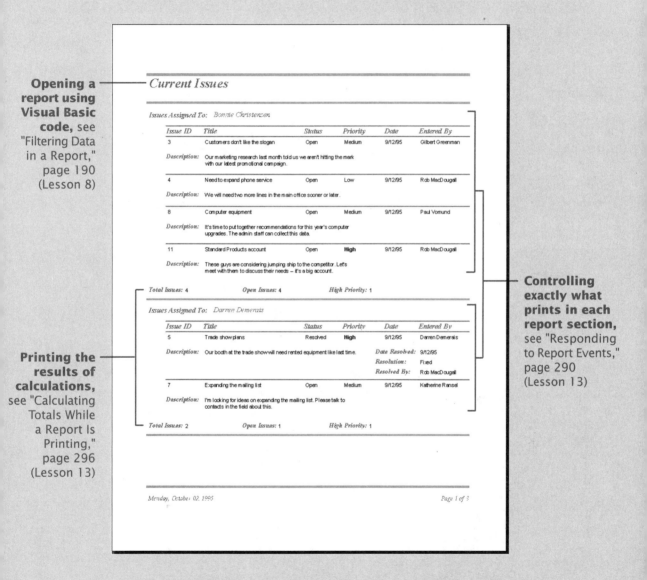

Opening a report using Visual Basic code, see "Filtering Data in a Report," page 190 (Lesson 8)

Printing the results of calculations, see "Calculating Totals While a Report Is Printing," page 296 (Lesson 13)

Controlling exactly what prints in each report section, see "Responding to Report Events," page 290 (Lesson 13)

Current Issues

Issues Assigned To: Bonnie Christenzen

Issue ID	Title	Status	Priority	Date	Entered By
3	Customers don't like the slogan	Open	Medium	9/12/95	Gilbert Greenman
Description:	Our marketing research last month told us we aren't hitting the mark with our latest promotional campaign.				
4	Need to expand phone service	Open	Low	9/12/95	Rob MacDougall
Description:	We will need two more lines in the main office sooner or later.				
8	Computer equipment	Open	Medium	9/12/95	Paul Vomund
Description:	It's time to put together recommendations for this year's computer upgrades. The admin staff can collect this data.				
11	Standard Products account	Open	**High**	9/12/95	Rob MacDougall
Description:	These guys are considering jumping ship to the competitor. Let's meet with them to discuss their needs – it's a big account.				

Total Issues: 4   Open Issues: 4   High Priority: 1

Issues Assigned To: Darren Demerais

Issue ID	Title	Status	Priority	Date	Entered By
5	Trade show plans	Resolved	**High**	9/12/95	Darren Demerais
Description:	Our booth at the trade show will need rented equipment like last time.		Date Resolved:	9/12/95	
			Resolution:	Fixed	
			Resolved By:	Rob MacDougall	
7	Expanding the mailing list	Open	Medium	9/12/95	Katherine Ransel
Description:	I'm looking for ideas on expanding the mailing list. Please talk to contacts in the field about this.				

Total Issues: 2   Open Issues: 1   High Priority: 1

Monday, October 02, 1995   Page 1 of 3

About This Book

In "About This Book" you will learn:

- How to find your best path through the lessons in this book, based on your experience.
- How to use this book to teach a class, if you're an instructor.
- What the terms and notational conventions used in this book mean.
- Where to find additional information about Microsoft Access.

This book teaches you how to create database applications in Microsoft Access for Windows 95. If you're using Microsoft Access and are ready to move on to Visual Basic programming, this is the book for you.

Microsoft Access has taken the database world by storm with its ease of use for storing and retrieving information. As you'll see, it's also quite possibly the most productive tool available for creating database applications. With the newest version for Windows 95, Microsoft Access has moved to an even more powerful programming language, Visual Basic for Applications—the same language found in Microsoft Excel and Project, and soon to be the standard for all Microsoft applications. Using the programming techniques you'll learn in these lessons, you'll be able to take advantage of Microsoft Access in new ways, creating your own custom solutions in a short time. What's more, if you're working on databases for others to use, you'll learn to create a foolproof user interface to help them get their work done easily.

Microsoft Access/Visual Basic Step by Step walks you through tasks one at a time, keeping you on track with clear instructions and frequent pictures of what you should see on the screen. In each lesson, you'll solve a new puzzle and become familiar with another important area of Microsoft Access or Visual Basic. The disk you'll find in the back of the book contains practice files specially designed for you to use while learning—and the examples they provide will give you plenty of ideas for your own work in Microsoft Access. You'll find instructions for installing the practice files in "Getting Ready," the next section in this book.

Finding the Best Starting Point for You

Microsoft Access is a complex application with many areas to learn, and your background may determine how quickly you'll want to jump in. Fortunately, the steps in this book are designed for anyone to follow, regardless of prior experience. Whatever your background and plans for programming in Microsoft Access, this book has a good place for you to start.

This book is designed for Microsoft Access users who are learning programming for the first time, and for programmers who are moving to Microsoft Access from another programming system, such as dBASE or QuickBasic. You'll get the most from this book if you're already familiar with the basic capabilities of Microsoft Access, such as designing and using forms. You can complete the steps in this book even if you're new to Microsoft Access, but to create your own databases, you'll also need to pick up basic skills not covered in this book.

The book is divided into four parts:

Part 1: Automating Database Tasks starts you off with practical, straightforward solutions for customizing your Microsoft Access databases. It also introduces Visual Basic for Applications—the programming language in Microsoft Access—and teaches the basic concepts you'll need along the way. In this part, you'll use Microsoft Access wizards and simple programming code to create and customize a contact management database.

Part 2: Programming in Visual Basic teaches you to use the programming tools built into Microsoft Access to write and debug Visual Basic code. In this part, you'll continue using the contact management database, adding additional features as you go.

Part 3: Creating a Custom Application walks you through the process of creating a custom user interface for a database application. In this part, you'll work with a new database that manages subscriptions to a journal, preparing it to be delivered to users. Along the way, you'll create a dialog box, make forms and reports work together seamlessly, and add custom menus and toolbars.

Part 4: Working with Data and Objects takes you further into the underlying structure of Microsoft Access. It will teach you how to take direct control of objects such as forms, reports, and databases—and how to manipulate objects in another application, such as Microsoft Word. In this part, you'll use advanced programming techniques to add features to an issue-tracking application.

Start by reading "Getting Ready," the next section in this book, and then install the practice files you'll use in the lessons. Find where you fit in the following table to determine where to go from there.

If you are	Follow these steps
New to Microsoft Access and Visual Basic programming	Work through all the lessons in the book, consulting online Help along the way when you have questions about basic features of Microsoft Access. Before you start, you may want to become familiar with basic Microsoft Access skills using another book, such as the *Getting Results* manual included with Microsoft Access.
Experienced with Microsoft Access but new to Visual Basic programming	Skim Lesson 1, which introduces wizards you can use in creating applications. Then work through the remaining lessons in the book.
Experienced with Visual Basic but new to Microsoft Access	Work through Lessons 1, 3, and 4 in Part 1, which introduce Microsoft Access features you'll need to know, but just skim Lesson 2 along the way. Also skim the lessons in Part 2. Then work through all the lessons in Parts 3 and 4.
Experienced with a previous version of Microsoft Access and Access Basic	Skim Lessons 1 and 2. Then read the remaining lessons more carefully. Depending on your experience, you may not want to work through all the lessons; however, note that Lessons 3, 5, 6, 11, and 12 in particular cover areas that are new to Microsoft Access for Windows 95.

Using This Book as a Classroom Aid

If you are an instructor, you can use *Microsoft Access/Visual Basic Step by Step* for teaching Microsoft Access programming to beginners, and for teaching specific programming concepts to advanced developers. If students aren't already familiar with the basic features of Microsoft Access, however, you might want to cover the basics at the beginning of the class or recommend that students take a less advanced class.

In planning to teach a class using this book, you might want to select certain lessons that meet your students' particular needs. You might also want to extend the lessons by incorporating your own review exercises or programming assignments at the end of each lesson. The bulleted list at the beginning of each lesson offers good lecture and homework topics, and the Lesson Summary table at the end of each lesson might provide ideas for questions on a quiz.

If you plan to teach the entire contents of this book, you should set aside at least five days of classroom time to allow for discussion, questions, and any customized review or practice you might create.

Conventions Used in This Book

Before you start the lessons, you should take a look at the terms and conventions used throughout the book.

Typographic Conventions

- Characters for you to type appear in **boldface**.
- New terms and the titles of books appear in *italic*.
- Program code (on its own line or lines) appears in monospace type:

```
Me.AllowEdits = False    ' Return the form to its read-only state.
```

- Names of keyboard keys for you to press appear in SMALL CAPITAL LETTERS.

Procedural Conventions

- Numbered lists (1, 2, 3, and so on) indicate steps you should follow.
- A single triangular bullet (▶) indicates a single task for you to do.

Other Features of This Book

Database Window button

- You can perform many operations in Microsoft Access by clicking a button on the toolbar or a tool in the toolbox. When the instructions in this book tell you to click a toolbar button, a picture of the button is shown in the left margin next to the instructions. The Database Window button in the margin next to this paragraph is an example.
- Screen capture illustrations show sample user interfaces and the results of your completed steps, and frequently include text that calls out the part of the illustration you should notice.
- Sidebars—short sections printed on a shaded background—introduce special programming techniques, background information, or features related to the information being discussed.
- The Lesson Summary table at the end of each lesson provides a list of the important new commands and programming techniques introduced in the lesson.

How to Find Out More About Microsoft Access

At the end of each lesson, references to online Help and the *Building Applications with Microsoft Access* manual direct you to specific topics and chapters in the documentation for additional information. These and other resources will help you take full advantage of Microsoft Access:

Online Help   The Help system in Microsoft Access provides how-to information for almost any task you need to do—including many programming tasks—as well as reference information on every function, method, property, and other element you can use in Microsoft Access. You'll learn more about using Help in "Getting Ready," the next section in this book.

Getting Results with Microsoft Access* or *Getting Results with Microsoft Office   The book you received depends on whether you have Microsoft Access by itself or as part of Microsoft Office, Professional Edition. Both help introduce you to practical solutions you can achieve by using standard features of Microsoft Access.

Building Applications with Microsoft Access   This manual contains information about programming and creating applications in Visual Basic. It also covers advanced topics, such as client-server programming.

Orders and Solutions sample applications   These two sample applications are provided with Microsoft Access, and may help you gather ideas for your own projects. They include Help topics to explain their features. Note that these databases aren't installed by default with Microsoft Access; for information on installing them, see "Installing All the Microsoft Access Tools You Need," in the next section of this book.

Getting Ready

In "Getting Ready" you will learn how to:

- Install and use the Step by Step practice files.
- Make sure your Microsoft Access installation is complete.
- Use the Microsoft Access online Help system.

This section prepares you to get started creating applications in Microsoft Access. You'll install the Step by Step practice files and check to make sure your Microsoft Access installation includes the necessary tools. You'll also learn how to use the extensive online Help system in Microsoft Access to get more information as you work.

Using the Practice Files Disk

The disk attached to the inside of the back cover of this book contains practice files that you'll use as you work through the lessons in the book. Most of the files on the disk are Microsoft Access database files—they contain partially completed programming projects that you'll work on to learn programming techniques.

Install the practice files

The practice files are compressed on the disk, so you must run the Setup program on the disk to install them.

> **1** Remove the disk from the package inside the back cover of this book and insert it in drive A or drive B of your computer.

2   On the Windows 95 taskbar, click the Start menu, and then click Run.

3   In the Run dialog box, type **a:\setup** (or **b:\setup** if you put the disk in drive B) and press ENTER.

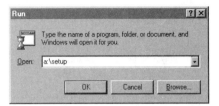

4   Follow the instructions on your screen to complete the Setup process. If possible, be sure to install the practice files in the default folder (C:\Access VBA Practice).

5   Remove the disk from the disk drive and replace it in the package inside the back cover of the book.

Because the practice files are now on your computer's hard disk, you won't need the practice files disk again as you work through the lessons unless you want to reinstall all of the practice files later.

After it copies files, the Setup program also creates a shortcut icon for them on the Windows 95 desktop. Double-clicking this icon opens the practice files folder.

The practice folder contains 14 files, most of them Microsoft Access database files. The steps in each lesson will tell you how to open and work with the files. You'll notice that the name of each file begins with the number of the lesson in which it is used (02 Contacts, for example). Each file is used in just one lesson, with one exception—you'll use the same database file, 12 Issues, for all three lessons in Part 4.

Notice that many of the practice database files are similar—you use the same type of sample database in Lessons 1 through 7, for example—however, because the practice files have slight differences from lesson to lesson, always be sure to open the correct one.

Create copies of the practice files

Although an optional step, it's a good idea to create backup copies of the practice files before you get started. That way, if you want to redo a lesson or start it over again, you can restore the necessary file without reinstalling all practice files.

1 Open the Access VBA Practice folder (use Windows Explorer or click the folder's shortcut icon on the Desktop).

2 On the Edit menu, click Select All.

3 On the Edit menu, click Copy.

4 On the Edit menu, click Paste.

Windows creates a copy of each file with the name "Copy of [existing file name]."

Now that you have copies of the files, you can easily restore a practice file if something goes wrong. Before you restart a lesson, just delete the practice file you were using for that lesson and then rename the copy to the original name. (You may also want to create another copy at that point.)

Installing All the Microsoft Access Tools You Need

To permit you to complete the steps in this book, the Microsoft Access installation on your computer must include the Developer Tools component, which includes builders and other add-in tools to help you create and maintain applications. Unfortunately, these tools are not included by default when you run Setup to install Microsoft Access. If you selected the Typical or Minimal option in Setup, you don't have all the necessary tools. Before you begin the lessons, it's best to check your installation by running Setup again.

Fortunately, you don't have to reinstall Microsoft Access to check your installation or add the developer tools. When you run Setup, it will detect that Microsoft Access is already installed and allow you to add the necessary components.

Install Microsoft Access developer tools

1 Start Microsoft Access Setup (or Microsoft Office Professional Setup).

2 When Setup asks what you want to do, click the Add/Remove button.

3 In the Options list, make sure the following components are checked:

- Help Topics
- Wizards
- Developer Tools

NOTE If you want to install the Orders and Solutions sample applications, which include many useful programming examples, now's the time to do it. Select the Sample Databases option, click Change Option, make sure the Orders Database and Solutions Database options are selected, and then click OK.

4 If you did make changes to your installation, click Continue. Otherwise, click Cancel and then exit Setup.

Now you can be sure you have everything you need to complete the lessons.

Using the Microsoft Access Help System

Microsoft Access has a vast online Help system that you can use to learn new topics or get answers to your individual questions. There isn't only reference information in Help—it also includes how-to information for nearly every task, graphical introductions to areas of Microsoft Access, and additional topics that help you find the information you need by answering questions. Additionally, there is a complete reference topic on every function, method, property, and other element you can use in Microsoft Access. And as you'll see, Help has several innovative ways for you to locate the topics you need.

If you're new to Microsoft Access or to the Windows 95 version, you may want to explore the product and its online Help before you start the lessons in this book. Additionally, as you work through the lessons, you'll frequently want more information about a topic.

Search for a topic in online Help

In these steps, you'll discover ways to search for online Help, and then find a specific topic.

1 On the Help menu, click Microsoft Access Help topics.

The Help Topics window appears. This window has four tabs, each of which helps you perform a different type of search.

Contents The Contents feature groups topics into logical order, which makes it a great place to browse Help, discover what's there, and begin your exploration of a new area in Microsoft Access.

Index The Index feature works like a book index. You can look up any topic covered in Help and jump directly to that topic. You'll use this method in steps 2 through 5 of this procedure.

Find While the online index includes the most important words in a topic, the Find feature lets you search the complete text of every single topic to find what you want. You may want to avoid this feature, however, since it requires Microsoft Access to set up a special index file the first time you use it—which takes time and disk space.

Answer Wizard The Answer Wizard may be the best tool of all for searching Help, since you can find topics by typing in a question or phrase *in your own words*—you don't have to guess the exact words that are in the index. This capability makes the Answer Wizard the most useful method for getting help if you have a question while you work. For example, if you wanted to know about displaying a list of values, you could simply type **looking up values** The Answer Wizard would interpret your text and diplay a range of topics.

The Answer Wizard finds how-to information...

...topics for additional learning...

...and programming topics.

At the end of each lesson in this book, there are references to online Help that you can use to find more information on the topics covered in that lesson. To find the information referred to, you'll use the online index.

2   Click the Index tab.

To find a topic, you type the keyword you want to find. For example, in Lesson 5, you'll learn about predefined constants in Microsoft Access. For more information, you can search for "constants" in the index.

3   Type **consta**

As you type, Help searches the index. When you finish typing these six letters, the Help index displays the index list for the keyword "constants."

4 Underneath the list of topics for constants, click "declaring," and then click the Display button.

Because there are several topics for this keyword, Help displays the Topics Found box.

5 Click "Const statement," and then click the Display button.

Microsoft Access displays the Help topic for the Const statement.

After you read a topic, you can close the Help window, click Help Topics to search for another topic, or click any underlined text in the Help topic to display a related topic. Most programming topics, for instance, have an underlined Example link in the top line of the topic, which you can click to view a Visual Basic code example.

6 Close the Help window (click its Close button at the right side of the title bar—the one with the "X").

In addition to the technique shown here, it's also handy to know that pressing the F1 key at any time brings you Help. This method is especially useful when you're working in the Module window—if the insertion point is on any Microsoft Access or Visual Basic keyword, pressing F1 takes you directly to its reference topic. In Lesson 2, you'll learn to do this when writing Visual Basic code.

Automating Database Tasks

Get Started Quickly with Wizards

Estimated time
30 min.

In this lesson you will learn how to:

■ Create a database with the Database Wizard.

■ Add an additional object to a wizard-created database.

■ Create a command button with a wizard.

Ever try to write a letter or a report, but you just can't get the first word down on the page? A blank page is a big obstacle to progress. This is why we often seek help from others, and why brainstorming is such a good technique—ideas good or bad help you come up with other ideas, and next thing you know, you have a good start.

Like working from a blank page, creating a database application from scratch is a difficult task. In fact, before you can do any customization or programming, you have to get most of your database in place and working! Fortunately, Microsoft Access includes several *wizards* that can help you get started quickly. Wizards ask you questions about databases or objects you want to create, then create them for you. For example, new to Microsoft Access for Windows 95 is the Database Wizard, which can create all the basic elements of a database application—tables, forms, reports, and other objects. After the wizard does its work, you can start using the application right away, or modify the user interface it creates, add new objects, even delete some of the objects it creates and replace them with your own.

In this lesson, you'll create an entire database application from scratch using the Database Wizard, and customize the application in various ways. Then, as you progress through Part 1, you'll learn how to use Visual Basic for Applications—as well as a number of other Microsoft Access wizards—to further customize the way the database works.

Start the lesson

▶ Start Microsoft Access for Windows 95. (In Windows 95, click the Start button on the taskbar, point to Programs, and then click Microsoft Access. In Windows NT, open the Microsoft Office program group, and then double-click Microsoft Access.)

Using Wizards for Application Development

It seems like wizards are popping up all over the place these days—usually to help end users perform difficult tasks without needing to know all the ins and outs of the software. But there are several wizards included in Microsoft Access that help make your job as an application developer much easier as well. In this book, you'll try out the following wizards:

■ Database Wizard

■ Import Text Wizard

■ Command Button Wizard

■ Combo Box Wizard

■ Option Group Wizard

■ Database Splitter Wizard

These wizards will not only help you get work done faster, they'll help you learn more about application development as you work. Even so, it's important to remember that anything you accomplish with a wizard you could do on your own in Microsoft Access. In fact, the wizards themselves are written in the Visual Basic programming language and use ordinary Microsoft Access forms for their interface, just like the applications you'll create.

 IMPORTANT To complete the steps in these lessons, all Microsoft Access wizards, developer tools, and online Help must be installed. If you didn't install these components, or if you chose the Typical option when you installed Microsoft Access, run Setup again, choosing the Custom option and selecting all wizards and online Help as well as the Developer Tools component.

As you learn to program Microsoft Access using Visual Basic, you'll go much further than wizards can take you. But there's no sense turning down the help wizards have to offer.

Creating a Database Using the Database Wizard

The Database Wizard can create several common types of databases for business and personal use, including:

- Asset tracking
- Contact management
- Donations
- Event management
- Expenses
- Inventory control
- Ledger
- Membership
- Order entry
- Resource scheduling
- Service call management
- Students and classes
- Time and billing
- Various personal and home databases, including ones that store information about your address book, household inventory, and music, book, and video collections

NOTE Even if the Database Wizard doesn't have just the database you need, the databases it creates may provide you with ideas for your own applications. Additionally, all the techniques you'll use to modify the wizard-created database apply equally to tables and forms you create on your own. In fact, in Part 3, you'll bypass the Database Wizard entirely to create the elements of a user interface from scratch.

Create the Contacts database

New Database button

1 In the opening Microsoft Access dialog box, click Database Wizard and then click OK. Or, if you've already closed the opening dialog box, click the New Database button.

Microsoft Access displays the New dialog box.

2 Click the Databases tab.

Microsoft Access displays icons for each type of database the Database Wizard can create for you.

A few of the databases the Database Wizard can create

3 Double-click the Contact Management icon.

4 In the File Name box type **01 Contacts** and then click Create.

The Database Wizard starts up and lists the types of information that the Contact Management database will include.

5 Click Finish.

The Database Wizard gets busy creating the Contacts database, which may take a minute or two. It then opens the Main Switchboard form, which shows up each time the database opens and guides users through the database. A *switchboard* form provides buttons and text that open other forms and reports in an application—providing a sort of control center for users.

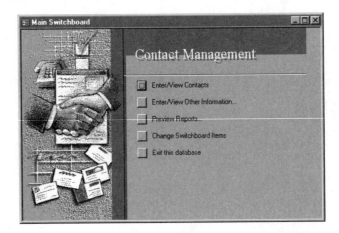

What Is a Database Application?

The Contacts database you've created is more than an ordinary Microsoft Access database—with its Switchboard form and the other forms and reports it contains, the Contacts database is an *application*. This term refers to the fact that the database has its own custom-built user interface, designed especially to help users of the database navigate through its forms and reports and get work done with the database. Database applications range from those as simple as the Contacts database, which has a very specific job in life, to complete business solutions that contain many objects and large amounts of Visual Basic code.

Developing custom applications is the central purpose of programming Microsoft Access with Visual Basic—and the central topic of this book. Throughout the book, you'll learn to tailor Microsoft Access databases to solve specific user problems and make information easier to get in and out of the computer. Because its simple interface leaves plenty of room for customization, the Contacts database is a great place to start.

View the Contacts form

The first item on the Switchboard form allows users to open the Contacts form, the main form in the application, where they can view and enter contact information in the database.

1   On the Switchboard form, click Enter/View Contacts.

The Contacts form opens, ready to accept new records. In addition to text boxes and other controls for all the information stored in the Contacts table, the form includes a footer with command buttons that users can click to perform common actions.

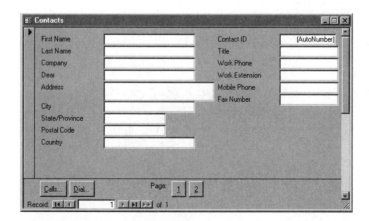

2   Close the Contacts form (click the Close button—the one with the "X"—in the upper right corner of the Form window).

What Else Did the Wizard Create?

The Database Wizard creates all the bare essentials of a database application, along with a few goodies to help users navigate in the application. Here's a list of everything the Contacts database includes:

- Tables that store information about contacts, contact types, and phone calls. The wizard automatically sets table properties and creates relationships between the tables.

- Forms for entering contact information and phone call information.

- Reports that summarize information about contacts and phone calls.

- The Switchboard form and the Switchboard Items table, which make up the application switchboard you see when you open the Contacts database.

NOTE The Switchboard form the wizard creates is a special form which you shouldn't try to change directly. It contains Visual Basic code that, along with the Switchboard Items table, displays the text you see on the form and makes the buttons work. Although you can't easily modify the way the Switchboard form works, you can add or remove buttons from the form, as you'll see later in the lesson. Alternatively, you could replace the Switchboard form with your own custom startup form, a technique you'll learn in Lesson 11.

View the objects in the Contacts database

A quick look at the Database window shows all the objects the Database Wizard created for the application. This should help you see that there's nothing magical about the database the wizard creates—it's just a few objects pulled together with a nice cover sheet.

Database Window button

1 Click the Database Window button.

2 Click the Tables, Forms, and Reports tabs to view the five tables, seven forms, and two reports the wizard created.

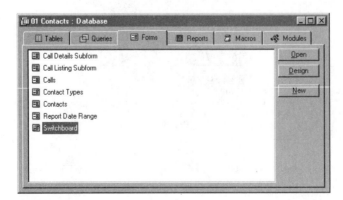

For many Microsoft Access users, the tables, forms, and reports created by the Database Wizard are just right as they are. But as a custom database developer, you'll want to customize these objects and add new objects. Now that the Database Wizard has done its work, you can choose to keep all or part of the wizard-created database, adding or modifying objects to meet the needs of your users.

3 Minimize the Database window.

Click the Minimize button
to minimize the window.

Entering Information into the Database

The first thing you need to do after creating a database is get some data into it. The Contact Management application lets you keep a list of the *types* of contacts you have, so that you can categorize each contact you enter in the database. Before going any further, it makes sense to enter this preliminary information.

Enter contact types

You can use the Switchboard form to open a form for entering contact types.

1 On the Switchboard form, click Enter/View Other Information.

2 Click Enter/View Contact Types.

The Contact Types form opens, ready for a new record.

3 Type **Client**

4 Click the New Record button.

New Record button

Microsoft Access saves the record and moves to a new record.

5 Type **Contractor**

6 Click the New Record button, and then type **Personal**

7 Close the Contact Types form (click the Close button in the upper right corner of the Form window).

8 Click Return To Main Switchboard.

This returns you to the initial switchboard menu.

Now when you enter contacts, you'll be able to select one of these three types for each contact record.

Using Existing Data with a New Database

As you've seen, the Contacts form is empty—it doesn't display any records. But suppose you already have some contact information that you've been storing in another program, and you don't want to retype it into your Microsoft Access application. One of the sample files included on your disk is 01 Clients, a comma-delimited text file containing names, addresses, and phone numbers you can add to the Contacts table. This file could easily have been exported from another spreadsheet or database system in order to move it into Microsoft Access.

Before you import data into an existing table, you should make sure it's in a format that Microsoft Access can accept. For example, you can import an Excel worksheet, a dBASE file, or a text file. Additionally, the data in the file you want to import must be compatible with the structure of the table you're adding it to. If it isn't, you may need to edit the file before importing it, to get it ready for Microsoft Access. For example, the 01 Clients text file already has the correct field names for the Contacts table in the first row of the file, so Microsoft Access can determine which fields to store data in.

TIP If you don't have any existing data to import, you may want the Database Wizard to include a few sample records in each of the applications' tables. Just select the Include Sample Data check box when creating an application. You can delete sample records from tables when you're ready to enter real data.

Import data into the Contacts table

1 On the File menu, point to Get External Data and then click Import.

Microsoft Access displays the Import dialog box, where you can select from a variety of data formats to import.

2 In the Files Of Type box, select Text Files.

The Import dialog box shows the 01 Clients text file, which is provided with the practice files you installed.

3 Select 01 Clients, and then click Import.

Microsoft Access starts the Import Text Wizard, which helps you select options for importing delimited or fixed-width text files. The wizard automatically detects that the 01 Clients text file is in Delimited format.

The wizard shows you the fields in the text file as Microsoft Access will import them.

4 Click Next.

5 Select the First Row Contains Field Names option, and then click Next.

6 Select the In An Existing Table option, select the Contacts table from the drop-down list, and then click Finish.

Select the Contacts table here.

Microsoft Access appends records from the text file to the existing Contacts table, and then displays a message indicating that it's finished successfully.

7 Click OK.

View new records in the Contacts form

Now, when users open the Contacts form, they'll see the client records you've added, and they'll be all set to start logging calls or adding additional contacts. You can also check to see that the contact types you added to the database are available on the form.

1 On the Switchboard form, click Enter/View Contacts.

The form displays the first record you imported into the Contacts table. Because the text file includes only a subset of the fields in the table, many of the text boxes are blank.

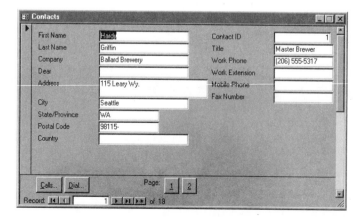

2 Click the Page 2 button in the form footer.

3 Click the drop-down arrow next to the Contact Type box, and click Client.

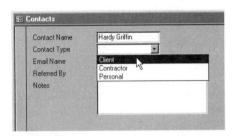

As you can see, the three types of contacts you added are available in the list.

4 Close the Contacts form.

Adding an Object to Your Application

Although the Database Wizard creates several useful forms and reports for the Contacts database, you're sure to need additional ones in your application. Suppose users need to print an up-to-date phone list for current contacts, organized by the city they're located in. You can create this form easily by using the Report Wizard.

Create a contact list report organized by city

Database Window button

New Object button

1 Click the Database Window button.

2 Click the Tables tab.

3 Click the Contacts table to select it.

4 Click the arrow next to the New Object button on the toolbar (which displays the button face for the last button you selected here), and then click New Report.

5 Click Report Wizard in the list, and then click OK.

6 In the Available Fields box, double-click the City field, followed by the LastName, FirstName, CompanyName, Title, and WorkPhone fields.

The Report Wizard adds the fields to the Selected Fields list.

Double-click a field to add it to the report.

7 Click Next.

The wizard asks what fields you want to use to group data in the report.

8 Double-click the City field in the list, and then click Next.

The wizard asks what fields you want to sort in the report.

9 Select the LastName field from the first sorting box, select the FirstName field from the second sorting box, and then click Next.

The wizard asks how you want to lay out your report.

10 In the layout box select Outline 1, and then click Next.

11 Choose a style for your report (or accept the default style), and then click Next.

The wizard asks what title you'd like for the report.

12 Type **Contacts By City** and then click Finish.

The Report Wizard creates the Contacts By City report and displays it in Print Preview.

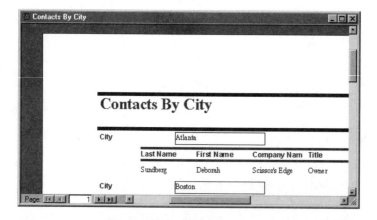

13   Close the report.

14   Minimize the Database window.

Add the new report to the Switchboard form

After you create new objects, you can add them to the Switchboard form that the Database Wizard created.

1   On the Switchboard form, click Change Switchboard Items.

Microsoft Access starts the Switchboard Manager, which helps you modify the items available on the Switchboard form.

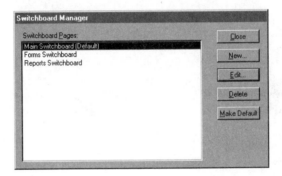

2   Select Reports Switchboard Page, and then click Edit.

3   Click New.

4   In the Text box, type **Preview the Contacts By City Report**

5   In the Command box, select Open Report.

6   In the Report box select Contacts By City, and then click OK.

7   Click Preview The Contacts By City Report, and then click Move Up.

8   Click Close.

9   Click Close again.

The Switchboard Manager updates the Switchboard Items table so that your new item appears in the Switchboard form.

Try the new Switchboard button

1   On the Switchboard form, click Preview Reports.

2   Click Preview The Contacts By City Report.

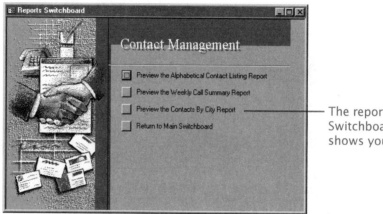

The reports page of the Switchboard form now shows your new option.

The button opens your report.

3   Close the report window.

4   On the Switchboard form, click Return To Main Switchboard.

Adding a Command Button to a Form

You've seen how the buttons on the Switchboard form help users open the forms and reports they need to use. In this way, buttons can help users navigate, tying objects together into a powerful application.

Once users get to the forms in your application, you want to put common tasks at their fingertips, so your forms are easy to use. One way to do this is by creating command buttons to automate tasks on your application forms. As you've seen, the Database Wizard already created some useful command buttons on the Contacts form.

Open the Contacts form and try a command button

1   On the Switchboard form, click Enter/View Contacts.

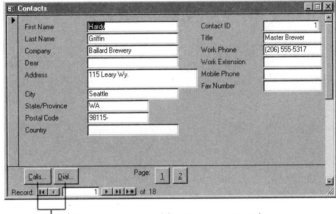

These command buttons open other
forms or perform common actions.

2   Click the Calls button.

The Calls form appears. When you click the button, it runs a few lines of Visual
Basic code programmed by the Database Wizard. Next, you'll add your own
button to the Contacts form, which will work in much the same way.

3   Close the Calls form.

Create a command button that moves to the new record

When you open the Contacts form, it displays the first existing contact record. If you
want to enter a new contact, you can move to the new record at the end of the recordset
by clicking the New Record button at the bottom of the form window. Or, you can use
the Insert Record command with the same effect.

But suppose you want to make this command more accessible to other users, so they
won't have to find it on the menu or know about the navigation buttons—after all, new
users won't be as familiar with Microsoft Access as you are. To bring this command to
the forefront, you'll go into the form's Design view and place another button in the form
footer that performs this action whenever you click it. The Command Button Wizard
makes the button work automatically by writing Visual Basic code for you.

1   Click the Design View button on the toolbar.

*Design View
button*

2 Scroll down in the form to display the Form Footer section.

The command buttons appear in the footer section of the Contacts form.

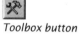

Toolbox button

3 If the toolbox isn't displayed, click the Toolbox button on the toolbar.

4 In the toolbox, make sure the Control Wizards tool is selected, and then click the Command Button tool.

Control Wizards tool

Command Button tool

5 In the form footer, click just to the right of the Page 2 button.

Click here to create the new button.

The Command Button Wizard starts, asking what actions you want to perform.

6 In the Categories list, select Record Operations.

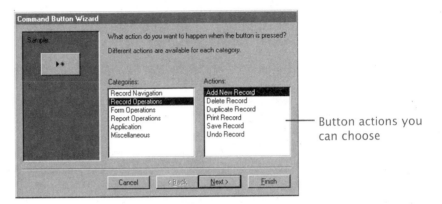

Button actions you can choose

7 In the Actions list select Add New Record, and then click Next.

The wizard asks whether you want a picture or text on your button.

8 Select the Text option, and then click Next.

When you create your own buttons, you may want to use the pictures that the wizard provides for them—there's an extensive library of icons available to choose from. The wizard even shows you a preview of the picture for the button you've chosen. In this case, however, the existing buttons on the Contacts form have text on them, so for the sake of consistency it makes sense to go with text on the Add Record button.

9 Type **AddRecord** as the button name, and then click Finish.

The wizard finishes creating the button and places it on your form. Behind the scenes, it also writes several lines of Visual Basic code and attaches them to the button for you.

Try the new command button

Let's make sure the Add Record button does what you intended.

Form View button

1 Click the Form View button on the toolbar.

2 Click the Add Record button.

Microsoft Access moves to the new record in the Contacts table, displaying a fresh form for you to enter data into.

How Does the Button Work?

If you create a button without using the Command Button Wizard, the button won't *do* anything when you click it. What did the wizard do to make the button perform as you asked?

Here's how it works: whenever you perform any action in a form—click a button or change a field's value, for example—an *event* occurs. Every event is a chance for your application to perform some action, such as running a macro or a Visual Basic procedure. When the Command Button Wizard created the button, it attached an *event procedure* to the button's Click event. This way, every time the button is clicked, the Visual Basic code in the event procedure runs, causing Microsoft Access to perform the desired action—in this case, moving to the new record.

Creating Other Command Buttons

You can see how easy it is to customize your forms by adding command buttons. And as you saw when using the Command Button Wizard, adding a record is just one type of operation you can create a button for—the Command Button Wizard can create buttons for all kinds of other tasks as well. Here are some other common operations you can create buttons for:

- Navigating between records
- Finding and filtering data
- Opening forms and reports
- Printing and other miscellaneous tasks

Using the Command Button Wizard is like "programming without programming"— even after programming with Microsoft Access becomes second nature, you still may want to rely on the Command Button Wizard to give you a head start.

Close the Contacts form

1   Close the form window.

2   When Microsoft Access asks if you want to save changes to the Contacts form, click Yes.

 NOTE   When you save the form, Microsoft Access saves not only the new button, but also the Visual Basic code that the wizard created for it. Because a form's module is stored along with the form, you don't have to save the Visual Basic code separately.

Close the application and exit Microsoft Access

1   On the Switchboard form, click Exit This Database.
2   On the File menu, click Exit.

Moving from Macros to Visual Basic

In the lessons to come, you'll learn to perform many database tasks using Visual Basic for Applications. Some of these tasks can also be accomplished with Microsoft Access macros. However, macros are much less flexible and powerful than Visual Basic—and because there are Visual Basic equivalents for just about every macro action, you can do nearly all the same things in Visual Basic that you can in macros. Because of Visual Basic's power and flexibility, the Database Wizard and the Command Button Wizard create Visual Basic event procedures, not macros.

If you have existing macros in your databases, it will soon be time to convert them to Visual Basic—this way, you'll have a consistent strategy for customization in your applications. Microsoft Access makes the move to Visual Basic easy by including a tool called the Convert Macros To Visual Basic Add-In. When you run this add-in procedure on a database, Microsoft Access goes through all the macros in the database, replacing them with Visual Basic procedures. To do this, just open the database that contains macros, click Add-Ins on the Tools menu, and then click Convert Macros To Visual Basic. Microsoft Access not only creates procedures for all the macros, it attaches them to the same events, so that your application works just as before.

Lesson Summary

To	Do this	Button
Create a database using the Database Wizard	Click the New Database button and double-click the type of database you want.	🗋
Import data into an existing database	On the File menu, click Get External Data, and then click Import. Select the Append option when importing.	
Modify the Switchboard form in a database created by the Database Wizard	Click the Change Switchboard Items button on the Switchboard form.	
Create a command button on a form	In Form Design view, click the Command Button tool and click on the form where you want to place the button.	▣

For online information about	On the Help menu, click Microsoft Access Help Topics, click the Index tab, and then
Creating database applications	Search for "databases, creating"
Getting started with Visual Basic	Search for "Visual Basic"
Creating command buttons	Search for "command buttons"

For more information on	In *Building Applications with Microsoft Access*, see
Creating database applications	Chapter 1, "Creating an Application"
Getting started with Visual Basic	Chapter 2, "Introducing Visual Basic"
Creating command buttons	Chapter 3, "Using Forms to Collect, Display, and Filter Information"

Preview of the Next Lesson

In this lesson, you learned that wizards can create useful objects for you, complete with Visual Basic code. In the next lesson, you'll learn to view and make changes to the Visual Basic code the wizard creates, and to write your own simple event procedures to perform tasks that the wizards don't do.

Customize an Application with Visual Basic

In this lesson you will learn how to:

Estimated time
40 min.

- View and understand the Visual Basic code created by the Command Button Wizard.
- Edit Visual Basic code in the Module window.
- Set form and control properties using Visual Basic.
- Display a message box.

When you take the city bus around town, trip planning is of the utmost importance. Where does the bus stop? How close does it get me to my destination? Like it or not, the bus follows a predetermined route. But wouldn't it be nice if you had complete control of the bus route? You could just sit near the bus driver and say, "Take a left at the next light, then head that way for half a mile or so—I'll get off at the second building on the right."

We all love to be in control of our situation—a characteristic especially true of computer users and programmers. If there's one type of complaint you'll hear from computer users, it's along the lines of: "This machine doesn't let me do what I want it to," or "I sure wish I could make the software work a different way." Working with Microsoft Access is no exception. Sure, you can get lots of work done without too much extra work, and you can even customize the way your application looks and behaves. But if you want it to work a specific way, or if you're developing an application for others who have specific needs, it's time to get into Visual Basic. It's more work to customize an application, but there are unlimited possibilities when you make the effort to program your own solutions in Visual Basic.

In this lesson, you'll start taking control—telling the application how to work, rather than following the rules built into Microsoft Access.

Start the lesson

▶ Start Microsoft Access and open the 02 Contacts database in the practice files folder.

Customizing a Command Button

In the first lesson, you created a button using the Command Button Wizard, and the button worked just as planned—it moved to the new record in the Contacts form. But what if you create a button with a wizard, and it doesn't work quite right? Or what if the wizard doesn't offer a button that does what you want? You've probably guessed by now: the answer lies in the Visual Basic code that makes the button work.

In this section, you'll open the Visual Basic event procedure for the Add Record button. After exploring the Visual Basic code in the procedure, you'll write your first line of code, making a small improvement to the code the wizard created.

Open the Contacts form

▶ On the Main Switchboard form, click Enter/View Contacts.

The Contacts form displays the first record in the recordset.

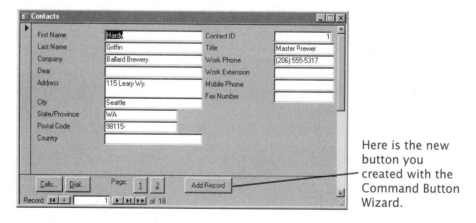

Here is the new button you created with the Command Button Wizard.

Next, you'll take a look at the event procedure that makes the Add Record button work.

Viewing the Visual Basic Code Behind a Command Button

Visual Basic code, such as the code that the Command Button wizard creates, is stored in *modules*. Each form and report in a database has its own attached *form module* or *report module* for storing Visual Basic code—for example, the code that the wizard created for your button is stored in the form module for the Contacts form. Most Visual Basic code you'll write will belong to an individual form or report; however, if you write code that applies to more than one form or report, you can store it in one or more *standard modules*, which are separate objects in the Database window.

Visual Basic code comes in units called *procedures*, each performing a single task—for example, the code that responds to the clicking of the Add Record button is one procedure. A module can contain many procedures, one for each event you want to respond to or task you want to perform.

The following diagram illustrates the relationships among all these objects, and shows where your Visual Basic procedures can live:

Form

Form Module

| Procedure |
| Procedure |
| Procedure |

Report

Report Module

| Procedure |
| Procedure |
| Procedure |

Module

| Procedure |
| Procedure |
| Procedure |
| Procedure |

Open the button's Click event procedure

Let's take a look at a procedure—for starters, you can view the event procedure that the Command Button Wizard created for the Add Record button. Because the button belongs to the Contacts form, the wizard stored the procedure in the form module for that form, which you can get to from the form's Design view.

Design View button

1   Click the Design View button.

2   Scroll down in the form to display the form footer.

3   With the right mouse button, click the Add Record button.

4   Click Build Event.

The Build Event command tells Microsoft Access to open the Visual Basic module for the current form and display the default event procedure for the selected object. For a command button, the default event procedure is the Click event procedure, so the module window shows the AddRecord_Click procedure.

Form module for the Contacts form

Click event procedure for the Add Record button

The Visual Basic code in this procedure runs automatically each time you click the Add Record button. The main attraction in the procedure is the following line of Visual Basic code, which tells Microsoft Access to move to the new record:

```
DoCmd.GoToRecord , , acNewRec
```

How does this code work? Let's take apart this line piece by piece to understand how it works. Along the way, you'll learn a few important terms.

- The first keyword in the line is DoCmd (pronounced "DO-command"), which you'll be seeing quite a bit when programming Microsoft Access. DoCmd is an *object*—it shares this honorable position with other objects you're already familiar with, such as forms, reports, and controls. You use the DoCmd object to perform common actions in the Microsoft Access interface, such as opening a form, printing a report, or choosing a menu command.

- The second keyword is GoToRecord, which is a *method* of the DoCmd object. Each object that Microsoft Access recognizes has its own set of methods that you use with that object. The methods of the DoCmd object are all the actions it allows you to perform—in fact, if you've created macros in Microsoft Access, you'll recognize the things you can do with the DoCmd object as the macro actions available in the Macro window. The GoToRecord method, as its name suggests, tells Microsoft Access to move to a specified record in the current recordset.

  To perform a method on an object, such as the DoCmd object, you type the object immediately followed by its method, separating the keywords with a period.

- What follows the GoToRecord method are its *arguments*, which provide any information that's necessary to carry out the method. The arguments for the GoToRecord method, for example, allow you to specify such critical options as which record you want to go to. You specify arguments by typing a space after the method, then typing the argument values separated by commas. If you don't need to specify one or more of the argument values, you can leave them out by simply typing a comma for each—for example, the line above skips the first two arguments, supplying only the third argument.

Some methods, such as GoToRecord, have specially-defined *constant* values that you can enter as arguments. The argument acNewRec is a constant that tells the GoToRecord method to move to the new record at the end of the recordset (other options include moving to the next record or the first record in the recordset). The constant acNewRec actually stands for the number 5—but the constant name is much easier to remember and makes your code easier to understand.

To sum up, this line of code uses the GoToRecord method of the DoCmd object to move to the specified record—in this case, to the new record.

Get Help on arguments

With all the objects, methods, and other keywords you'll use when programming in Visual Basic, there's no way you can remember all their arguments. But there's a quick way to find the information you need using the language reference material in online Help.

1   Click to position the insertion point on the GoToRecord keyword in the Module window.

2   Press the F1 key.

Microsoft Access displays the Help topic for the GoToRecord method.

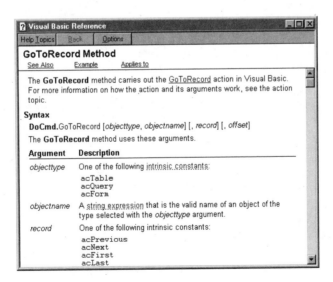

In the syntax section of the Help topic, you'll find an explanation of each of the arguments you can specify for the GoToRecord method, including their constant values, where appropriate. As you can see, the line of code that the Command Button Wizard wrote leaves out the first two arguments, *objecttype* and *objectname*, but specifies the third argument, *record*. It also leaves out the fourth argument, *offset*.

TIP Seeing an example of a keyword in Visual Basic code is often the best way to figure out how to use it. To see a code example for a keyword in Help, you can always click Example in the top line of the Help topic.

3 Close the Help window.

Unless you have a perfect memory for details, you'll find the F1 key to be a very good friend. Anytime you can't remember the syntax for a method or object, or the values for a property you're using, just click the keyword and press F1.

What About the Other Code the Wizard Created?

Although the DoCmd line we dissected and discussed is what really does the job in the AddRecord_Click procedure, you may be wondering about the rest of the code the Command Button Wizard created. Here's the complete procedure:

```
Sub AddRecord_Click()
On Error GoTo Err_AddRecord_Click

    DoCmd.GoToRecord , , acNewRec

Exit_AddRecord_Click:
    Exit Sub
Err_AddRecord_Click:
    MsgBox Err.Description
    Resume Exit_AddRecord_Click
End Sub
```

The Sub and End Sub lines designate the beginning and end of the procedure. You'll see similar lines at the beginning and end of every event procedure—but because Microsoft Access adds them to event procedures automatically, you won't usually have to think about them.

The remaining lines in the procedure—other than the DoCmd line—provide *error handling* for the procedure. The Command Button Wizard includes these error handling lines so that in case an error occurs, your application won't come to a halt. In Lesson 7, you'll learn how to add your own error handling code to procedures; for now, rest assured that the wizard took care of it for you.

Modifying a Command Button Created Using the Wizard

The Command Button Wizard is a great tool for customizing your applications, but it isn't perfect. Although it creates buttons for a variety of tasks, it can't anticipate everything you'll want your buttons to do. Fortunately, if the wizard doesn't get it quite right, you can modify the buttons it creates to suit your application's needs. That's just what you'll do with the Add Record button in this section.

There's nothing really *wrong* with the Add Record button—when you click it, you jump to the new record in the recordset—but it could use some polishing. To get it just right, you'll first change a property and then add a line of Visual Basic code to the button's event procedure.

Add an accelerator key for the command button

The Add Record button is missing a handy feature that the other buttons on the Contacts form already possess. The other buttons have *accelerator keys*—underlined characters that let you "press" the buttons using the keyboard. Because many users like to have the option of using the keyboard instead of the mouse, it's always wise to make your applications work as well with the keyboard as with the mouse. For the Add Record button, you'll make the "A" into an accelerator key.

To provide an accelerator key for a button, all you have to do is edit the Caption property of the button—which determines the actual text shown on the button—to include the ampersand (&) symbol. This symbol in a button's caption tells Microsoft Access that the next character in the caption is the accelerator key for the button.

1 On the Window menu, click Contacts : Form.

The Contacts form, still in Design view, comes to the front. Note that you don't have to close the form module in the Module window to continue working on the form itself.

2 With the right mouse button, click the Add Record button, and then click Properties on the shortcut menu.

Microsoft Access displays the property sheet for the Add Record button.

3 Click the All tab in the property sheet.

4 In the Caption property box, click the left edge of the Add Record text (before the "A"), and then type &

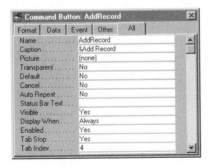

Adding the ampersand (&) symbol tells the wizard to make the "A" in Add Record the accelerator key for the button. The button won't actually show the ampersand, but the "A" will appear underlined on the button. This way, the user can press ALT+A to achieve the same effect as clicking the Add Record button.

5 Close the property sheet.

Use the accelerator key to press the command button

1 Click the Form View button on the toolbar.

2 Press ALT+A.

Microsoft Access moves to the new record in the Contacts table just as if you'd clicked the button using the mouse.

Add a line to your event procedure to change the focus

The Add Record button needs one other modification. Notice that after you press the button, the *focus* is still on the Add Record button—there's no current field or insertion point for typing data. In order to begin entering data, the user must first click the First Name field on the form. Ideally, you'd like the focus to move automatically to the first field in the record.

After you click the Add Record button...

...you want the focus to be on the first
field so the user can begin entering data.

1 On the Window menu, click Form_Contacts : Module.

The form's module comes back to the front, still displaying the AddRecord_Click event procedure.

2 Click the blank line underneath the DoCmd line in the event procedure, press TAB, and then type the following line of Visual Basic code:

```
FirstName.SetFocus
```

This line has two parts:

- *FirstName* is the name of a control object on your form. (Be sure not to separate FirstName with a space between words—the underlying control name doesn't contain a space.)

- *SetFocus* is a method—and like the method you used with the DoCmd object earlier in the lesson, it's separated by a period from the FirstName object to which it belongs. The SetFocus method tells Microsoft Access to set the focus to the specified form or control object.

Here's the procedure with the new line of code:

Test the command button

1 Close the Module window.

2 Click the Add Record button.

Microsoft Access moves to the new record in the Contacts table. This time, however, you'll notice that the insertion point is flashing in the FirstName field, ready for the user to enter data.

As you continue to polish your application, you'll want to use the SetFocus method whenever you can anticipate what users will want to do next. Moving to a form or control with SetFocus is a great way to save extra clicks—which makes your application easier to use.

Save your changes to the Add Record button

Now that you've finished modifying the button, save your changes.

Save button

▶ Click the Save button on the toolbar.

Microsoft Access saves your changes to the form and its form module.

Editing a Form's Module While in Form View

You may have noticed that you were able to make your addition to the Click event procedure while the Contacts form was in Form view—in a sense, you changed the underlying design of the form without switching to Design view. This is a unique feature of Visual Basic as compared to many programming languages: you can edit a code module "on the fly"—while the code in the module is potentially being used by the form. You'll soon discover how useful this can be, because you won't usually have to restart a complex application in order to make minor changes.

As you'll learn in later lessons, you can even edit code in a Visual Basic procedure while it's running. In cases where you make a significant change, however, Microsoft Access may need to reset your code and start over. For the time being, however, you can appreciate the fact that you don't have to constantly switch between Form view and Design view to examine and edit code.

Making a Form Read-Only by Default

If you type in any of the fields in the Contacts form, you begin editing the recordset. This is one of the great advantages of Microsoft Access over many other database systems— data is almost always available for both viewing and updating. However, business users are commonly worried about "messing up" the information in a database—their data is important, and they don't want it to be too easy to make changes to data.

In this section, you'll modify the Contacts form to provide a solution to this common data-entry request. The idea is to make the default mode for a form *read-only*, so users can't make changes unless they specifically ask to. This way, users can open the form and look at contact information without worrying about accidentally making a change.

The first step is easy: to make a form read-only, you simply set the AllowEdits property for the form to No. But you also need a way for users to tell you when they *do* want to make changes. What you want is an additional two buttons on your form—one for indicating that they want to edit data, one for saving the record they've edited. For one of these buttons, you won't use the Command Button Wizard at all—instead, you'll create the button on your own, and then write a custom Visual Basic event procedure to make the button work.

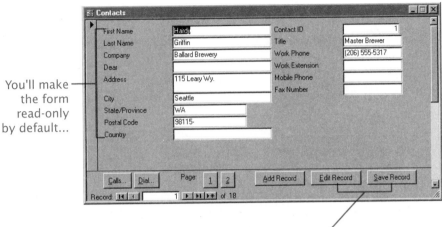

You'll make the form read-only by default...

...and then provide buttons that users can click to begin and finish editing a record.

Make existing records in the Contacts form read-only

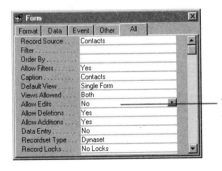

Design View button

1 Click the Design View button on the toolbar.

2 Double-click the form selection box at the upper left corner of the form window (at the intersection of the rulers).

Double-click here to select the form and display its properties.

Microsoft Access displays the form's properties in the property sheet.

3 Click the AllowEdits property, and then set the property to No.

The AllowEdits property controls whether you can change existing records in the form.

That's all it takes to solve the problem of accidentally editing data; now when you open the form to an existing record, you won't be able to change data. Note that we're leaving the other two "Allow" properties—AllowDeletions and AllowAdditions—set to Yes, so users can still delete or add records. Accidental deletions shouldn't be a problem, because Microsoft Access warns users automatically before deleting records.

4 Close the property sheet.

Form View button

5 Click the Form View button on the toolbar.

6 Try to type a few letters in the First Name text box.

Nothing happens, because the record is read-only—and the existing data is safe.

Creating a Command Button Without a Wizard

Now that the form is read-only, you need a command button that sets the AllowEdits property back to Yes. But the Command Button Wizard doesn't offer a button that changes the value of a property. It's time to up the ante and push beyond where the wizard goes!

First, you'll create the button and set its properties. Then, you'll use the Build Event command to create your own event procedure for the button's Click event.

Create the Edit Record command button

You want to place the Edit Record button in the form footer along with the existing buttons.

Design View button

1 Click the Design View button on the toolbar.

2 Scroll down in the form to display the form footer.

Toolbox button

3 If the toolbox isn't displayed, click the Toolbox button on the toolbar.

4 In the toolbox, click the Control Wizards tool to deselect it, and then click the Command Button tool.

Control Wizards tool

5 In the form footer, click just to the right of the Add Record button.

Command Button tool

Place the new button here.

Without the Control Wizards tool selected, the button appears immediately, but with a default name (such as Command45) and no associated event procedure.

Properties button

6 Click the Properties button on the toolbar.

7 In the Name property box, type **EditRecord**

8 Press ENTER, and then in the Caption property box type **&Edit Record**

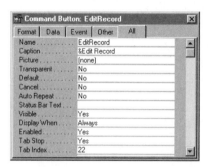

The ampersand (&) character in the button's caption tells Microsoft Access to make the "E" in Edit Record the accelerator key for the command button.

NOTE   Be sure to include a space in the button's caption, but *not* in the underlying control name. None of the fields or controls on the Contacts form contain spaces in their names, because spaces make fields and controls more difficult to work with (every time you type the name, you have to enclose it in brackets).

9 Close the property sheet.

Create the button's Click event procedure

As it stands, the new button won't *do* anything when you click it. You need to write a Visual Basic event procedure to make it work.

1 With the right mouse button, click the Edit Record button, and then click Build Event on the shortcut menu.

Microsoft Access displays the Choose Builder dialog box. (If you wanted to create an expression or a macro rather than Visual Basic code, you could choose Expression Builder or Macro Builder.)

2 Select Code Builder, and then click OK.

Microsoft Access opens the form module for the Contacts form and creates an event procedure for the button's Click event.

The procedure that Microsoft Access creates is called EditRecord_Click. The name of an event procedure has two parts, separated by an underscore character: the name of an object, and the event that the procedure responds to. You can think of the name EditRecord_Click as meaning "the code that runs when you click the EditRecord control."

3 Press ENTER, press TAB, and then type the following line of Visual Basic code:

```
Me.AllowEdits = True
```

The equal sign (=) in Visual Basic code means "assign the value of the expression on the right to the thing identified on the left." This code tells Microsoft Access to assign True to the expression on the left. The expression *Me.AllowEdits* refers to the AllowEdits property of the form—to refer to a property of the current form in the form's module, you use the Me keyword, followed by a period, followed by the property name. It's as if the form is telling Microsoft Access, "Set my AllowEdits property to True."

Setting a property to True in Visual Basic code is the same as setting the property to Yes in the form's property sheet. (To set a property to No in code, you assign it the value False.)

4 Press ENTER, and then type the following line so that the focus will move back to the first control on the form—just as in the Add Record event procedure:

```
FirstName.SetFocus
```

Your event procedure should look like this:

Try the Edit Record button

1 On the Window menu, click Contacts : Form.

The form window, still in Design view, comes to the front.

*Form View
button*

2 Click the Form View button.

3 Click the Dear field, and try to type in it.

You can't type anything—the record is still read-only.

4 Click the Edit Record button you just created.

Although it happens so fast you couldn't have seen it, Microsoft Access ran your event procedure when you clicked the button. The AllowEdits property should now be set to Yes. Also, you'll notice that the focus is on the First Name field as you specified using the SetFocus method in the event procedure. But you want to edit the Dear field to add this contact's nickname to the record.

5 Click the Dear field, and then type **Red**

You can now edit data, which means that the button's event procedure successfully changed the AllowEdits property to True.

 NOTE If you typed anything incorrectly when creating your event procedure, clicking the button will most likely cause an error message to appear. If this happens, don't worry—Microsoft Access brings up the Module window so you can recheck it. After making corrections to the procedure, click the Continue button on the toolbar.

Add comments to your event procedure

When you first take a look at any given Visual Basic procedure—even if you wrote it yourself—it's really tough to figure out what the procedure does and why it's there. To help make your applications easier to understand, it's extremely important to include *comments* embedded in your code. Comments are like notes to yourself, helping to explain what you were thinking of when you wrote the code.

To add a comment to the code in the Module window, simply precede the text of your comment with an apostrophe (').

1 On the Window menu, click Form_Contacts : Module.

This brings the event procedure back up.

2 Click the blank line underneath the Sub statement in the procedure, and then type the following line:

```
' Make the Contacts form editable.
```

Now when you look at this event procedure later on, you won't need to figure out what it does or why you wrote it. If you have a color display, you'll notice that Microsoft Access displays the comment text in green.

3 Press ENTER.

4 Click the far right side of the line that includes the SetFocus method, press TAB twice, and then type the following text:

```
' Move to the FirstName field.
```

As you can see, a comment can either begin on a new line, or explain the line of code to the left. A comment on a line by itself often gives information about several lines of code or a whole procedure, while a comment to the right of a line of code generally explains what that one line does.

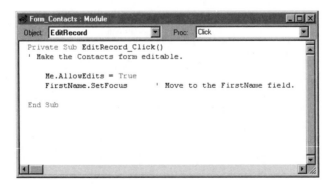

5 Close the Module window.

Create a command button that saves the current record

With the two buttons you've created, users can either add new records or edit existing ones. But there's one more button you need to add.

When entering or editing data about a contact, you can save data by either moving to a new record or closing the form. Or, you can use the Save Record command (on the File menu) to explicitly save the current record. But you want to make this command more accessible to users, so they won't have to find it on the menu. Because the Command Button Wizard creates such a button, you may as well use it.

Design View button

Control Wizards tool

Command Button tool

1   Click the Design View button on the toolbar.

2   Scroll down in the form to display the form footer.

3   In the toolbox, click the Control Wizards tool to select it, and then click the Command Button tool.

4   In the form footer, click just to the right of the Edit Record button.

Click here to create the new button.

The Command Button Wizard starts, asking what actions you want to perform.

5   In the Categories list, select Record Operations.

6   In the Actions list, select Save Record, and then click Next.

The wizard asks whether you want a picture or text on your button.

7   Select the Text option.

8   In the Text box, click the left edge of the Save Record text, and then type &

Adding the ampersand (&) symbol tells the wizard to make the "S" in Save Record the accelerator key for the button.

9   Click Next.

10   Type **SaveRecord** as the button name, and then click Finish.

The wizard finishes creating the button and its event procedure and places it on your form.

11   If necessary, resize and align the buttons in the footer so that they're uniform. (When you create buttons by different methods, it's easy for them to end up with different shapes or sizes.)

Save button

12   Click the Save button on the toolbar.

Microsoft Access saves both the form and its module.

Creating Event Procedures for Form Events

Up to this point, you've worked only with procedures for the Click event—code that runs when you click a button. But there are many other events you can respond to. In this section, you'll work with event procedures for two form events.

When a user clicks the Edit Record button you created, your code makes the form editable. When the user saves the record or moves to another record, you need to return the form to its read-only state, so that records won't be vulnerable to accidental changes until the Edit Record button is clicked again.

Much of the trick in programming with Microsoft Access is figuring out which event to attach code to. You could have added code to the Save Record button that would set the form's AllowEdits property back to False. But there are other ways the user could save an edited record—using a menu command, for example—and your application needs to anticipate all these possibilities. Additionally, the user could move to another record without saving the record at all, in which case you also want to return the AllowEdits property to False.

The two cases you need to catch are:

■ Whenever the user moves to another existing record

■ Whenever the user saves the current record using any method

For the first case, you'll add a line of code to the event procedure for the form's *Current* event, which occurs whenever Microsoft Access displays an existing record in a form procedure (the Database Wizard already created this event procedure). For the second case, you'll create your own event procedure for the form's *AfterUpdate* event, which occurs whenever a record is saved in a form. Between the two, you'll be sure to return the form to its read-only state at the appropriate times.

Edit the procedure for the form's Current event

Earlier in this lesson you used the Build Event command on the shortcut menu to create or open the Click event procedure for a button. But the Build Event command always opens the *default event* for the object you choose. Because the Current event isn't the default event for a form, you'll have to use the more general method to open the event procedure—you'll create the procedure by setting an event property in the property sheet.

1   Double-click the form selection box at the upper left corner of the form window (at the intersection of the rulers).

Microsoft Access displays the form's properties in the property sheet.

2   Click the Event tab in the property sheet.

3 Click the OnCurrent property, and then click the Build button to the right of the property box.

Build button

4 Select Code Builder, and then click OK.

Microsoft Access creates the Form_Current event procedure and displays it in the Module window.

5 Press ENTER, and then type the following line of Visual Basic code:

```
Me.AllowEdits = False    ' Return the form to its read-only state.
```

By setting the form's AllowEdits property to False, this line of code returns the form to its read-only state each time you move to an existing record in the form.

6 Press ENTER.

Copy the procedure to the form's AfterUpdate event

You need the same code to run when the AfterUpdate event occurs, but the AfterUpdate event doesn't yet have any event procedure. Rather than retype the Form_Current code in the Module window, you can just copy the code from one procedure to another.

1 In the Module window, select the line of code you added (click the left margin of the line of code to highlight the whole line).

2 On the Edit menu, click Copy.

3 On the Window menu, click Contacts : Form.

4 Click the AfterUpdate property, and then click the Build button to the right of the property box.

5 Select Code Builder, and then click OK.

Microsoft Access creates the Form_ AfterUpdate event procedure and displays it in the Module window.

6 Press ENTER.

7 On the Edit menu, click Paste.

Displaying a Message to the User

It's important to communicate with users of your application. One way to do this is by using a message box. Using the MsgBox statement, you can give some feedback in response to events in your application.

The same users who worry about accidentally changing data are equally concerned that their changes get registered when they finish editing a record. For these users, you can display a message in response to the AfterUpdate event, confirming that the record was saved.

Add a line to the AfterUpdate procedure that displays a message box

1 Press TAB, and then type the following line of code:

```
MsgBox "Record saved."
```

This line uses the Visual Basic MsgBox statement, passing as an argument the message that you want to display to the user. Because it is a string argument, you enclose the message in quotation marks. (In Visual Basic, any text data or combination of text and numbers is referred to as a *string*.)

2 Press ENTER.

Here's the complete code for the AfterUpdate event procedure.

3 Close the Module window.

4 Close the property sheet.

Save your changes to the Contacts form

Now that you've finished adding all the buttons to the form and editing their event procedures, save your changes to the form.

Save button

➤ Click the Save button on the toolbar.

Microsoft Access saves your changes to the form and its form module.

Try the buttons with your changes

Let's make sure the Edit Record and Save Record buttons work together as you intended. Suppose you found out the mobile phone number of the first contact, and want to enter it in the Contacts form.

Form View button

1 Click the Form View button on the toolbar.

2 Click the Edit Record button.

3 Click the MobilePhone field, and then type **206 555 2365**

When you change data in a record and haven't yet saved the new information, the record selector at the left side of the form displays a pencil icon.

The pencil icon indicates that your changes haven't been saved.

Contacts			
First Name	Hardy	Contact ID	1
Last Name	Griffin	Title	Master Brewer
Company	Ballard Brewery	Work Phone	(206) 555-5317
Dear		Work Extension	
Address	115 Leary Wy.	Mobile Phone	(206) 555-2365
		Fax Number	
City	Seattle		
State/Province	WA		
Postal Code	98115-		
Country			

Calls... | Dial... | Page: 1 | 2 | Add Record | Edit Record | Save Record

Record: 1 of 18

4 Click the Save Record button.

Microsoft Access saves the record in the Contacts table and changes the pencil back to the current record indicator. Having saved the record, it fires the form's AfterUpdate event, which in turn runs your event procedure and displays your message.

Microsoft Access

Record saved.

OK

43

5 Click OK.

6 Click in the FirstName field, and then try to type a few letters.

Because the form's AfterUpdate event procedure set the AllowEdits property back to False, you can't edit data any longer. Everything's working as planned!

7 Close the Contacts form.

Close the application and exit Microsoft Access

1 On the Switchboard form, click Exit This Database.

2 On the File menu, click Exit.

Lesson Summary

To	Do this
Open or create the default event procedure for a control	In Design view, with the right mouse button click the control, and then click Build Event.
Open or create any event procedure for a control	In the property sheet for the control, click the event property for the event, and then click the Build button.
Add an accelerator key for a command button	In the button's Caption property setting, precede the accelerator key with an ampersand (&).
Use a method of an object in code	Type the name of the object followed immediately by a period (.) and the name of the method.
Set a property in code	Type the name of the property followed by the equal sign (=) and then the value you want to assign to the property.
Add a comment to a procedure	Type an apostrophe followed by your comment text.
Get Help on a keyword in the Module window	Click the keyword and press F1.

For online information about	On the Help menu, click Microsoft Access Help Topics, click the Index tab, and then
Editing code in modules	Search for "modules"
Setting form and control properties	Search for "setting properties"
Using methods in Visual Basic	Search for "methods"
Assigning values in Visual Basic	Search for "assigning values to controls"

For more information on	In *Building Applications with Microsoft Access*, see
Editing code in modules	Chapter 2, "Introducing Visual Basic"
Setting form and control properties	Chapter 3, "Using Forms to Collect, Display, and Filter Information"
Using methods in Visual Basic	Chapter 5, "Working with Objects and Collections"
Assigning values in Visual Basic	Chapter 3, "Using Forms to Collect, Display, and Filter Information"

Preview of the Next Lesson

Now that you've learned to create and edit simple event procedures, you're ready to discover other ways to customize forms using Visual Basic. In the next lesson, you'll explore ways to help users find and filter data. You'll start with simple code like the code you saw in this lesson, but you'll also write some longer procedures—and learn new elements of Visual Basic along the way.

Find and Filter Records in a Form

In this lesson you will learn how to:

Estimated time
45 min.

■ Create a combo box that moves to a specific record in a form.

■ Filter data to show a subset of records.

■ Use the Debug window to view and change properties.

■ Respond to filtering events.

■ Create an option group.

In the 19th century, scientists discovered the laws of thermodynamics, which govern all physical systems in nature. The second law, they said, is that every system tends toward entropy—in other words, that everything is becoming more and more disorderly. Sound familiar? These scientists didn't intend the law to apply directly to our daily lives—but nonetheless, the premise seems to hold true. The more information we have, the more difficult it is to find what we want—and the more important it is that we locate the details we need quickly.

"Where did I put that phone number? I know it's in here somewhere...." How many times have you filed some important information away, only to spend precious time looking for it later? And while this routine is especially commonplace in the world of the "paper" office, it isn't altogether solved when you put information in your computer—you can still spend plenty of time wading through files and records trying to find what you need.

The key to a useful database is being able to find the information you need quickly. As an application developer, you need to consider what information users will need, and help them get to it as quickly as possible. In the first two lessons, we concentrated on getting data into the database; in this lesson, we'll work on getting it back out.

Start the lesson

➤ Start Microsoft Access and open the 03 Contacts database in the practice files folder.

Creating a Combo Box to Find Records

Perhaps the most common task you'll perform in any database application is to look up an existing record. In the Contacts database, when you need someone's phone number or address, you want to jump to the person's record quickly. The standard way users can find a record in a form is by using the Find command: first click the LastName field, then click the Find button, and then type the name you're looking for and click OK. Not only does this method require several actions for a common task, it assumes that you know the exact last name and can spell it correctly.

There are much better methods you can provide for finding records in your applications. One was is to create a combo box on the form where users can select a contact name from a list. This type of combo box requires setting quite a few properties, as well as writing a macro or event procedure that moves to the record. Fortunately, the Combo Box Wizard can do just about all of this for you—you need only put on the final touches to make it work just right.

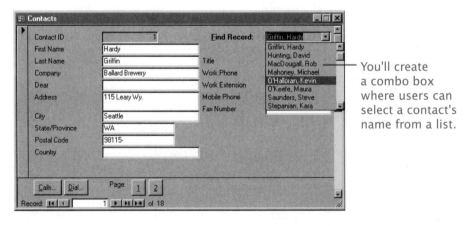

You'll create a combo box where users can select a contact's name from a list.

Open the Contacts form and switch to Design view

1 On the Main Switchboard form, click Enter/View Contacts.

2 Click the Design View button on the toolbar.

Design View button

Create a combo box that finds records

To create the Find Record combo box, you'll use the Combo Box Wizard.

Control Wizards tool

Combo Box tool

1 In the toolbox, make sure the Control Wizards tool is selected, and then click the Combo Box tool.

2 Click the top of the form above the left side of the Title field.

Click here to create the combo box.

The Combo Box Wizard starts, asking how you want the combo box to get the values it will display in the list.

3 Select the third option, Find A Record On My Form Based On The Value I Selected In My Combo Box, and then click Next.

The wizard asks which fields you want to include in the combo box.

4 Double-click the LastName field to add it to the Selected Fields list, and then click Next.

Add the LastName field to the list.

The wizard displays the list of last names.

5 Drag the right side of the field selector in the LastName column to make it about half again as wide, and then click Next.

The wizard asks what label you want for your combo box.

6 Type **&Find Record:** and then click Finish.

The wizard creates the combo box and places it on your form. Behind the scenes, the wizard has set properties and added a Visual Basic event procedure so that the combo box can find records in the form.

Change the appearance of the combo box

Before you try out the combo box, you'll want modify its appearance just a bit. For starters, its label isn't big enough for the text. Additionally, because this is a special control on the form—it's a helpful tool, but users don't have to enter any data in it—you'll want it to stand out in appearance.

Bold button

1 Click the label to the left of the control, and then click the Bold button on the toolbar.

2 Move the mouse pointer to the right edge of the label until you see the sizing cursor, and then double-click.

The label changes to the correct size for the text.

3 Click the combo box itself, and then drag the right edge of the combo box to make it the same width as the controls below it.

Back Color button

4 On the toolbar, click the arrow next to the Back Color button, and then click the light gray box.

Try out the combo box

Now the Find Record combo box is ready to use.

Form View button

1 Click the Form View button on the toolbar.

2 Click the arrow next to the Find Record combo box.

Microsoft Access displays the list of contact's last names in the list.

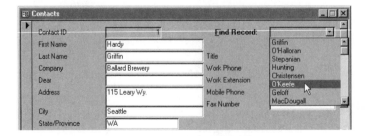

3 Click O'Keefe.

Microsoft Access moves to the record for Maura O'Keefe in the Contacts form.

Modify the combo box list

The Find Record combo box works as planned, but the list it displays isn't quite right. First of all, the list isn't alphabetized. Secondly, the list includes only last names. Ideally, you'd like it to display "last name comma first name"—such as Geloff, Kevin—so you can more easily find the record you want.

Design View button

1 Click the Design View button on the toolbar.

2 With the right mouse button, click the Find Record combo box, and then click Properties on the shortcut menu.

Microsoft Access displays the property sheet for the combo box.

3 Click the All tab in the property sheet.

4 Click the RowSource property, and then click the Build button to the right of the property box.

Click the Build button to display the Query Builder.

Microsoft Access displays the Query Builder window. In the window is the query that provides values for the combo box drop-down list.

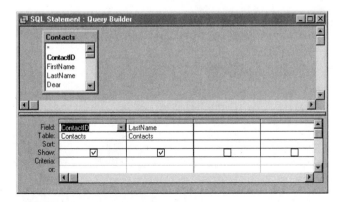

You want to modify this query so it displays last names combined with first names.

51

5   In the Query By Example (QBE) grid in the lower part of the window, click the box displaying the LastName field, and change the text to the following expression: **LastName & ", " & FirstName** (be sure to include a space after the comma in quotes).

This expression combines three string values with the ampersand (&) operator. When you want to put more than one string of text together in expressions or in Visual Basic code, you separate them with an ampersand. This is known as *concatenating* the strings. In this case, the expression concatenates each contact's last name and first name, separated by a comma and a space.

Note that when you click outside the expression, Microsoft Access automatically adds a label *(Expr1:)* for the expression and encloses field names in brackets. If you want to see the whole expression, you can make the column wider by dragging the right edge of its column selector to the right.

6   Click the Sort box underneath the expression you just entered, click the drop-down arrow, and then click Ascending.

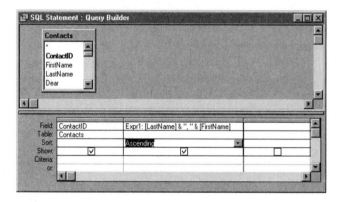

7   Close the Query Builder window, clicking Yes when Microsoft Access asks if you want to save changes to the query.

Try out the new list

Now the Find Record combo box should display complete names in alphabetical order.

Form View button

1   Click the Form View button on the toolbar.

2   Click the arrow next to the Find Record combo box.

Sure enough, Microsoft Access displays the list of names in order, last names followed by first names.

3   Click Geloff, Kevin (you may need to scroll up in the list).

Add code to keep the combo box synchronized

There's one last idiosyncrasy with the Find Record combo box—although it finds records well enough, it doesn't always display the name of the current contact. If you change records with some other method than using the combo box, the combo box doesn't stay synchronized—it may not display the current record. Because this could be misleading, you'll add a line of code to the form's module to fix the problem.

1   Click the Next Record button at the bottom of the form window.

As you can see, while the form changes to the next record, the Find Record combo box doesn't update to display the current name—it still shows Geloff, Kevin.

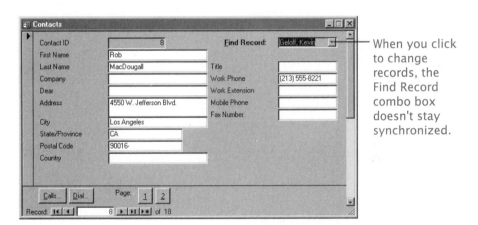

When you click to change records, the Find Record combo box doesn't stay synchronized.

This happens because this combo box, unlike all other controls on the form, is an *unbound* control. Unbound controls can be very useful in an application, because users can change them without changing any data, and the application can respond accordingly. The flip side, however, is that if you want an unbound control to display data, you have to set its value in code yourself.

Design View button

2   Click the Design View button on the toolbar.

The Find Record combo box should still be selected, its properties shown in the property sheet. Note the name of the combo box in the title bar of the property sheet—something like Combo54—which is a default name given to the control when the wizard creates it. You'll need to know this name for the code you'll write.

3   Click the form selection box at the upper left corner of the form window (you may need to move or close the toolbox).

4   Click the Event tab in the property sheet.

53

5   Click the OnCurrent property, and then click the Build button to the right of the property box.

Click the
Build button
to display the
Code Builder.

6   Select Code Builder, and then click OK.

Microsoft Access opens the form module for the Contacts form and displays the Form_Current event procedure.

7   Press TAB, and then add the following line of Visual Basic code to the procedure (substituting the actual number of the combo box on your own form):

```
Combo54 = ContactID    ' Update the Find Record combo box.
```

This code sets the value of the combo box control to the value of the ContactID control. This way, each time you move to a new contact, the combo box will change along with the rest of the form. As when you set a property, all you do to set the value of a control is type the control name followed by the equal sign and the value you want to set it to.

8   On the Window menu, click Contacts : Form.

9   Click the Form View button on the toolbar.

*Form View
button*

10   Click the arrow next to the Find Record combo box, and then click Geloff, Kevin.

11   Click the Next Record button at the bottom of the form window.

While the form changes to the record for Rob MacDougall, the Form_Current event procedure runs, and your code synchronizes the Find Record combo box: it displays MacDougall, Rob.

Save your changes to the Contacts form

It took a bit of work, but now the Contacts form has a highly visible, easy-to-use tool for jumping to a contact's record. Now save your changes to the form.

Save button

➤ Click the Save button on the toolbar.

Microsoft Access saves all changes to the form and its form module.

Filtering Data

The combo box you created jumps to an individual record in the recordset. However, all the rest of the records are still available—you can move to other records by clicking the record navigation buttons at the bottom of the form window. But when you're trying to locate certain contacts, you may not want all the records to be available. For example, suppose your company is located in New York City, and you want to place calls to local customers. To browse through contacts located in New York, excluding all contacts in other cities, you use a *filter*.

You can think of a filter as a funnel for data that lets through the specific records you ask for, but keeps all the rest out of view. In fact, the filter icon in Microsoft Access is a funnel—you can see it on the Apply Filter button on the toolbar.

Apply Filter button

There are three Microsoft Access filtering commands available to the user:

Filter By Selection limits data to records that have the currently selected value. For example, if you're viewing a contact in New York, you can click the City field and then the Filter By Selection button, and contacts from all other cities will be filtered out of the recordset.

Filter By Form displays a blank version of the current form, where you can select from existing field values and then apply the filter to view records that match the selected criteria. For example, you can click the Filter By Form button, select New York in the list of City values, and then click the Apply Filter button to show only contacts in New York. Using Filter By Form, you can specify criteria for more than one field at a time.

Advanced Filter/Sort displays a query window, where you can drag fields to the QBE grid and specify criteria for sorting. This type of filter is the most flexible, but requires an understanding of the Microsoft Access query window.

Unless you disable them, these standard filtering commands are available to users. Even if your application doesn't do any filtering of its own, users can choose these commands to browse through a subset of data in a table or form.

Filter records in the Contacts form using Filter By Form

Suppose you want to view contacts in New York City.

Filter By Form button

1 Click the Filter By Form button on the toolbar.

The form changes to display the Filter By Form view, where users can specify criteria for the records they want to see.

2 Click the City field, and then click the down-arrow next to the text box.

Microsoft Access displays all the cities where contacts are located.

3 Click New York.

4 Click the Apply Filter button.

Apply Filter button

The form displays only contacts in New York. Note that the text at the bottom of the form window indicates that the recordset in the form is filtered.

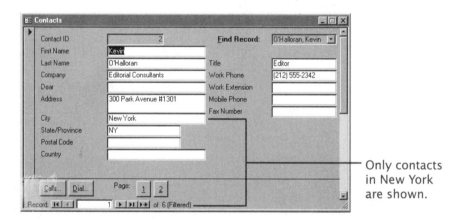

Only contacts in New York are shown.

Responding to Filtering Events

Although the filtering interface in Microsoft Access is very flexible, there's always room for improvement. If you want to control or customize filtering in your application, you can write Visual Basic event procedures that respond to one of two filtering events. The first of these events is the Filter event, which is triggered whenever a user chooses the Filter By Form or Advanced Filter/Sort command. You can respond to the Filter event to customize these commands.

The other filtering event is the ApplyFilter event, which occurs when the user finishes specifying a filter and clicks the Apply Filter button, or when the user clicks the Filter By Selection button, which applies a filter immediately. This event also occurs when the user removes a filter—basically, whenever the set of records displayed is about to be changed. You can respond to the ApplyFilter event to change filtering behavior when the user chooses these buttons or commands.

To start, you'll provide a simple customization of the Filter By Form command by responding to the Filter event with an event procedure.

Display a message when the user filters

For beginning users, the Filter By Form interface can be confusing—when a user clicks this button, the form changes slightly in appearance and goes blank, and a user might not know what to do next. It would be helpful to display a simple message, providing the user with a hint explaining what to do next.

1 On the Window menu, click Form_Contacts : Module.

Microsoft Access brings the Contacts form's module back to the front, still showing the Form_Current event procedure. Because you're already viewing an event procedure for the form, the easiest way to create the procedure is by using the Module window's Proc box (short for "procedure or event box").

2 In the Proc box at the top of the Module window, select Filter from the list of events.

Select the Filter event in the Proc box.

Microsoft Access creates the Form_Filter procedure for you—you don't have to go back to the property sheet. Behind the scenes, Microsoft Access also automatically attaches the procedure to the control's Filter event by setting the control's OnFilter property to [Event Procedure]. (The OnFilter property is the event property that corresponds to the Filter event.)

3 Enter the following Visual Basic code for the procedure:

```
' Display instructions for Filter by Form.

    MsgBox "Select field values, then click the Apply Filter button."
```

This code displays the message whenever the user chooses a filtering command.

Using the If...Then Statement to Check a Condition

There's just one problem with the Filter event procedure—there's more than one filtering command that can trigger the Filter event. Because your message is applicable only if the user chose the Filter By Form command, you want to check in your code and make sure this was the command. Fortunately, it's easy to find out which command the user chose—Microsoft Access provides this information using the FilterType argument of the event procedure.

Check whether the user chose Filter By Form

To perform steps in code only when a condition is met, you use the Visual Basic If...Then statement. In this case, the condition you want to check is whether the FilterType argument of the event procedure is equal to the constant value acFilterByForm. If it is, that's when you want to display your message.

> Add lines of code before and after the existing line in the procedure, so that it reads as follows (you'll also want to add a tab before each line to indent it properly):

```
If FilterType = acFilterByForm Then
    MsgBox "Select field values, then click the Apply Filter button."
End If
```

The code between the If...Then and End If statements gets run only if the condition is true—in this case, if the FilterType argument is equal to the value of the constant acFilterByForm. In plain English, you can read these three lines of code as saying, "If the filter type the user chose is Filter By Form, then please display this message—otherwise, please do nothing." (Of course, you should always say please.)

Try the event procedure

Now that you've fixed it up, let's make sure the event procedure works as planned.

1 On the Window menu, click Contacts.

Filter By Form button

2 Click the Filter By Form button on the toolbar.

The Filter event occurs, triggering your event procedure. Because you chose the Filter By Form button, the condition in the If...Then statement is true, and the MsgBox statement runs and displays your message.

3 Click OK.

After your procedure finishes, the form appears in Filter By Form view.

4 Click the Cancel button on the toolbar.

Using conditional code as you've done here makes your application "smart"—it provides logic to your procedures, and is the first step toward powerful Visual Basic programming. This simple use of the If...Then statement performs just one action—but that's only the beginning of what you can do using conditional statements in Visual Basic. Soon, you'll use the If...Then statement to perform several lines of code depending on the value of a condition.

Understanding Filtering Properties

Whenever the user filters data using any of the standard filtering commands, Microsoft Access sets two form properties that reflect the filtering status of the form: the Filter property and the FilterOn property. The Filter property describes the criteria for the current filter—for example, the criterion for contacts in New York can be expressed as:

```
City = "New York"
```

The FilterOn property setting determines whether the filter is currently applied. When there's no filter, the FilterOn property is set to False; when the user applies a filter, it gets set to True.

In Visual Basic code, you can use the Filter and FilterOn properties to determine what the current filter is and whether it's in effect. More importantly, you can set these properties to affect the current filter on a form—actually changing the records that are displayed. This allows you to provide a custom filtering interface, setting the filtering status behind the scenes whenever you want. In this section, you'll see how these properties work on the Contacts form, and then provide a custom method for changing the filter on the form.

Using the Debug Window to View and Set Properties

In programming lingo, a "bug" is an error or mistake in programming code. Microsoft Access has several tools that help you find bugs or problems. The most important of these tools is the Debug window. In later lessons, you'll learn many techniques for *debugging* Visual Basic code with the Debug window and other tools. But there are also simple uses for the Debug window—one of which you'll try out in this section as you learn more about filtering data.

The Debug window is a great place to test properties and the way they work in Visual Basic. Usually, you place Visual Basic code in a module, and the code runs later on—for example, in response to an event. But in the Debug window, when you type Visual Basic code, it runs right away—as soon as you press ENTER.

Try out the Debug window

Because it's so convenient, the Debug window is a great place to try things out. It's also a good place to find out the current value of a property or expression. If you want to know the value of any Visual Basic expression, you can display it in the Debug window by typing a question mark (?) followed by the expression.

1   On the Window menu, click Form_Contacts : Module.

Debug Window button

2   Click the Debug Window button on the toolbar.

Microsoft Access displays the Debug window, ready for you to enter Visual Basic commands.

3   Type **Beep** and press ENTER (and listen closely).

Your computer beeps—Beep is a Visual Basic statement, and when you type it in the Debug window, it runs immediately.

4   Type **?1+1** and press ENTER.

Typing this statement asks Microsoft Access a question: "What is the value of 1+1?" Microsoft Access displays the answer directly underneath your statement in the Debug window—it's 2. Bet you didn't know that Microsoft Access was such a fancy calculator!

Use the Debug window to view and set filtering properties

Making your computer beep (or add) is hardly a powerful use of the Debug window. Now that we've established what it does, let's put the Debug window to work. First, you'll use the Debug window to find out the value of the filtering properties for the Contacts form. Then, you'll actually change the value of these properties from the Debug window—in just the same way you've set properties in your event procedures.

1   Type **?Forms!Contacts.Filter**

This statement asks Microsoft Access to tell you the value of the expression to the right of the question mark—an expression that refers to the Filter property of the Contacts form. This expression is like an address to someone's house, describing to Microsoft Access exactly what property you're talking about. Here's how the expression works: the keyword *Forms* refers to the collection of forms in the current database; you follow it with an exclamation point and the name of a form, such as Contacts. Then, to indicate a property of the form, you follow the form reference with a period and the name of the property.

In short, this statement asks the question, "What is the value of the Filter property for the Contacts form?"

2   Press ENTER.

Microsoft Access displays the value of the expression—the filter you applied earlier to see only contacts in New York.

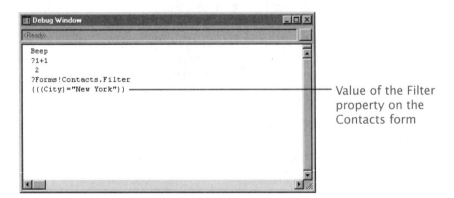

Value of the Filter property on the Contacts form

3   Type **?Forms!Contacts.FilterOn** and press ENTER.

The window displays the value of the FilterOn property for the Contacts form, which is -1. In Visual Basic, negative one (-1) is the numeric equivalent of True, while zero (0) is the equivalent of False. Because the filter is currently applied on the Contacts form, the value of the FilterOn property is True (-1).

4   Type **Forms!Contacts.FilterOn = False** and press ENTER.

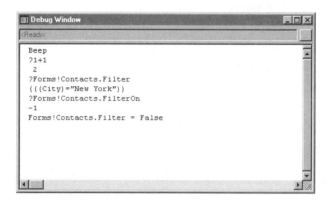

This statement sets the FilterOn property of the Contacts form to False, effectively removing the filter from the form—just as if the user had clicked the Remove Filter button.

5   Close the Debug window.

6   On the Window menu, click Contacts.

As you can see, the form now displays all contact records—you successfully removed the filter using the Debug window.

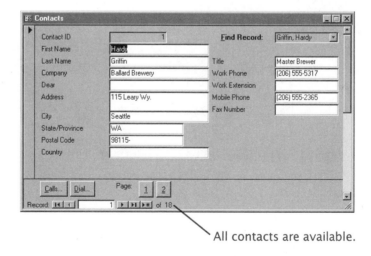

All contacts are available.

By viewing and setting the Filter and FilterOn properties in code, you can monitor or change the filter of any form. Now that you've seen how these properties work in the Debug window, it's time to use them to customize the Contacts form.

Creating an Option Group to Filter Data

Suppose the filter you've set—to view contacts in New York—is very common in your application. You should make it easy for users to filter records, even if they don't know how to use Filter By Form. A good way to do this is by adding an *option group* to the form—a group of buttons from which users can choose the records they want to see.

In this section, you'll add an option group to the Contacts form with two options for viewing records: all contacts, or just New York contacts. Whenever the user clicks a different option in the group, an event procedure that you write will respond by changing filtering properties to affect which records are displayed in the form.

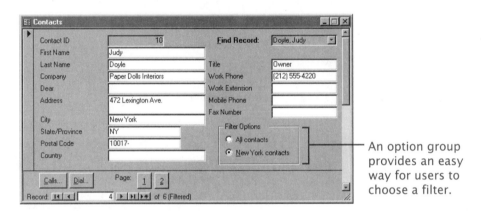

An option group provides an easy way for users to choose a filter.

Create the option group

An option group has many parts—but you can create them all at once using the Option Group Wizard. The wizard lets you specify all the options in the group, and it takes care of the details.

*Design View.
button*

Toolbox button

*Option Group
tool*

1   Click the Design View button on the toolbar.

2   Close the property sheet.

3   If the toolbox isn't displayed, click the Toolbox button on the toolbar.

4   In the toolbox, click the Option Group tool.

5 Scroll down a bit in the form window, and click the open space below the Fax Number field.

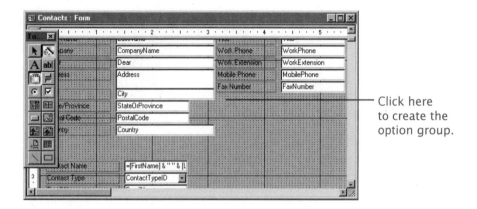

Click here to create the option group.

The Option Group Wizard starts, asking what option buttons you want in the option group.

6 Type **A&ll contacts** and then press TAB.

7 Type **&New York contacts** and then click Next.

The wizard asks if you want a default button to be selected automatically when you open the form, suggesting the All Contacts button.

8 Click Next.

The wizard shows you the values that each of the options will have. The All Contacts option corresponds to the number 1, the New York Contacts option to the number 2.

9 Click Next.

The wizard asks whether you want to use the value later or store the value in a field—that is, whether you want your option group to be an unbound or a bound control. You want the default option—Save The Value For Later Use—making the option group an unbound control.

10 Click Next.

The wizard asks about the style you want for your option group and buttons. Change it if you want to be fancy—the wizard shows you an example of what your choice will look like—or just accept the default style.

11 Click Next.

The wizard asks what label you want for the option group.

12 Type **Filter Options** and then click Finish.

The wizard creates the option group and its two buttons, and then places it on your form.

Unfortunately, the wizard doesn't give the option group a very sensible name (something like Frame58). Because you want to refer to the option group in Visual Basic code, you should rename it in the property sheet.

Properties button

13 Click the Properties button on the toolbar, and then click the Other tab in the property sheet.

14 In the Name property box, type **FilterOptions**

Add an event procedure to make the option group work

The option group you've created is an unbound control, like the Find Record combo box you created earlier. To make it work, you need to write an event procedure that sets the filter properties for the Contacts form. Each time you click an option in an option group, its AfterUpdate event occurs, so you can respond accordingly. In the event procedure, you'll perform a different action depending on which option button the user clicks.

1 Click the Event tab in the property sheet.

2 Click the AfterUpdate property box, and then click the Build button to the right of the property box.

3 Select Code Builder, and then click OK.

Microsoft Access opens the Module window and creates the AfterUpdate event procedure for the option group.

4 Enter the following code for the procedure (except the Sub and End Sub lines, which are already there):

```
Private Sub FilterOptions_AfterUpdate()
' Apply or remove the filter for the option the user chose.

    If FilterOptions = 2 Then
            Me.Filter = "City = 'New York'"
            Me.FilterOn = True      ' Apply the filter.
    Else
            Me.FilterOn = False     ' Remove the filter.
    End If
End Sub
```

Let's walk through this code line by line:

■ As you've seen, the If...Then structure lets you perform an action only if a certain condition is true. But before, you added only one line of code between the If...Then and End If statements. This code uses If...Then in a powerful new way—if the condition is true, Microsoft Access runs all the indented lines under the If...Then statement. This is known as a *block* of code, indented to show that it all belongs within the same If...Then...End If structure.

The condition here tests whether the value of the option group is 2: the number of the New York Contacts option. If the user clicks the second option in the group, the condition will be true, and Microsoft Access will run the code in the block.

■ The first statement in this block of code sets the Filter property for the form. The Filter property accepts a string setting, which means you surround the setting in quotation marks. This setting says that you only want the form to show records for which the City field is equal to the value 'New York'— which you surround with single quotation marks, because it's also a string value.

■ The second statement in the block sets the form's FilterOn property to True, applying the filter. When Microsoft Access runs this statement, it will requery the records in the form, displaying only those that meet the filter criteria.

■ The If...Then structure in this procedure uses another new feature—the Else keyword, which allows you to add a line or block of code that runs if the condition is false. You can think of this If...Then statement as saying, "If the option group value is 2, do this block of code—otherwise do this other block of code."

■ The other block in this case is a single line that sets the FilterOn property to False. This way, if the user clicks the All Contacts option, your event procedure will remove the filter.

■ The End If statement marks the end of the Else code block. Any lines after this one would run regardless of whether the condition is true. Every If...Then statement must have a corresponding End If statement.

Try the option group

It's time to test the code by clicking values in the option group.

1 On the Window menu, click Contacts : Form.

2 Close the property sheet.

Form View button

3 Click the Form View button on the toolbar.

The option group shows its default value—the All Contacts option—and all records are available in the form.

4 Click the New York Contacts button in the option group.

The AfterUpdate event occurs for the option group, and your event procedure runs. Because the option you selected is option number 2, your code sets the Filter property to show only New York contacts and applies the filter.

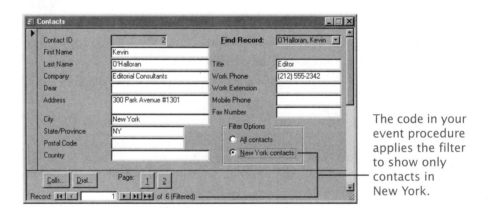

The code in your event procedure applies the filter to show only contacts in New York.

5 Click the All Contacts button in the option group.

This time, your event procedure removes the filter.

Add an event procedure to respond when the user filters

The option group works great, but there's still one problem with this strategy—it doesn't take into account the fact that other standard filtering commands are still available. What if the user changes the filter in another way? Will the option group update automatically?

As you customize your applications, it's important to anticipate conflicts like this. Let's take a look at this problem, and add another event procedure to solve it.

1 Click the City field.

For this contact, the value of the City field is Seattle.

Filter By
Selection button

2 Click the Filter By Selection button on the toolbar.

The form now displays only contacts in Seattle. But the option group still shows All Records—which is no longer true! To avoid misleading users, you should update the option group control whenever users filter data.

The easiest way to indicate that the user's filter is in effect is for the option group to show neither option in the group as selected. To do this, you want to set the value of the option group control to Null any time the user applies a filter. If the user removes the filter, on the other hand, you might as well set the option group value to 1 (the All Contacts option), because removing the filter is the same as clicking the All Contacts option.

3 On the Window menu, click Form_Contacts : Module.

4 In the Object box at the top of the Module window, select Form from the list of objects.

5 In the Proc box, select ApplyFilter from the list of events.

Select the Form object...

... and then select the ApplyFilter event procedure.

6 Enter the following code for the procedure:

```
Private Sub Form_ApplyFilter(Cancel As Integer, ApplyType As Integer)
' Set the option group value to match the user's filtering action.

    If ApplyType = acShowAllRecords Then
        FilterOptions = 1
    Else
        FilterOptions = Null
    End If

End Sub
```

Here's what this code does:

- The If...Then statement checks to see whether the ApplyType argument to the event procedure is equal to the constant value acShowAllRecords. This ApplyType value would indicate that the user removed the filter to show all contact records.

- If the condition is true—the user did remove the filter—the line of code after the If...Then statement sets the FilterOptions control value to 1, automatically selecting the All Contacts button in the option group.

- If the condition is false—the user applied another filter—the line of code after the Else statement sets the FilterOptions control value to Null, causing the control to show neither option as selected.

7   On the Window menu, click Contacts.

8   Select the New York Contacts option.

    The form displays only those records for which the city is New York.

Remove Filter button

9   Click the Remove Filter button on the toolbar.

    When you remove the filter, the ApplyFilter event procedure runs, automatically returning the option group to the All Records option.

Filter By Selection button

10 Click the City field, and then click the Filter By Selection button on the toolbar.

    The form now displays only contacts in Seattle, just as you requested. Even better, because of your event procedure, the option group now appears without either option selected, indicating that you have applied your own filter.

As you can see, filtering is a powerful feature—but you'll need to consider carefully how the various filtering commands interact. Fortunately, between the Filter and ApplyFilter events and the Filter and FilterOn properties, Microsoft Access provides all the tools you need to control filtering in your Visual Basic code.

Close the application and exit Microsoft Access

1   Close the Contacts form, clicking Yes when Microsoft Access asks if you want to save changes.

2   On the Switchboard form, click Exit This Database.

3   On the File menu, click Exit.

Lesson Summary

To	Do this
Create a combo box to find records	Choose the Find A Record On My Form... option in the Combo Box Wizard.
Concatenate (combine) string values in an expression	Separate each string value with the ampersand (&) character.
Set a control's value in code	Type the control reference followed by the equal sign (=), then the value you want to assign to the control.
Run a block of code conditionally	Surround the block of code with the If...Then and End If statements, specifying a true or false condition to determine whether the code runs. To include a block that runs if the condition is false, add the Else statement.
Run a Visual Basic command immediately	Type the command in the Debug window and press ENTER.
View the value of an expression, property, or control	In the Debug window, type a question mark (?) followed by the expression, and then press ENTER.
Perform actions when a user chooses the Filter By Form or Advanced Filter/Sort command	Write an event procedure for the form's Filter event.
Perform actions when the user chooses to apply or remove a form's filter	Write an event procedure for the form's ApplyFilter event.
Change the filter of a form	Set the form's Filter property. To apply or remove the filter, set the FilterOn property.

For online information about	On the Help menu, click Microsoft Access Help Topics, click the Index tab, and then
Creating and using combo boxes	Search for "combo boxes"
Finding and filtering records in a form	Search for "finding records"
Referring to forms and controls in an expression	Search for "expressions"
Using the Debug window	Search for "Debug window"

For more information on	In *Building Applications with Microsoft Access*, see
Creating and using combo boxes	Chapter 3, "Using Forms to Collect, Display, and Filter Information"
Finding and filtering records in a form	Chapter 3, "Using Forms to Collect, Display, and Filter Information"
Referring to forms and controls in an expression	Chapter 5, "Working with Objects and Collections"
Using the Debug window	Chapter 8, "Handling Run-Time Errors"

Preview of the Next Lesson

In the next lesson, you'll explore the common events that occur on a form during data entry, and create event procedures to respond to many of those events. Along the way, you'll make some final enhancements to the Contacts form, and learn new ways that your application can interact with the user.

Lesson

4

Respond to Data Entry Events

Estimated time
40 min.

In this lesson you will learn how to:

■ Set the value of a control in code.

■ Respond to users' actions as they move around in a form.

■ Make sure that the data a user enters is valid.

■ Ask a question and perform different actions based on a user's choice.

Data entry can be time-consuming and monotonous, especially with a database system that's poorly designed. But data entry is also an art—when you get on a roll, you can surprise yourself with how quickly you enter information. The key to a successful data entry system lies in anticipating what information gets entered; providing shortcuts; and avoiding unnecessary clicking, typing, and moving around. With an efficient data entry form, there's time to concentrate on getting the information right, rather than just getting the job done.

As a database developer, one of your primary concerns is to facilitate this job of getting information into the database—after all, a database is not worth much more than the data you can put in and get out of it. Your goal is to make the job of data entry personnel as easy and fast as possible. At the same time, you want to ensure that the data they enter is complete and accurate. It's a big challenge. In this lesson, you'll learn how to enhance a data entry form by anticipating the way users will enter data and writing Visual Basic code to respond to events.

Start the lesson

▶ Start Microsoft Access and open the 04 Contacts database in the practice files folder.

Understanding Form and Control Events

Events are happening on your forms and controls all the time. Every time you press a key, use the mouse, or change data, an event occurs. Click the mouse—event! Change a field—event! And each event gives you a chance to make something happen in your application by attaching code to the event procedure.

Open the Contacts form

▶ On the Main Switchboard form, click Enter/View Contacts.

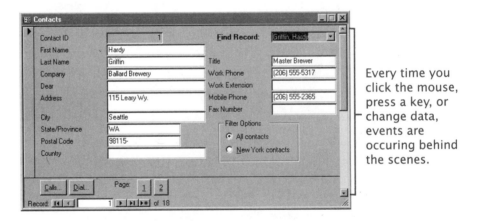

Every time you click the mouse, press a key, or change data, events are occuring behind the scenes.

From the point of view of your application, the events on a form occur randomly. You have no way of knowing *why*, for example, the user enters a certain control, or what the user will do next—you have to take each event as it comes. In some ways, events are like little fires popping up here and there, and your application is the fire department, running in to put them out. And like the fire department, your application must be prepared for anything.

The trick to programming events is figuring out which events to respond to and how. After you set up the responses, your application works automatically. Here's a list of the most common things users do on a data entry form, along with the events that you can respond to.

User actions	Associated event procedures
Opening and closing the form	Open, Close, Load, Unload
Moving to and from the form	Activate, Deactivate
Moving from control to control	Enter, Exit, GotFocus, LostFocus
Moving from record to record	Current
Pressing keys	KeyDown, KeyUp, KeyPress
Clicking the mouse	Click, DoubleClick, MouseDown, MouseUp
Changing data and saving records	BeforeUpdate, AfterUpdate
Adding records	BeforeInsert, AfterInsert
Deleting records	Delete, BeforeDelConfirm, AfterDelConfirm
Filtering records	Filter, ApplyFilter

These are only the most common events you might want to respond to in code—there are still others. In this lesson, you'll write Visual Basic code to respond to just a few of these events.

Performing Actions as the User Moves in a Form

Microsoft Access provides some cues to the user moving through a form: the title bar changes color when a form is active, the blinking insertion point indicates the current field, and the record indicator shows the current record, just to name a few. But you may want to customize this behavior or add additional cues for the user. You do this by responding to certain events. For example, when the user switches to a form, the Activate event occurs. To change something about the form or the Microsoft Access interface when a form becomes the active window, you write an event procedure for the Activate event. To return the interface to its previous state when the user moves to another form, you write code for the Deactivate event that reverses the effect.

You can also respond as the user moves within a form. As you saw in lessons 2 and 3, each time the user moves from one record to another, the Current event occurs. In addition, several events occur each time the user moves between controls on a form. When the user moves from one control to another, the Exit and LostFocus events occur for the control the user leaves, and the Enter and GotFocus events occur for the control the user moves to.

Suppose you want to change the color of a control whenever it is the active control on a form. You can do this by creating event procedures for the control's Enter and Exit events.

NOTE The Enter and Exit events occur when the user moves into or out of a control, but not when the user switches between windows in Microsoft Access. If you only care which control is current on the form, you can use Enter and Exit; if you also want to run the same code each time a control gets the focus from another window, use GotFocus and LostFocus.

Change the background color of a combo box

In Lesson 3, you created the Find Record combo box and set its background color to light gray to show that entering data in the control isn't required. But you'll want to make this control appear white again whenever it's the active control—after all, it seems a bit strange to select data from a control that's gray, as if it were disabled. To do this, you'll write a simple procedure for the control's Enter event.

You'll change the background of this control to white.

Design View button

1 Click the Design View button.

2 With the right mouse button, click the Find Record combo box, and then click Properties on the shortcut menu.

3 Click the Event tab in the property sheet.

4 Click the OnEnter property, and then click the Build button next to the property box.

Click the Build button.

5 Select Code Builder, and then click OK.

Microsoft Access opens the form module for the Contacts form and creates the event procedure for the combo box.

Remember, the name of the combo box is actually a default name—something like Combo54—that the Combo Box Wizard assigned when you created the control. You can see the actual name by looking at the event procedure's name (in the Sub statement at the top of the window).

6 Press TAB and type the following line of Visual Basic code for the procedure (substituting the actual number of your combo box for "54"):

```
Combo54.BackColor = 16777215    ' Change background to white.
```

This code sets the BackColor property to color 16777215—the code for the color white. As when you set a property of a form, you set a control property by typing the property name followed by the equal sign and the value you want to set it to. With a control property, however, you have to let Microsoft Access know which control you have in mind. To do this, you type the control name and a period before the property name.

Add a procedure to change the color back

The combo box will now change to white when you enter it—but you want to leave it the way you found it. To change the color back to gray when you leave, you'll write another procedure for the control's Exit event.

1 In the Proc box at the top of the Module window, select Exit from the list of events.

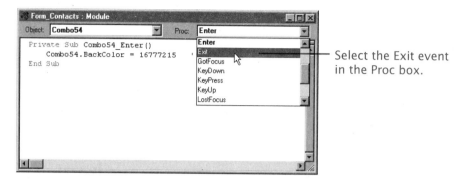

Select the Exit event in the Proc box.

Microsoft Access creates the Exit event procedure for you—and also sets the control's OnExit property to [Event Procedure] so the procedure will run when you exit the control.

2 Press TAB and type the following Visual Basic code for the procedure (again substituting the number of your combo box):

```
Combo54.BackColor = 12632256     ' Change background to gray.
```

This code sets the BackColor property of the combo box to the code for gray.

TIP Want to use other colors? You can find out the code for another color easily by setting a color using the palette in Form Design view, and then looking in the property sheet to see the corresponding code number for the color you chose.

Try out the new event procedures

*Form View
button*

1   On the Window menu, click Contacts : Form.

2   Click the Form View button.

3   Click the drop-down arrow next to the Find Record combo box.

  The Enter event for the combo box occurs, and your code changes the control's background to white.

4   Click the First Name field again.

  Back to an inconspicuous gray!

Performing Actions as the User Changes Data

Each time you change the value of a control, several events occur. Most of the events have to do with pressing keys and changing the focus, but two events deal specifically with changes to data: BeforeUpdate and AfterUpdate. BeforeUpdate occurs when the user tries to move out of a changed control or save a changed record; AfterUpdate occurs when the change is successfully completed.

In this section, you'll respond to the AfterUpdate event to perform an action after the user changes a control. Later in the lesson, you'll respond to the BeforeUpdate event to perform an action when the user tries to save a record.

Setting the Value of a Control "Auto-magically"

When entering data, there's nothing better than having the database enter information for you wherever it can. One way you can do this is to set the DefaultValue property for fields in your tables, so that when you add a new record, Microsoft Access fills in the field's value automatically. But this strategy doesn't work well if you want to fill in a field "on the fly" in response to an entry in another field. In this case, you can use an event procedure to respond to the user updating the one field, and provide Visual Basic code that updates the other field.

For example, the Contacts form has a Dear field that stores an informal name or nickname to be used in the salutation of a letter. For someone named Thomas, you might want to set this value to Tom, so that a letter you send out can use the familiar name in its greeting. Thing is, you'll want to address most people by their first name—so during data entry, you'd like the Dear field to get filled in automatically with the value the user enters in the FirstName field. Then, if necessary, you can always change the Dear field to something else.

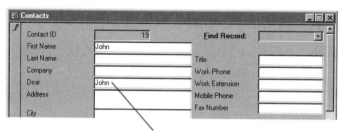

You want to fill in this field automatically.

Add an event procedure that sets the Dear control's value

The event that occurs when the user moves out of a field after changing its value is the AfterUpdate event. You'll place code in the AfterUpdate event procedure for this event to copy the FirstName value to the Dear field.

Design View button

1 Click the Design View button.

2 Click the FirstName control.

The property sheet shows event properties for the FirstName control.

3 Click the AfterUpdate property, and then click the Build button.

Click the Build button.

4 Select Code Builder, and then click OK.

Microsoft Access opens the form module for the Contacts form and creates the FirstName_AfterUpdate event procedure.

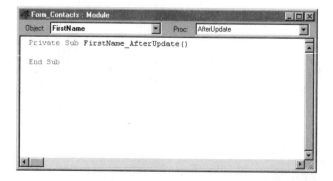

5 Type the following Visual Basic code for the procedure:

```
' Copy the FirstName value to the Dear control.

    Dear = FirstName
```

This line of code sets the value of the Dear control to the same value as the FirstName control.

Try out the event procedure

Form View button

New Record button

1 On the Window menu, click Contacts : Form.

2 Click the Form View button.

3 Click the New Record button on the toolbar.

4 In the FirstName field, type **John**, and then press TAB.

When you move out of the field, the AfterUpdate event occurs. Your code runs, setting the value of the Dear field. At this point, you could continue entering the record, either skipping the Dear field or manually changing its value if necessary. Instead, now that you know it works, undo the new record without saving it.

5 Press ESC.

Add code that checks whether the Dear field is blank

There's a minor glitch with our plan for the Dear field. Imagine this scenario: you enter a record for a Thomas Blanque, the first name Thomas gets copied to the Dear field, but you then change the Dear field to Tom. Then you realize you misspelled Thomas, so you go back and spell it correctly. Can you guess what happens? Your event procedure copies over the Dear field containing Tom—which really isn't what you want. Instead, you want the Contacts form to be smarter—you want it to copy the first name to the Dear field only when the Dear field is blank.

1 On the Window menu, click Form_Contacts : Module.

2 Add two lines of code before and after the existing line in the procedure, so that it reads as follows (you'll also want to add a tab before the word Dear to indent the line):

```
If IsNull(Dear) Then
    Dear = FirstName
End If
```

The IsNull function in Microsoft Access returns True if the item in parentheses is null (contains no value), False if it contains a value—so in this line, the code after the Then keyword gets run only if the Dear control is blank.

79

3   On the Window menu, click Contacts.

4   In the First Name field, type **Tomas**, and then press TAB.

Your event procedure runs. Because the Dear field is null, it copies the first name value to the Dear field just as it did before.

5   In the Last Name field, type **Blanque**

6   Press TAB twice, and then in the Dear field, type **Tom**

7   In the First Name field, click between the "T" and the "o" and type the **h** in Thomas.

8   Press TAB.

Your event procedure runs. This time, however, it doesn't copy the first name value to the Dear field because you've already filled it in—which means the expression *IsNull(Dear)* is false.

Responding to Keyboard Events

One way to provide shortcuts for users of your application is by giving them special keys that perform common actions. Keyboard shortcuts aren't as visible as command buttons—but you can have only so many command buttons on a form. In this section, you'll write an event procedure that responds to keyboard events and sets the value of several controls on the Contacts form.

Every time you press a key on a form, three events occur: KeyDown, KeyPress, and KeyUp. You use KeyPress to respond to normal characters—such as letters and numbers—as the user types them. You use the KeyDown and KeyUp events to handle the exact keys that are being pressed on the keyboard—including combinations that use special keys like SHIFT, ALT, and CTRL.

Add a KeyDown event procedure that sets control values

Most of your contacts are in New York City, so you want a quick way to enter values for New York in a contact's record. To do this, you'll create a KeyDown procedure for the City field that detects when a user presses the CTRL key and the number 1 key at the same time.

Design View button

1   Click the Design View button.

2   Click the City field to select it.

The property sheet should display the Event properties for the City field.

3 Click the OnKeyDown property, and then click the Build button.

Click the
Build button.

4 Select Code Builder, and then click OK.

Microsoft Access opens the form module for the Contacts form and creates the City_KeyDown event procedure.

5 Enter the following Visual Basic code for the procedure (the Sub and End Sub lines are already present):

```
Private Sub City_KeyDown(KeyCode As Integer, Shift As Integer)
' If key is CTRL+1, enter values for New York.

    If KeyCode = 49 And Shift = 2 Then     ' CTRL+1 was pressed.
        City = "New York"
        StateOrProvince = "NY"
        Country = "USA"
    End If
End Sub
```

The code in this procedure runs whenever a key or combination of keys is pressed. Using the KeyCode and Shift arguments, which contain numbers representing the key that was pressed and the status of the SHIFT and CTRL keys at the time it was pressed, the procedure determines whether the key combination was in fact the number 1 key along with the CTRL key. (The KeyCode value for the number 1 key is 49, and the Shift code of 2 indicates that the CTRL key was pressed.) If the key combination is CTRL+1, the three statements in the block assign values for New York to the three controls on the Contacts form.

6 On the Window menu, click Contacts : Form.

Form View button

New Record button

7 Click the Form View button on the toolbar.

8 Click the New Record button on the toolbar.

9 Click in the City field, and then press CTRL+1.

Your event procedure runs, filling in the three fields.

10 Press ESC.

Make the keyboard handler work anywhere on the form

As it stands, your keyboard shortcut works only if the focus is on the City field. If you want it to apply anywhere on the form, you'll have to modify the code to respond to the KeyDown event for the form instead of just for the City control. There's also another step you'll need to know about. Normally, keyboard events all occur for the control that has the focus, but they don't occur for the form. If you want all key events to be available to the form's event procedures, you can set the KeyPreview property for the form.

Design View button

1 Click the Design View button.

2 Click the form selection box (it's in the upper left corner of the window, at the intersection of the rulers).

The property sheet should display form properties.

3 Set the KeyPreview property to Yes.

Now all key events, regardless of which control they belong to, will fire the form's keyboard-handling procedures first, followed by those for the control that has the focus.

4 On the Window menu, click Form_Contacts : Module.

The Module window returns to the front, still displaying the previous event procedure.

5 In the procedure header (the Sub statement), select the word City, type **Form**, and then click on another line of code in the procedure to register the change.

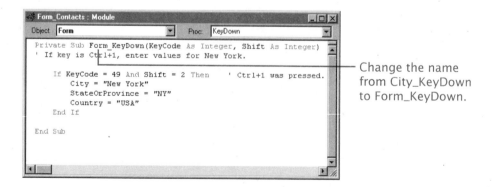

Change the name from City_KeyDown to Form_KeyDown.

Now the same code responds to the *form's* KeyDown event, so it will apply from anywhere on the form.

Form View button

6   On the Window menu, click Contacts : Form.

7   Click the Form View button on the toolbar.

8   Click the New Record button on the toolbar.

9   Press CTRL+1.

Your event procedure runs, filling in the three fields.

New Record button

10   Press ESC.

11   Click the Save button on the toolbar.

Microsoft Access saves your changes to the form.

Save button

The Contacts form is coming along very nicely—with code to set control values automatically, it's getting easier to use all the time. But we're not finished yet!

Validating Data

When entering data, it's easy to make mistakes or leave out important information. Errors or omissions in your data make your database less valuable and harder to use. One advantage of a database system is that it can check the data you enter, sometimes even refusing to save data that doesn't follow the rules. This process is referred to as *validation*, because it involves checking data to make sure it is valid.

There are several ways Microsoft Access checks data, most of which don't involve any programming. For a complex data-entry form, you'll typically use one or more of the following validation features:

Data types   This is the most simple form of validation, used in every database. Quite simply, Microsoft Access doesn't allow you to store data in a field if the data is inappropriate for the field's data type. For example, you can make sure a Date field always stores a date.

InputMask property   This property helps users enter data in fields that have formatting characters, such as the hyphens and parentheses in zip codes or phone numbers. Microsoft Access allows only values that fit the input mask. The phone number and postal code fields in the Contacts database have input masks (they were created automatically by the Database Wizard).

Required property   By setting this property for fields in a table, you can make sure they aren't left blank. If a user tries to blank a required field or save a record without entering a value for a required field, Microsoft Access displays a message.

ValidationRule property   By setting this property for fields, tables, or controls on forms, you can make sure data follows rules that you set. When the user updates a field or saves a record, Microsoft Access checks the data to make sure it fits with any validation expressions you've entered, and displays a message if it doesn't. You can specify the message that Microsoft Access displays by setting the ValidationText property.

BeforeUpdate event procedure   If you want to provide complex field validation that you can't write a validation expression for, you can write an event procedure that checks the data. Unlike other forms of validation in which Microsoft Access automatically displays a message, your BeforeUpdate event procedure must display a message and cancel the update.

The Contacts form already uses input masks. In this section, you'll add other validation, first setting properties in the Contacts table, and then creating a BeforeUpdate event procedure that checks data each time a user saves a record.

Require that each record have a complete name

To ensure that a field always has a value, you set the Required property in the table.

1 Close the Contacts form.

You have to close the Contacts form, because you can't modify the design of a table when the form is open.

Database Window button

2 Click the Database Window button on the toolbar.

3 Click the Tables tab, select the Contacts table, and then click Design.

Microsoft Access opens the table in Design view.

4 Click the FirstName field.

5 In the lower half of the window, set the Required property to Yes.

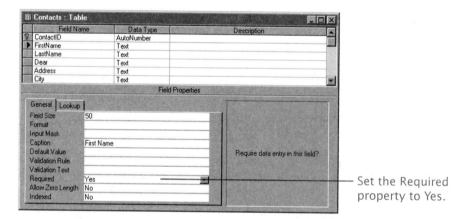

— Set the Required property to Yes.

6 Click the LastName field, and set the Required property to Yes.

Now Microsoft Access won't allow the user to save a contact without entering both a first and last name.

Require that each record include a phone number

Because you often print a phone list, you'd like to make sure that users enter either a work phone number or a mobile phone number for every contact. If you wanted to require entry in both fields, you'd set the Required property as you did for the name fields. But because either one or both of the phone numbers is acceptable, you'll need to use a different strategy. To provide a validation rule that involves more than one field in a table, you set the table's ValidationRule property.

Properties button

1 Click the Properties button on the toolbar.

2 In the property sheet, click the ValidationRule property, and then type **[WorkPhone] Or [MobilePhone]**

This validation expression uses the Or operator to test whether the phone fields contain text. Logical operators such as Or treat everything as either true or false: fields that contain text are true, fields that don't are false. You can think of this expression as asking, "Is it true that either the WorkPhone field or the MobilePhone field contains text?"

If both phone fields are blank, then the entire expression is false, which tells Microsoft Access that the record is invalid. Note that you must include the brackets around the field names you use in the validation expression, or else the property sheet will interpret them as string expressions instead of field names.

3 Click the ValidationText property, and then type **You must enter either a work phone or a mobile phone.**

This is the message Microsoft Access displays if the record is invalid.

4 Close the property sheet.

5 Close the Contacts table, choosing Yes when Microsoft Access asks if you want to save changes, and choosing No when it asks if you want to check whether existing data follows the rules you set.

6 Minimize the Database window.

Test the validation rules

New Record button

1 On the Contact Management Switchboard form, click Enter/View Contacts.

2 Click the New Record button on the toolbar.

3 In the First Name field, type **Carl**

4 On the Records menu, click Save Record.

Microsoft Access displays a message telling you that the Last Name field can't be null, and it doesn't let you save the record.

5 Click OK.

6 Click the Last Name field, and then type **Thorgerson**

7 On the Records menu, click Save Record.

This time, Microsoft Access displays your phone number validation message—and it still won't let you save the record.

8 Click OK.

9 Click the Work Phone field, and then type **212 555 1314** (because of the input mask, you don't have to enter the parentheses or the dash in the phone number).

10 On the Records menu, click Save Record.

This time, you can successfully save the record in the Contacts table.

Validating Data Using an Event Procedure

So far, the validation you've added hasn't required any code. But what if you want to provide validation that works differently in different situations? You may want to remind users that addresses should always have a zip code. You could set the Required property for the PostalCode field in the Contacts table; then, every record would have to have this field filled in. But this would be too restrictive—some contact records won't have an address at all, so you don't always want to require a zip code.

To provide this type of custom validation, you write an event procedure that runs each time a record is saved. The procedure will check for a postal code, and then display a message if necessary.

Create an event procedure that checks for a zip code

When the user tries to save a record in the Contacts table, the BeforeUpdate event occurs. In a BeforeUpdate event procedure, your code can either allow the record to be saved, or *cancel the event*, requiring the user to fix the problem and try again.

Design View button

1 Click the Design View button.

2 With the right mouse button, click the form selection box, and then click Properties on the shortcut menu.

3 Click the Event tab in the property sheet.

4 Click the BeforeUpdate property, and then click the Build.

5 Select Code Builder, and then click OK.

Microsoft Access opens the form module for the Contacts form and creates the Form_BeforeUpdate event procedure.

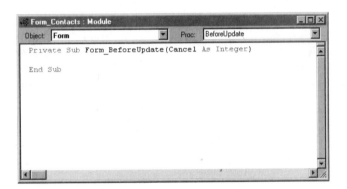

You'll notice that the header for the BeforeUpdate procedure includes a Cancel argument. You'll use this argument in your event procedure to tell Microsoft Access whether to allow the user to save the record.

6 Enter the following Visual Basic code for the procedure:

```
Private Sub Form_BeforeUpdate(Cancel As Integer)
' If the user entered an address, check for a zip code.

    If Not IsNull(Address) And IsNull(PostalCode) Then
        MsgBox "You must enter a postal code.", vbExclamation
        PostalCode.SetFocus    ' Go back to PostalCode field.
        Cancel = True          ' Cancel saving the record.
    End If

End Sub
```

Let's walk through the procedure line by line.

The first line uses a complex condition—*Not IsNull(Address) And IsNull(PostalCode)*—to determine whether or not the record that the user is saving is acceptable. This condition uses the IsNull function, which returns True if the field in parentheses contains a value, and False if it contains no value (also known as the Null value). You can read the statement like this: "If the Address field doesn't contain Null (if it has a value) and the PostalCode field does contain Null (it doesn't have a value), then do the statements in the block."

87

If the user enters an address without a zip code, the next three lines run:

■ The first line uses the MsgBox statement to display a simple message to the user. You've used this statement before, but here it has a second argument which you can use to tell Microsoft Access what type of box to display. The constant value vbExclamation tells Microsoft Access to display a message box with an exclamation point icon.

■ The user must return to the PostalCode field to enter a zip code before saving the record. For convenience, the second line uses the SetFocus method to return the focus to this field automatically, so the user can just type in the zip code.

■ The final statement sets the value of the Cancel argument to True to cancel the BeforeUpdate event. Every BeforeUpdate event procedure—like many other event procedures—includes the Cancel argument. Setting this argument to True is equivalent to saying, "Pretend that the user action that caused this event didn't happen." In this case, the user is trying to save the record, and canceling this event causes the record not to be saved. Instead, the user must enter a zip code and try again.

Test the new event procedure

1 On the Window menu, click Contacts : Form.

2 Click the Form View button on the toolbar.

Form View button

3 Click the New Record button on the toolbar.

4 Fill in the fields as follows:

New Record button

Field Name	Value
First Name	Karl
Last Name	Sigel
Address	200 Bourbon St.
City	New Orleans
State/Province	LA
Work Phone	404 555 3933

5 On the Records menu, click Save Record.

The BeforeUpdate event occurs, running the code in your event procedure. Because you filled in the Address field but not the Postal Code field, the code in the procedure displays the message—complete with exclamation point—telling you why the record can't be saved.

6 Click OK.

The code in your procedure continues, canceling the BeforeUpdate event. This returns you to the form without saving the record—you must now either undo the record or enter a zip code.

7 In the Postal Code field, type **70130**

8 On the Records menu, click Save Record.

Asking the User a Question

Your procedure works just fine—if the user types an address but doesn't have the zip code, it is impossible to save the record. This is still awfully restrictive. To be more flexible, it would be nice to simply warn the user that there's no zip code, and then allow the record to be saved.

To do this, you'll learn a very important technique: using the MsgBox function to get a response from the user, and performing different actions based on the response.

Give the user the option to leave the PostalCode field blank

1 On the Window menu, click Form_Contacts : Module.

2 Edit the code in the BeforeUpdate procedure to appear as follows:

```
Private Sub Form_BeforeUpdate(Cancel As Integer)
' If the user entered an address, check for a zip code.

    Dim strMessage As String
    Dim intOptions As Integer
    Dim bytChoice As Byte

    If Not IsNull(Address) And IsNull(PostalCode) Then
        strMessage = "You didn't enter a postal code. Save anyway?"
        intOptions = vbQuestion + vbOKCancel
        bytChoice = MsgBox(strMessage, intOptions)

        If bytChoice = vbCancel Then
            PostalCode.SetFocus    ' Go back to PostalCode field.
            Cancel = True          ' Cancel saving the record.
        End If
    End If
End Sub
```

The procedure now uses several new Visual Basic techniques:

■ The first three lines use Dim statements to tell Microsoft Access about three *variables* you're going to use in this procedure. A variable is a temporary place to store information in the computer's memory—similar to the memory function on a calculator. Each Dim statement includes the name of a variable, along with the type of data it will store. As the procedure continues, your code can assign values to the variables, retrieving the values at any time later in the procedure. The name of each variable has a prefix that indicates the type of data it stores—"str" for string data, "int" for integer data, "byt" for byte data.

■ The If...Then statement is the same as before, but the code block it runs if the user enters an address without a zip code is different. The first line in the block assigns a values to the strMessage variable. This variable stores the message you want to display, warning the user about the postal code and asking for a response. When you assign a value to a string variable, you surround the string data with quotation marks.

■ The next line assigns a value to the intOptions variable. This variable stores a number representing options for the MsgBox function. You can add the values of several constants to specify more than one option—here, for example, you've specified that you want the question-mark icon to appear in the box (vbQuestion), and that you want the box to include OK and Cancel buttons (vbOKCancel).

■ The next line uses the MsgBox function to display the question to the user. When you used the MsgBox statement previously, you placed the arguments to the statement—the message and options—after the statement, separated by a comma. Using the function, you do the same, but because it's a function, you surround the arguments with parentheses. In addition, the function returns a value that you want to store in the bytChoice variable. To assign the value of the function to the variable, you've put it after the variable name, separated by an equal sign (=). In effect, this line of code says, "Display the message text from the strMessage variable using the options from the intOptions variable, and put the result in the bytChoice variable." The result that the MsgBox function returns is a number representing which button the user chose in the message box, either OK or Cancel.

■ The next few lines use another If...Then structure to perform an action based on the user's response to the question. If the user responds by clicking the Cancel button, the value that gets stored in the bytChoice variable will equal the constant value vbCancel, and the block of code runs.

■ If the user responds by clicking Cancel, you want to move back to the PostalCode field and cancel the event so the user still has to enter a zip code. If the user responds with OK, the procedure skips this block of code, allowing the record to be saved without a zip code. Note that each If...Then structure ends with its own End If statement to indicate the end of that structure.

TIP You may wonder how you can find out which constant values to use for specifying options for the MsgBox function and interpreting the response. You can read about all these constants in the Help topic for the MsgBox function, by clicking on the MsgBox keyword in the Module window and pressing F1.

Test the procedure again

1 On the Window menu, click Contacts.

2 Click the Postal Code field's label, and press the DELETE key to delete the zip code.

3 On the Records menu, click Save Record.

The BeforeUpdate event occurs, running your new code. This time, the code in the procedure displays the question—and includes OK and Cancel buttons so you can indicate a response.

4 Click Cancel.

The code in your procedure continues, canceling the BeforeUpdate event. But suppose you realize that you don't have the zip code, and want to save the record anyway.

5 On the Records menu, click Save Record.

6 Click OK.

This time, your response causes the code that cancels the BeforeUpdate event to be skipped, allowing the record to be saved as if the procedure weren't there at all.

As you can see, validation can be as simple or complex as necessary in your application. Even this procedure could be expanded to cover several different scenarios: if you had other rules for entering contacts in records, you would simply add additional blocks of code to the same BeforeUpdate event procedure to check all your rules before allowing the record to be saved.

Close the form and exit Microsoft Access

1 Close the Contacts form, clicking Yes when Microsoft Access asks if you want to save changes.

2 Close Microsoft Access.

Lesson Summary

To	Do this
Change a control's properties when a user moves to and from it	Write event procedures for the control's Enter and Exit events.
Perform actions after a user changes a control's value	Write an event procedure for the control's AfterUpdate event.
Perform actions when the user presses a key combination on a form	Write an event procedure for a form's KeyDown event, and set the form's KeyPreview property to Yes.
Validate data in code before a control value is accepted or a record gets saved	Write a BeforeUpdate event procedure for the control or form event. To cancel the update, set the Cancel argument to True.
Ask the user a question	Use the MsgBox function, along with constants that define its options. Store the value of the user's choice in a variable.

For online information about	On the Help menu, click Microsoft Access Help Topics, click the Index tab, and then
Declaring and using variables	Search for "variables"
Creating and using combo boxes	Search for "combo boxes"
Referring to fields, controls, and properties in Visual Basic code	Search for "expressions"

For more information on	In *Building Applications with Microsoft Access*, see
Declaring and using variables	Chapter 4, "Variables, Constants, and Data Types"
Creating and using combo boxes	Chapter 3, "Using Forms to Collect, Display, and Filter Information"
Referring to fields, controls, and properties in Visual Basic code	Chapter 5, "Working with Objects and Collections"

Preview of the Next Lesson

In this lesson, you explored many events and learned a lot more about Visual Basic along the way. You've already used many Visual Basic programming techniques, but there are still quite a few you haven't explored. In the next part of the book—lessons 5 through 7—you'll learn much more about the ins and outs of the Visual Basic language, and the tools you can use to get the most from it.

Programming
in Visual Basic

Write Your Own Functions

Estimated time
40 min.

In this lesson you will learn how to:

- Create a standard module.
- Write general Sub and Function procedures.
- Provide information to a procedure by adding arguments.
- Use general procedures in code and expressions on a form.

Watching small children learn to speak is fascinating. Long before they're aware of grammar or sentence structure, they manage to build sentences. Without any under-standing of the rules of language, they nevertheless communicate. Of course, before you can read or write, you need to learn *something* about the language—still, you can get by pretty well with a rudimentary understanding of grammar and a limited vocabulary.

Although a far cry from anyone's native tongue, computer programming languages share many characteristics with human language. Both have an extensive vocabulary and complex rules of grammar to follow. But as you've seen in previous lessons, you can learn to get things done using Visual Basic, even create and customize applications, without bothering to learn much about the programming language. So far, you've been speaking the language without knowing the underlying rules.

You can get a good start with a language before studying any grammar, but you won't be likely to write *War and Peace*. In order to use a language with confidence, you need to understand how it works—the basic rules and components, and how to combine them effectively. Now that you've gotten a taste of what you can accomplish by programming Microsoft Access, it's time to discover the bigger picture.

97

In this lesson, you'll learn about the fundamental building blocks of Visual Basic for Applications—modules and procedures—and how you fit them together to build flexible, well-organized applications. You'll pick up new vocabulary along the way, and you'll try using it in several different contexts. Then, throughout Part 2, you'll continue to explore the underlying rules of Visual Basic programming and try out all the tools Microsoft Access provides for crafting your modules.

Start the lesson

 Start Microsoft Access and open the 05 Contacts database in the practice files folder.

Understanding Modules and Procedures

In Part 1, you worked exclusively with event procedures on existing forms. Because forms are so central to Microsoft Access applications, this type of procedure is probably where you'll add most of the code you write. However, there is another important type of procedure you'll create in this lesson, called a *general* procedure. General procedures don't run automatically in response to events—instead, you have to run them yourself, either by referring to them in an expression on a form or report or by using them in Visual Basic code. General procedures come in two types: Sub procedures and Function procedures. Event procedures, by contrast, are all Sub procedures.

You can think of general procedures as having a supporting role in your applications— while event procedures are the central force in Microsoft Access programming, general procedures are helpers along the way. You could accomplish most anything in Microsoft Access with event procedures alone; but as you'll see, using general procedures will provide much better solutions as the complexity of your application increases.

Why Create General Procedures?

You can use general procedures to:

Perform complex operations that don't fit in an expression. If you've used expressions as property settings on forms and reports, you know that they can quickly become unwieldy. You can hide this complexity by creating your own function to perform the operation you need, and then referring to it in your expressions. Additionally, Visual Basic code can perform complex operations that aren't possible using expressions.

Reuse program code to repeat a task. Your event procedures often perform the same or similar actions at various times. For example, you might often display a message to the user. While you could copy the same code into every event procedure that uses it, this would be extremely inefficient. Instead, you can create a general procedure that performs a common task, and reuse it in every procedure that performs that task.

Break up programming tasks into manageable units. If you were to put all your code into event procedures, they could become very long, complicated, and difficult to understand. By creating separate procedures to perform each part of a large task, you can simplify your work and make each individual procedure easier to read and understand.

Standard Modules and Form Modules

You can put general procedures in one of two places: in a form or report module, where they share space with any event procedures you write, or in a *standard* module. Standard modules are separate database objects containing one or many procedures. They most often contain "utility" functions, so named because they are useful in many different circumstances. For example, one standard module might contain several general functions for working with dates in Visual Basic—you can copy such a module to any application in which you use dates.

If you add a general procedure to a form or report module, it belongs to that form or report. Most often, you'll use this type of procedure only in the form or report itself, either in expressions on the form or in other procedures in the same module. Create this type of procedure to perform a task that applies directly to the form—for example, to work with information in the fields on that form.

General procedures that you add to standard modules usually belong to the application as a whole. Create this type of procedure to perform a task that applies to more than one form or report—often, a task that could apply to any form or report.

Creating General Procedures in a Standard Module

A database can contain one or more standard modules, each of which can hold many procedures. You'll usually group all the procedures for a specific purpose into one module. In this section, you'll create a module to store two procedures that are used to display messages to the user.

Create a new standard module

1   In the Database window, click the Modules tab.

   Standard modules are regular objects in the Database window, just like tables and forms.

2   Click the New button.

   Microsoft Access creates a new standard module and displays it in the Module window. From here, you can enter Visual Basic code and create general procedures.

Using the Declarations Section

A new module doesn't contain any procedures—however, like all modules, it has a special section called the *Declarations section*. In this section, you declare variables and constants, and enter other preliminary code that applies to the entire module. In a standard module, code in the Declarations section can even apply to all modules in the application.

As you can see, Microsoft Access automatically added two statements to the Declarations section of your module:

```
Option Compare Database
Option Explicit
```

These statements use the Option keyword to set options for the whole module. They are two of several available statements that begin with the Option keyword.

The Compare option determines the method Microsoft Access uses for comparing strings in your module, and can be set to Database, Text, or Binary. Using the Database option tells Microsoft Access to compare strings using the sort order set in your database, as opposed to the traditional Visual Basic sort order, which distinguishes between upper-case and lowercase letters. Because Option Compare Database makes sense for most applications in Microsoft Access, you should just leave this statement alone in your modules.

The Explicit option tells Microsoft Access to check all the variable names you use in the module, to make sure you've declared them. If you remove this option from the Declarations section of a module, Microsoft Access lets you enter just about anything in code—but doing this makes your code much more prone to errors, because a misspelling won't be caught before you run your code. Having the Option Explicit statement in your modules will help you avoid many headaches down the road.

Declaring Constant Values

One of the statements you can place in the Declarations section is the Const statement, which declares a *constant* for use in your code. A constant is like a variable, except that you can't change its value after you declare it. You've already used predefined constants in previous lessons. Your own constants work the same way, except that you decide what name and value to give them. You can think of a constant as being a placeholder for a value, making it easier to refer to in your code.

Declare a constant for the name of your application

You might want to declare a constant to store the name of your application, which you plan to use in procedures in the module.

 Press ENTER, type **Const conAppName = "Contact Management"** and press ENTER again.

This tells Microsoft Access that each time conAppName appears in code, it should be replaced with this string value. If you want to change the application name later, you'll only need to change it in one place, not throughout the module.

Here's what the completed Declarations section looks like:

 NOTE   Declaring a constant in the Declarations section makes the constant available throughout the module. If you plan to use a constant value in only one procedure, it makes more sense to declare it in the procedure itself.

On the other hand, if you plan to use a constant value in more than one module, you can make it available to the entire database by using the Global Const statement instead of Const. Place this statement only in the Declarations section of a standard module.

Creating a Sub Procedure

You've already seen how to create event procedures and write code for them in the Module window. Creating general procedures is much the same, except that you have more flexibility. While the attributes of an event procedure—its name, type, and arguments—are predefined by Microsoft Access, you choose all these attributes for the general procedures you create.

Create the DisplayMessage procedure

You'll create a general procedure that you can use to display a message to the user—a common task that the procedure will help make easier.

1   Click the Insert Procedure button on the toolbar.

Insert Procedure button

Microsoft Access displays the Insert Procedure dialog box, where you specify the name and type of the procedure you want to create.

2   In the Name box, type **DisplayMessage**

3   In the Type box, select the Sub option.

4   Click OK.

Microsoft Access creates the new procedure and displays its Sub and End Sub lines in the Module window.

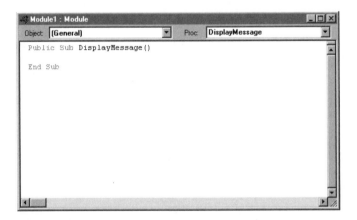

Although the code in the Declarations section is still in the module, it has disappeared. This is because the Module window displays only one procedure (or Declarations section) at a time.

Add code to the procedure

1   Enter the following code for the procedure:

```
' Display an important message to the user.

    MsgBox "This is important.", vbExclamation, conAppName
```

This code uses the MsgBox statement to display your message. It specifies a MsgBox option by including the vbExclamation constant as the second argument, so that the message box will include the exclamation point icon. Additionally, it specifies a title for the message box by including the third argument—the constant value that provides the name of the application.

Save button

2 Click the Save button on the toolbar.

3 Type **Messages** in the Module Name box, and then click OK.

Microsoft Access saves the module in the Contacts database.

Test your procedure using the Debug window

You can test general procedures such as the DisplayMessage procedure by using the Debug window.

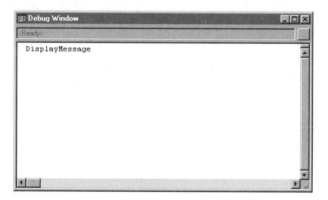

Debug Window button

1 Click the Debug Window button on the toolbar.

2 Type **DisplayMessage**

3 Press ENTER.

Your procedure runs, displaying a message on the screen.

4 Click OK.

Adding Arguments to a Procedure

Your procedure works well so far, but it leaves something to be desired. The message it displays is always the same—and the user will get pretty tired of seeing it if it stays this way. What you want is a flexible procedure that allows you to specify which of several messages you want to display. You can achieve this by adding an argument to the procedure.

Add an argument to the DisplayMessage procedure

1 Close the Debug window.

2 Type **strMessage As String** within the parentheses in the Sub statement:

```
Public Sub DisplayMessage(strMessage As String)
```

This tells Microsoft Access that you want to be able to give some information to the DisplayMessage procedure: namely, the message you want to display. You're also saying that the piece of information you'll provide to the procedure will be a string, and that it will be called strMessage.

3 Edit the MsgBox line, replacing the message string with this argument:

```
MsgBox strMessage, vbExclamation, conAppName
```

Now, when Microsoft Access runs the MsgBox statement, it will use the value of strMessage instead of a string that's always the same.

Run your procedure using an argument

When you run a procedure and provide an argument value, it's referred to as *passing* the argument to the procedure.

Debug Window button

1 Click the Debug Window button on the toolbar.

2 Type **DisplayMessage "I can say anything I like!"** and press ENTER.

Your procedure runs, using the string value you passed for the strMessage argument.

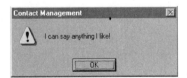

3 Click OK.

Creating a Function

The procedure you created performs an action, but it doesn't provide any information back to the program—this is the nature of a Sub procedure. A much more common type of general procedure is a *function*. Using a function procedure allows you to *return* a value to the procedure that runs the function. You've probably already used lots of built-in functions in Microsoft Access—such as the IsNull function—to get information back about something. Now you'll create your own function.

Create a procedure that asks a question

In Lesson 4, you used the MsgBox function to ask for confirmation before saving a record. Now you'll create a general function, called Confirm, that performs this same task for any action that needs confirmation. The function returns a different value depending on the choice the user makes in the message box.

Insert Procedure button

1   Close the Debug window.

2   Click the Insert Procedure button on the toolbar.

3   Type **Confirm** in the Name box, and then click OK.

Because the default type of procedure is Function, Microsoft Access creates a new function and displays its Function and End Function statements.

4   Type **strMessage As String** within the parentheses of the Function statement, and type **As Boolean** at the end:

```
Public Function Confirm(strMessage As String) As Boolean
```

Let's take a close look at this function declaration:

- The Public keyword before the Function statement says that this function can be used from anywhere in the application. If you had used the Private keyword instead, you could only run the Confirm function from within the Messages module.

- The argument declaration in parentheses tells Microsoft Access that you'll pass the message you want to display to the procedure, as you did for the DisplayMessage procedure.

- The As clause at the end of the Function statement tells Microsoft Access that you want the function to return a certain type of value. Because you want the Confirm function to return either True or False depending on the user's choice, you'll use the Boolean data type for the function—variables of the Boolean type can have one of only two values, True (-1) or False (0).

5 Type the following code into the procedure between the Function and End Function statements:

```
' Ask the user to confirm an action, returning True or False.

    Dim bytChoice As Byte

    bytChoice = MsgBox(strMessage, vbQuestion + vbOKCancel, conAppName)

    If bytChoice = vbOK Then
        Confirm = True
    Else
        Confirm = False
    End If
```

Here's what the code does:

- First, it uses the Dim statement to declare the variable bytChoice, in which it will store the number returned by the MsgBox function.

- Next, it calls the MsgBox function, passing it the strMessage argument provided to the function, and specifying options using the predefined constants vbQuestion and vbOKCancel, which tell Microsoft Access to display the message with a question mark icon and to include OK and Cancel buttons.

- Finally, the function uses an If...Then structure to check whether the user chose OK—the condition in the If...Then statement compares the bytChoice variable to the predefined constant vbOK. If the condition is true, the return value of the Confirm function gets set to True; otherwise, it gets set to False. To specify the value you want a function to return, all you have to do is type the function name followed by the equal sign and the value you want it to return. Of course, the value it returns must be consistent with the data type of the function, in this case Boolean.

Test the Confirm function

Now you can try out the Confirm function. To display the value of a function in the Debug window, you type a question mark (?) before the function name. Also, remember to enclose the arguments to a function in parentheses.

Debug Window button

1 Click the Debug Window button on the toolbar.

2 Type **?Confirm("Is it OK?")** and press ENTER.

Your procedure runs, using the string value you passed for the strMessage argument and displaying the message box according to the options you specified in your function.

3 Click OK.

The Debug window displays the return value of the Confirm function.

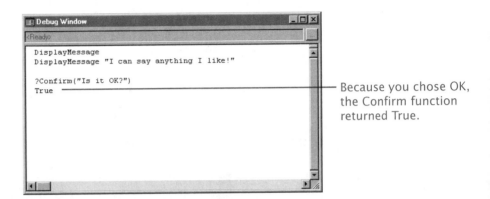

Because you chose OK, the Confirm function returned True.

4 Press the BACKSPACE key six times to move back to the end of the line that calls the Confirm function, and then press ENTER.

5 Click Cancel.

This time, the function returns False, indicating that you didn't confirm the action.

6 Close the Debug window.

7 Close the Module window, clicking Yes when Microsoft Access asks if you want to save changes to the Messages module.

You've created two useful general procedures, DisplayMessage and Confirm, that you can use in code throughout your database. Moreover, you could copy the Messages module to other databases you create, so you wouldn't have to redo this work in future applications. This is the advantage of standard modules—they're like a box of tools you can use when you need them, and you can carry them around wherever you go, increasing your programming productivity.

Using General Procedures on a Form

The next step is to put your new procedures to work. And because they're general procedures, declared as public, you can use them anywhere in your application. In this section, you'll simplify the code in the Contacts form's module by using general procedures where appropriate.

Open the Contacts form's module

In Part 1, you opened the Contacts form's module by setting event properties in the property sheet. However, an easy way to view the Visual Basic code for a form is to click the Code button.

1 In the Database window, click the Forms tab, and then click the Contacts form.

Code button

2 Click the Code button.

Microsoft Access opens the Contacts form in Design view, and then opens its module and displays the Declarations section of the module. From here, you can browse through existing procedures or add new Visual Basic code.

3 Press the PAGE DOWN key several times.

Paging down moves you to other procedures in the module. So far, the only procedures the module contains are event procedures.

4 Click the drop-down arrow next to the Object box, and select Form.

5 Click the drop-down arrow next to the Proc box, and click BeforeUpdate.

The Module window displays the Form_BeforeUpdate event procedure, which you added code to in Lesson 4.

The event procedure displays a message if a user fails to enter a zip code for an address. If the user clicks Cancel in the message box, it cancels the update so the record isn't saved.

Edit the code to use the Confirm function

This procedure performs a simple action, but it uses several variables and lines of code that aren't really related to the task at hand—they're related to the problem of displaying a message box that asks the user a question. Now that you have a general function that does this for you, you can simplify this event procedure.

1 Replace the three Dim lines with a single Dim statement:

```
Dim blnOK As Boolean
```

This line of code declares a variable called blnOK, which stores the response you get from the Confirm function. Because the Confirm function returns a Boolean value (either True or False), you declare the variable with the Boolean data type.

2 Replace the three lines that set up and display the message (after the If...Then statement) with the following line:

```
blnOK = Confirm("You didn't enter a postal code. Save anyway?")
```

This line calls the Confirm function, passing it the message you want to display and storing its return value—True if the user chose OK, False if Cancel—in the blnOK variable.

3 Replace the second If...Then statement, which tests what button the user chose, with the following line:

```
If Not blnOK Then        ' User chose Cancel.
```

This line checks to see whether the user chose the OK or the Cancel button. Because the value of blnOK is True if the user chose OK, the condition *Not blnOK* is True if the user chose Cancel. If the user chose Cancel, the code in the If...Then block runs, moving the focus to PostalCode and canceling the update.

The following illustration shows the much simplified BeforeUpdate event procedure:

Try the procedure

Form View button

1 Switch to the Contacts form.

2 Click the Form View button on the toolbar.

3 Click the Postal Code field's label, and press DELETE to delete the zip code.

4 On the Records menu, click Save Record.

The BeforeUpdate event occurs, running your new version of the event procedure. The event procedure works just as it did before, displaying the message that asks if you want to save. This time, however, your general Confirm procedure displays the question.

5 Click OK.

Creating General Functions in a Form Module

You've created general functions, and you're using one of them on the Contacts form. Now, suppose you have some ideas for functions that would be useful on the Contacts form, but that would apply only to the form itself. For example, you might want to write functions that manipulate text values on the form.

There's no reason to put this type of procedure in a standard module, because no other form could use it. Additionally, from a standard module, it would be harder to work with values on the form: every time you referred to it, you'd have to specify the form name so that Microsoft Access would know which controls you were referring to. Instead, you should put this type of procedure in the form module.

In this section, you'll create two general functions designed specifically for the Contacts form.

Create the FullName function

The Contacts table has separate fields for last name and first name—and for good reason: in a database that has a single field for names, it's very difficult to search and sort by last name. But suppose you're finding that you often need a way to refer to the full name of the current contact, either in expressions or in code. You can write a very simple general function for the form that returns the full name, so you'll have a simple way to refer to it.

1 Switch to the Contacts form's module.

Up to now, you've created a procedure by clicking a toolbar button. But you don't have to use a command to create a new procedure—you can also create a procedure by typing its header in the Module window.

2 Press the DOWN ARROW key several times, until the insertion point is positioned below the End Sub statement at the end of the BeforeUpdate event procedure in the module.

3 Type the following function header:

```
Private Function FullName() As String
```

When you press ENTER, the new procedure gets created and is displayed by itself in the Module window. As its header declares, the FullName function returns a string value. The function is private to the Contacts form module, because you won't need to call the function from outside the form.

4 Type the following line of code for the function:

```
FullName = FirstName & " " & LastName
```

This line concatenates the value of the FirstName field with a space, followed by the LastName field, and specifies that this is the value for the function to return.

Use the FullName function in an expression on the form

The Contacts form has a calculated field that displays the full name of the contact—it's at the top of page 2 of the form. The ControlSource property of this field is set to an expression that combines the two name fields. But now that you have a function to perform this task, you can refer to the function as the source of the control. This is one of the common situations for including a private function in a form module—when you need to refer to a calculation in expressions on the form.

1 Switch to the Contacts form window.

2 Click the Page 2 button in the form footer.

This field displays the full name of the current contact in the form.

Now you'll change the control to use your new function.

3 Click the Design View button on the toolbar.

Design View button

4 Scroll down a bit in the form, and then click the Contact Name text box.

5 If the property sheet isn't open, click the Properties button on the toolbar.

6 In the property sheet, click the Data tab.

Properties button

The ControlSource property has a long setting, which you can simplify by using your new function.

111

7   Change the ControlSource property setting to **=FullName()**

This setting tells Microsoft Access to run your function each time it refreshes this control, and display the return value of the function in the control.

8   Close the property sheet.

9   Click the Form View button on the toolbar.

Form View button

10   Click the Page 2 button in the form footer.

The Contact Name control still shows the full name, but now it uses your function to fill in the name.

In this case, you could have done without the function—after all, the wizard wrote the control's expression for you. But now that you have a function, you can use it in expressions or code throughout the form.

Create the FullAddress function

You might want to combine the address fields for a contact into a single value, such as the full address you'd type on an envelope. But unlike the FullName function, which you'll only use on the Contacts form itself, you may want to call this function from outside the form—to put the address on another form or report, for example. To make a function available outside the form, you declare it using the Public keyword.

1   Switch to the Contacts form's module.

2   Click below the End Function line in the FullName function, and then type the following function (except the End Function line, which Microsoft Access enters automatically after you type the function header):

```
Public Function FullAddress() As String
' Return a string containing the full name and address.

    Dim strNewLine As String

    strNewLine = Chr(13) & Chr(10)

    ' If no name or address, return an empty string.
    If IsNull(LastName) Or IsNull(Address) Then
        FullAddress = ""
    Else
        ' Build the address string.
        FullAddress = FullName & strNewLine & _
            Address & strNewLine & _
            City & ", " & _
            StateOrProvince & " " & PostalCode
    End If
End Function
```

Microsoft Access enters the End Function line automatically after you type the function header.

Here are some things to notice in the function:

- First, the function declares a string variable *strNewLine*, and then sets the value of the variable to the two characters that make up a new line in Visual Basic: a carriage return character and a line feed character. To represent string values like these, which you can't type using the keyboard, you use the Chr function, entering the ASCII code number for the character you want (the code number for a carriage return is 13, while line feed is 10). The function uses this combined value to separate the lines in the address.

- Next, the function uses the If...Then structure to determine whether there are LastName and Address values on the form. If there aren't, it returns an empty string (""). If there are, it builds the address string by concatenating the contact's name, address, city, state, and postal code.

- Take a closer look at the Else statement, which builds the address string. Because the code is much too long to fit on a single line, it's broken up into four lines using the Visual Basic line-continuation character, the underscore (_). Any time you want to continue a line of code on a second line, you can type a space followed by this character, and then continue on a new line—Microsoft Access interprets the code as if it were all on one line.

- The Else statement uses the FullName function you already created to represent the first and last names. You'll recall that in the expression for the ContactName control, you had to include an equal sign before the function, and then follow the function name with a pair of parentheses; in code, by contrast, you can run a function that has no arguments by simply entering its name.

- The code then goes on to concatenate the fields in the address, separating them with correct formatting. It places the strNewLine value after the name and address, places a comma and a space after the state, and includes a space before the postal code. This whole string value gets assigned to the return value of the FullAddress function.

Try the FullAddress function from the Debug window

Now that the function is complete, you can use it in expressions or code throughout the form. For example, you could create a control on the form that displays the full address. But because you declared the FullAddress function using the Public keyword, you should also be able to use it from outside the Contacts form—for example, from the Debug window.

Debug Window button

1   Click the Debug Window button on the toolbar.

    The Debug window still displays the text you assigned earlier.

2   Type **?Forms!Contacts.FullAddress**

    The expression *Forms!Contacts* refers to the Contacts form. To use a public function of a form, you enter the form reference, followed by a period (.), followed by the function name (and its arguments, if any, in parentheses).

113

3 Press ENTER.

The FullAddress function runs, combines the address fields for the current record on the Contacts form, and displays the function's return value in the Debug window.

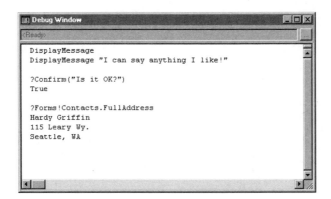

```
Debug Window                                    _ □ X
<Ready>

DisplayMessage
DisplayMessage "I can say anything I like!"

?Confirm("Is it OK?")
True

?Forms!Contacts.FullAddress
Hardy Griffin
115 Leary Wy.
Seattle, WA
```

Try the FullName function from the Debug window

There's no problem running a public function from outside the form. But what about the FullName function, which you declared using the Private keyword?

1 Type **?Forms!Contacts.FullName** and press ENTER.

An error message appears, telling you that there was an object-defined error. In plain English, this means that you asked the form to do something it isn't allowed to do—and it responds, "Sorry, that's private!"

2 Click OK.

As you can see, you can't refer to a private function from outside its module. Note, however, that if a public function in the module uses the private function, you can end up running the private function from elsewhere. This is the case with the FullAddress function, which uses the FullName function in its code—so although FullName isn't directly available from the Debug window, we actually ran it courtesy of the FullAddress function, because FullName is available to any of its siblings in the Contacts form's module.

So Many Options, So Few Rules

Microsoft Access gives you nearly unlimited freedom as a programmer to put code all over the place—in standard modules, form and report modules, and event procedures—and to specify various options, such as public and private procedures. How do you decide where to put your code and how to declare it? Here are some guidelines:

Break procedures into separate tasks. Try to follow the rule of one procedure per task—your applications will be much easier to maintain. If you're writing code for an event procedure and it's getting complex, consider writing a general function for each subtask.

Generalize procedures whenever possible. If you can write a procedure so that it could apply to any form or report, do so—and put it in a standard module. One way to achieve this is to add arguments to the procedure, so you can provide the specifics when you call the procedure.

Put object-specific procedures in the object's module. For object-specific tasks or procedures that you know will only be used by a single form or report, be sure to put them in the form or report modules where they belong. You'll avoid having stray procedures, and it will be easier to refer to objects, properties, and controls on the form.

Choose private over public to avoid conflicts. In a form or report module, declare procedures using the Private keyword unless you have a reason to call them from outside the form. In a standard module, most procedures will need to be declared using Public, because you'll want to use them throughout your database; however, if they're only used to perform subtasks for other procedures in the module, be sure to declare them using Private. Making procedures private whenever possible uses less memory, and can help avoid conflicts.

Close windows and exit Microsoft Access

1 Close the Debug window.

2 Close the Contacts form's Module window.

3 Close the Contacts form, clicking Yes when Microsoft Access asks if you want to save changes.

4 Close Microsoft Access.

The Many Ways to Declare Variables

Like procedures, the variables you use can be public or private, and can live in various places in your database. How variables work depends entirely on where and how you declare them. So far, all the variables you've used have been private variables, declared using the Dim keyword inside a procedure—and used only in that procedure. When the procedure finishes running, a variable declared in this way disappears, along with its contents.

There are several other ways to declare variables that you'll want to keep in mind:

Module-level   To declare a variable that you'll use throughout a module, use the Dim statement in the Declarations section of the module—outside any one procedure. The variable will keep its value between procedure calls. Use this type of variable when several procedures in the module all work with the same data.

Public   To declare a variable that you'll use throughout your application, use the Public statement instead of the Dim statement, placing it in the Declarations section of any module. The variable will keep its value during the entire time your application is running. You can declare a public variable in a form or report module, but you'll have to include the object's name in every reference to the variable that occurs outside that object. Public variables are useful for application-wide information, such as the names of the application users.

Static   Variables you declare within a procedure normally lose their values when the procedure ends. However, if you want Microsoft Access to preserve the value of a variable between calls to the procedure, replace the Dim keyword with the Static keyword. This is useful for a procedure that accumulates a value each time it is called.

In later lessons, you'll use some of these techniques. However, except in special cases, you should stay in the habit of using only private, procedure-level variables—they take up space in memory only while their procedure is running, and they don't conflict with variables of the same name in other procedures.

Lesson Summary

To	Do this
Create a standard module	In the Database window, click the Modules tab, and then click the New button.
Add a general procedure to a module	In the Module window, click the Insert Procedure button. Or, click anywhere outside a procedure and type a Sub or Function statement declaring the procedure.
Provide information to a procedure	Include arguments, along with their data types, in parentheses in the Sub or Function statement declaring the procedure.
Return information from a function	Include the return data type of the function in the declaration. In the function, assign the value you want to return to the function name.
Call a Function procedure and pass arguments	Assign the function name to a variable, including arguments, if any, in parentheses after the function name.
Call a Sub procedure and pass arguments	Type the procedure name followed by the arguments (without parentheses).
Use a general function in a property setting	Type an equal sign followed by the function name, including arguments in parentheses (or just parentheses if there aren't any arguments).
Declare a constant	Type the Const statement, followed by a name, the equal sign, and the value of the constant. To use the constant, simply include its name in place of its value.

For online information about	On the Help menu, click Microsoft Access Help Topics, click the Index tab, and then
Using variables	Search for "variables"
Using constants	Search for "constants"
Declaring Sub and Function procedures	Search for "declaring procedures"
Working with string values and other data types	Search for "data types, Visual Basic"

For more information on	In *Building Applications with Microsoft Access,* see
Using variables and constants	Chapter 4, "Variables, Constants, and Data Types"
Declaring Sub and Function procedures	Chapter 2, "Introducing Visual Basic"
Working with string values and other data types	Chapter 4, "Variables, Constants, and Data Types"

Preview of the Next Lesson

Up to this point, you've written code and seen the results of your efforts, but you haven't actually *seen* the code run. In the next lesson, you'll try out tools in the Module window that let you watch your Visual Basic code in action—and help you find any mistakes you've made along the way. Additionally, you'll learn how to deal with errors or unexpected events that occur while your application is running.

Monitor and Debug Your Code

Estimated time
35 min.

In this lesson you will learn how to:

■ Watch Visual Basic code run line by line.

■ View the values of variables and expressions in your code.

■ Compile procedures to ensure that they follow the rules.

■ Find and fix programming errors using Visual Basic debugging tools.

In trying to stay on course to reach a destination, a navigator uses various tools to keep track of the vessel's location and heading—and keeps a constant eye on the chart. Because of obstacles, wind conditions, or currents, changes in course are common, and a navigator has to anticipate problems and adjust accordingly. A change in course doesn't necessarily indicate a mistake—it's just part of the job.

When you program in Visual Basic, you have to anticipate that errors will pop up here and there, both while you're programming and when you run your application. Microsoft Access comes equipped with many tools that, like a ship's compass or direction finder, help you keep track of where your application is and where it's heading. In this lesson, you'll learn to monitor your Visual Basic code as it runs, and to understand what's really happening inside that computer when your application is running. You'll use tools in Microsoft Access to find bugs and then fix them and test to make sure they're taken care of.

Start the lesson

▶ Start Microsoft Access and open the 06 Contacts database in the practice files folder.

Stepping Through Code Line by Line

In previous lessons, you've written quite a bit of Visual Basic code, and seen the results of running your procedures. But so far, you haven't actually *seen* the code run—you've taken it on faith that your code was running behind the scenes. In this section, you'll see your code run for the first time.

The Visual Basic Module window provides tools that let you stop your code while it's running, and step through Visual Basic statements one by one. This way, you can see what's really going on in your code.

Open the Messages module

In order to watch code run, you first need to open it up and tell Microsoft Access where you want to start watching it. First, you'll open the Messages module and switch to the Confirm function, which you created in Lesson 5.

1 In the Database window, click the Modules tab.

2 Double-click the Messages module.

Microsoft Access opens the Module window and displays the Declarations section.

3 Press the PAGE DOWN key four times.

The Module window shows the Confirm function.

Setting a Breakpoint to Stop Running Code

When you want Microsoft Access to stop running your code midstream so you can take a look at it, you set a *breakpoint* at the line of code you want to check. A breakpoint tells Microsoft Access, "When you get to this line—but before you run it—stop everything and display the code." It's like calling time out in a basketball game: the action stops so you can regroup, consider what you're doing right or wrong, and make adjustments. Then, when the time-out is over, you allow your code to continue, letting the game go on as before.

Set a breakpoint at the beginning of a procedure

You'll set a breakpoint at the very beginning of the Confirm function, on the Function statement itself. This way, you can take a look at the function each time it runs.

Breakpoint button

▶ Click the Breakpoint button.

The current line changes to white text on red, indicating that Microsoft Access will stop when it encounters this code—in other words, as soon as it tries to run the Confirm function.

Code will stop running at this line.

Run the procedure

Now try running the Confirm function from the Debug window.

Debug Window button

1   Click the Debug Window button.

2   Move the Debug window to the lower right corner of the screen, out of the way of the code in the Module window.

The Debug window stays on top of other windows, so it's always easy to find. However, because you need to see the other windows behind it, you should try to position it as much out of the way as possible. (If you don't have enough screen space, you may need to have the two windows overlap as shown. If this is the case, you may also want to make the Debug window a bit smaller—but make sure you leave room to type commands in it.)

3   In the Debug window, type **?Confirm("Isn't it wonderful?")** and press ENTER.

The Confirm function runs, but as soon as it starts, Microsoft Access encounters the breakpoint you set. It then switches back to the Confirm function in the Module window. When you view running code, you'll notice that Microsoft Access displays a box outlining the current statement.

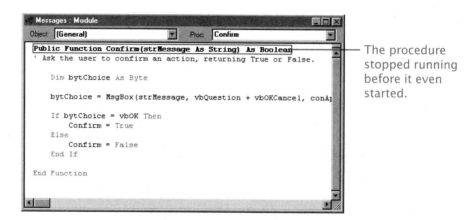

— The procedure stopped running before it even started.

Step through the code one line at a time

Nothing is happening right now because of the breakpoint—but in a sense, your code is still running. Information about the procedure, such as the values of local variables and arguments, is stored in your computer's memory. Microsoft Access is ready to continue running the function as soon as you say so. You'll use the Step Into command, which tells Microsoft Access to run one line of code, and then display the Module window again and return control to you.

Step Into button

1   Click the Step Into button.

When you click the button, Microsoft Access moves the current statement indicator—the outline around the line of code—to the statement that uses the MsgBox function. Note that Microsoft Access skips over two lines of code: the comment statement and the Dim statement. Because these lines of code don't actually *do* anything, they never become the current statement.

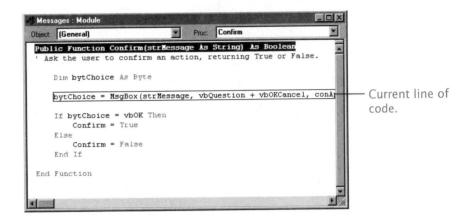

Current line of code.

This line of code uses the MsgBox function to display a message to the user, and assigns the return value of the function to the bytChoice variable. When you start the code running again, you can expect to see the message on the screen.

2 Click the Step Into button again.

Microsoft Access runs the current statement, which displays your message on the screen.

3 Click OK.

When you answer the question in the message box, Microsoft Access finishes running the statement by assigning your choice to the bytChoice variable. It then returns to the Module window and moves the current statement indicator to the next line of code: the If...Then statement that determines whether you clicked the OK button.

4 Click the Step Into button again.

Because the condition in the If...Then statement is true—the bytChoice variable is equal to the vbOK constant—Microsoft Access moves to the line of code directly underneath the If...Then statement.

When the If...Then condition is true, this line runs next.

5 Click the Step Into button again.

Microsoft Access sets the return value of the Confirm function to True, and then skips over the Else block, moving the current statement indicator to the End If statement.

Microsoft Access skips to this line.

Here's where you can really see the value of stepping through your code. If the condition in the If...Then statement were false—if you'd chosen Cancel instead of OK—Microsoft Access would have taken a different path through the code. By stepping through your code, you can see exactly which lines of code actually run, rather than trying to guess what's happening in your procedures.

6 Click the Step Into button two more times.

The last two statements in the function run. When you step past the End Function statement, the Debug window becomes active again. This is where you started running the code—before it was stopped by the breakpoint—so this is where control returns when the code finishes running.

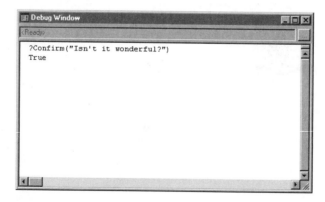

The Debug window displays the return value of the function, which is True.

7 Close the Debug window.

8 On the Run menu, click Clear All Breakpoints.

This command clears the breakpoint you set, so that Microsoft Access will allow the Confirm function to run without interruption in the future.

Stepping from One Procedure to Another

So far, you've stepped through code in just one procedure. But in Lesson 5, you learned to separate your code into a procedure for each task. When you step through code in your application, Microsoft Access can automatically step into each procedure you call so you can follow the progression of your code.

To see this, you'll step through the BeforeUpdate event procedure on the Contacts form. This event procedure calls the Confirm function, so you'll get to see how Microsoft Access runs both procedures.

Open the Contacts form's module and set a breakpoint

Before you can step through the code in an event procedure, you need to set a breakpoint in the function.

Database
Window button

Code button

1 Click the Database Window button on the toolbar.

2 In the Database window, click the Forms tab.

3 Select the Contacts form, and then click the Code button.

Microsoft Access opens the Contacts form in Design view, and displays the form's module in the Module window.

4 In the Object box, select Form.

5 In the Proc box, select BeforeUpdate.

The Module window shows the Form_BeforeUpdate event procedure.

6 Resize the Module window so it displays most of the code in the procedure (drag the upper left corner of the window to make it larger).

Now you'll set a breakpoint using a handy tool: the shortcut menu.

7 With the right mouse button, click the fifth line in the procedure—the one that calls the Confirm function—and then click Toggle Breakpoint on the shortcut menu.

This sets a breakpoint on the statement, so code will stop running there.

Set a breakpoint on this line of code.

Step through the event procedure

To run an event procedure on a form, you don't use the Debug window—instead, you make the event occur on the form, and the event procedure runs automatically.

Form View button

1 Switch to the Contacts form.

2 Click the Form View button.

3 Click the PostalCode field, and delete the value in the field.

4 On the Records menu, click Save Record.

The BeforeUpdate procedure runs, and when Microsoft Access encounters the breakpoint you set, it displays the event procedure in the Module window.

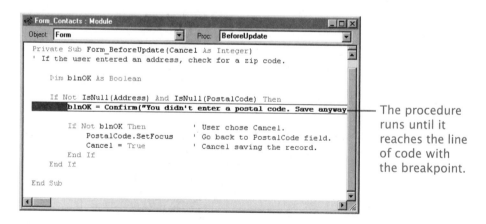

The procedure runs until it reaches the line of code with the breakpoint.

This line of code, the next statement that will run, calls the Confirm function in the Messages module. When you step through this statement, Microsoft Access will pass control to the Confirm function.

Step Into button

5   Click the Step Into button.

Microsoft Access switches to the Messages module window and displays the
Confirm function.

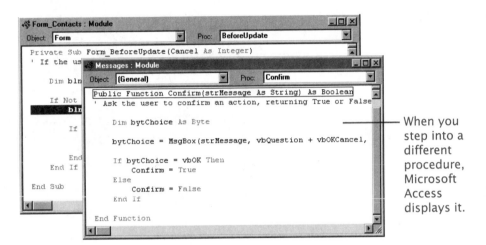

When you
step into a
different
procedure,
Microsoft
Access
displays it.

Now that you're in the Confirm function, you'll use another new technique to
run several lines of code at once.

6   With the right mouse button, click the line with the End Function statement, and
then click Step To Cursor on the shortcut menu.

This command tells Microsoft Access to run code until it reaches the line you
clicked. The code in the Confirm function displays your message, asking whether
you want to save the record without a postal code.

7   Click Cancel.

Microsoft Access displays the procedure again, showing the End Function statement as the current statement.

8   Click the Step Into button.

When the Confirm function ends, Microsoft Access returns control to the Form_BeforeUpdate event procedure—remember, this is the procedure that called the Confirm function. Starting up where it left off, it moves the current statement indicator to the If...Then statement after the line that called the function.

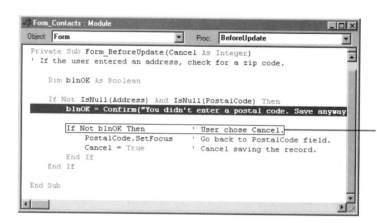

After Microsoft Access returns from another procedure, code continues running where it left off.

You can now continue stepping through the event procedure, or just tell Microsoft Access to continue.

Continue button

9   Click the Continue button.

The BeforeUpdate event procedure finishes running.

10   Switch back to the Contacts form.

Because you chose the Cancel button in the message box, your code didn't allow the record to be saved—the pencil icon is still displayed in the record selector. In the next section, you'll try to save the record again.

> **NOTE**   When you're stepping through code in an event procedure, you can't switch back to the form until the event procedure finishes running. If you want to stop code from running, use the End command (on the Run menu) to end the procedure. Additionally, if an error occurs while you're stepping through code, you may seem to be "stuck" in the procedure. If you can't fix the error and move on, use the Reset command (on the Run menu) to stop all code from running and reset all variables.

Monitoring Variables and Other Values

Stepping through your code can help you figure out where it's going. But as your application progresses, the values of variables and fields stored in the computer's memory change, affecting how your application works. To really understand what's happening as your code runs, you'll want to find out the values of variables and fields along the way. You need a window into the computer's brain.

Using the Debug window, you can find out the value of a variable, control, or other expression. In fact, you've already done this—in Lesson 3, you used the Debug window to find out the value of a property. However, there's a more efficient way to monitor values while your code is running, using the *Watch pane* of the Debug window. To use the Watch pane, you specify one or more expressions in your code that you want to watch, and Microsoft Access displays their values continuously in the Debug window.

Set a watch expression to appear in the Debug window

To see how the Watch pane works, you'll run the form's BeforeUpdate procedure again. But first, you'll specify a variable whose value you want to watch.

1 Switch to the Contacts form's module.

2 Click the Debug Window button.

Debug Window button

If necessary, position the the windows on the screen so you can see the event procedure in the Module window.

3 In the third line of the procedure (the Dim statement that declares the blnOK variable), click the string "blnOK" to position the insertion point on the variable.

Click here to position the insertion point.

4 Click the Instant Watch button on the toolbar.

Instant Watch button

Microsoft Access displays the Instant Watch dialog box, showing the expression you selected. If the expression were *in context*—if the BeforeUpdate event procedure were currently running—the dialog box would also show you the current value of the variable.

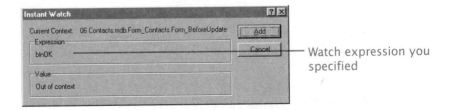

Watch expression you specified

5 Click the Add button.

129

When you added the watch expression, Microsoft Access split the Debug window into two panes. In the top pane, it added the blnOK variable. If you were to add additional watch expressions, they would be listed underneath this one.

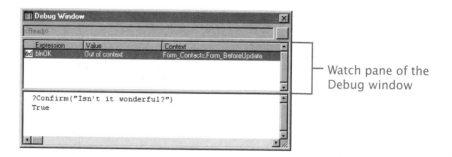

Watch pane of the Debug window

As your procedure runs, the Watch pane automatically reflects the current value of the variable.

Step through the event procedure again

To run the form's BeforeUpdate procedure one more time, you'll try to save the record again with the Postal Code field blank.

1 Switch to the Contacts form.

2 On the Records menu, click Save Record.

When Microsoft Access encounters the breakpoint you set in the BeforeUpdate event procedure, it displays the Module window. Now that the procedure is running, you can check the Debug window to see the value of the watch expression—it shows that the blnOK variable is currently set to False.

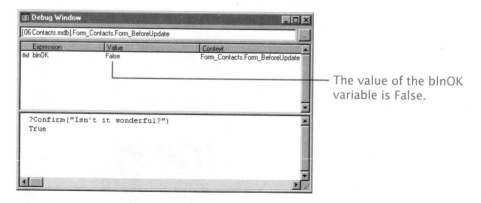

The value of the blnOK variable is False.

It's time to step through the rest of the procedure, starting with the current statement, which calls the Confirm function.

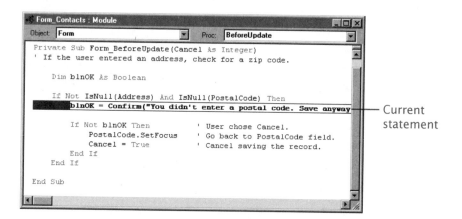

Current
statement

In the previous run through this code, you stepped *into* the code of the Confirm function. This time, you'll learn how to save time by skipping *over* procedures that you aren't interested in. To run a line of code without stepping into the procedure it calls, use the Step Over command—it works just like the Step Into command, except that it runs procedures without pause.

Step Over button

3 Click the Step Over button on the toolbar.

The Confirm function runs, displaying its message box.

4 Click OK.

Microsoft Access displays the BeforeUpdate event procedure again—although you stepped over the Confirm function, you are still stepping through code line by line. The Confirm function in the line you just stepped over should have set the blnOK value based on your choice in the message box. As you can see in the Debug window, the watch expression shows that the blnOK variable is now set to True—indicating that you chose OK in the message box.

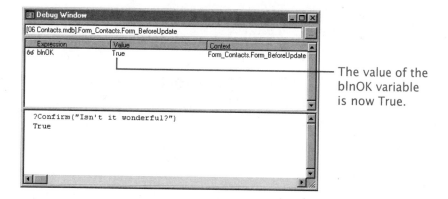

The value of the
blnOK variable
is now True.

You can now continue stepping through the event procedure.

5   Click the Step Over button again.

The current statement indicator skips to this line.

Because the value of the variable is True—which means that *Not blnOK* is False—the If...Then block doesn't run.

6   Click the Step Over button three more times.

The BeforeUpdate event procedure finishes running, allowing the record to be saved in the Contacts form.

Delete the watch expression

When you're finished with a watch expression, you can delete it from the Watch pane of the Debug window.

1   In the Debug window, click the line with the blnOK expression, and then press DELETE.

With no watch expressions listed, you no longer need to see the Watch pane.

2   Click the bar between the two panes of the Debug window, and then, holding down the mouse button, drag it to the top of the window.

Click here and drag to the top of the window.

The Watch pane disappears.

3 Close the Debug window.

Other Techniques for Monitoring Your Code

Watch expressions are useful when you want to monitor the value of a variable or other expression continuously while your code runs. But there are several other techniques you can use for monitoring the progress of your code.

Send values or messages to the Debug window. If there is a certain point in your code where you want to check the status of your procedure or the value of a variable, you can send a message to the Debug window by using the Print method of the Debug object. Anywhere you want to send output to the Debug window, insert a line and type **Debug.Print** followed by the expression you want to display. For example, you might add the following line of code in the BeforeUpdate procedure instead of using a watch expression:

```
Debug.Print "The Confirm function returned: "; blnOK
```

This way, each time the procedure runs, it reports the value of blnOK in the Debug window. You don't need to set a breakpoint or step through code at all—you can just check the Debug window after the procedure finishes running.

Display message boxes. If you want to report on the progress of a procedure while it runs, but you don't want to check the Debug window each time, you can instead display messages to yourself using the MsgBox function. For example, you could place the following line of code in the BeforeUpdate procedure:

```
MsgBox "The Confirm function returned: " & blnOK
```

Change code as it runs. In most programming systems, you can't change code while it's running. But in Microsoft Access, you have the flexibility to change the values of variables or code itself while you step through line by line. Suppose you're monitoring a variable and you notice it doesn't have the value you expect. If necessary, you can add a line of code to your procedure and continue running it.

Set the current statement. Normally, when stepping through code, you don't control the order in which Visual Basic statements occur. However, if you're stepping through code and would like to change which statement runs next, you can use the Set Next Statement command (on the Run menu). This is especially useful if you change a line of code that didn't work as expected, and you want to run it again without restarting the procedure.

The strategy you select to monitor and debug your code depends on what problems you're trying to diagnose and how often you need to check what's happening. As you program in Visual Basic, you'll learn which techniques are most appropriate for each debugging task.

Finding and Fixing Bugs in Your Code

The procedures you've stepped through so far aren't broken—although you've learned more about how they work by monitoring them more closely, they seem to be working just fine. But what if code isn't working as you'd planned? This is when Module window tools come in especially handy. In this section, you'll learn to check your Visual Basic code as you enter it, and then fix any errors you find.

Most of your contacts are in either New York or Seattle, and you'd like to make it easier for users to enter addresses from these cities. One approach is to write an event procedure that runs after you enter a postal code, filling in the correct City and State values. This way, users who know about the shortcut can skip over the City and State fields when they're entering New York or Seattle addresses. While you're at it, you'll also have the event procedure fill in the Country field if the user enters a U.S. postal code.

Write an event procedure that fills in values for you

You want to set the City, State, and Country fields each time the user enters a value in the PostalCode field. To do this, you need to create an event procedure for the control's AfterUpdate event.

1   In the Object box at the top of the Module window, select PostalCode.

2   In the Proc box, select AfterUpdate.

The Module window shows the PostalCode_AfterUpdate event procedure.

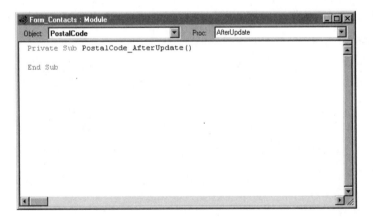

3 Type the following code for the event procedure:

```
' If New York or Seattle postal code, fill in city and state fields.

    Select Case PostalCode
        Case "10000" To "10200"
            City = "New York"
            State = "NY"
        Case "98100" To "98199"
            City = "Seattle"
            State = "WA"

End Select
```

So far so good! This code introduces a new Visual Basic statement for controlling the flow of code: the Select Case statement. You use this statement when you want to perform one of several different actions based on the value of a single variable or expression. Each Case statement underneath it introduces a different block of code—which block of code runs depends on which value the Select Case expression has. As you've seen before, indenting each block of code helps to show how the statement works.

In this example, you're telling Microsoft Access, "Okay, look at the value of the PostalCode field—if it's between 10000 and 10200 (New York), run this first block of code; if it's between 98100 and 98199 (Seattle), run this second block of code." You can set up as many "cases" as necessary—and if you want, you can finish with the Case Else statement followed by a block of code, which runs if none of the cases match the value of the Select Case expression.

Next, you'll add code that checks whether the postal code is a U.S. code, and fills in the Country field if the postal code is a U.S. code.

4 Just above the line with the End Select statement, enter the following line of code:

```
If PostalCode > "00000" And < "99999" Then
```

When you press ENTER, the text of this line turns red and a message appears. You made an error! (Of course, you were only following instructions.)

Microsoft Access highlights the spot where it identifies a problem.

135

The error message, "Expected: expression," tells you that Visual Basic requires an expression—such as a variable—at this point in the line.

You may not have known it, especially if you're a good typist, but every time you've entered a line of code in the Module window, Microsoft Access has checked to make sure it follows the rules. In this case, you've entered something that isn't allowed—even though it looks like it should work. The line seems to say, "If the PostalCode field is greater than five zeros and less than five nines, then..." Why doesn't it work? Unlike the English language, where you can skip the subject if it's repeated after a conjunction such as "and"—as in "Buzz went to the moon and returned"—the Visual Basic language requires you to repeat the subject. In other words, you have to say, "If the PostalCode field is this and the PostalCode field is that..."

Fix the error and finish the procedure

Before going any further, you should fix the error. Incidentally, if you don't fix a line of code that contains a syntax error, Microsoft Access continues to display the line in red text to indicate that it isn't valid.

1 In the message box, click OK.

2 Press the LEFT ARROW key, type **PostalCode** and then click the next line.

No error this time!

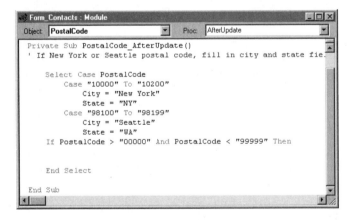

```
Form_Contacts : Module
Object: PostalCode          Proc: AfterUpdate

Private Sub PostalCode_AfterUpdate()
' If New York or Seattle postal code, fill in city and state fie.

    Select Case PostalCode
        Case "10000" To "10200"
            City = "New York"
            State = "NY"
        Case "98100" To "98199"
            City = "Seattle"
            State = "WA"
    If PostalCode > "00000" And PostalCode < "99999" Then


    End Select

End Sub
```

3 Enter the following two lines of code underneath the If...Then statement:

```
Country = "USA"
Title.SetFocus
```

These two lines set the value of the Country field and then move the focus to the Title field, because the user no longer needs to enter a value in the Country field.

Types of Errors

Errors are bound to occur when you write or run code—which is why Microsoft Access offers so many tools to help you deal with them. Still, it isn't always easy to figure out what's wrong. To know where to look, it helps to know the types of errors that can occur. Most errors fall into the following categories:

Syntax errors   When you type a keyword incorrectly or leave off punctuation in code, Microsoft Access displays a message as soon as you try to leave the line. Usually, the message tells you exactly what is wrong with the line of code. Until you fix a line of code with a syntax error, Microsoft Access displays the line in red.

Invalid references   If you misspell a variable, field name, or procedure, or if you forget to declare a variable you use, Microsoft Access displays an error when you try to run the code.

Incomplete code   If your code isn't logically complete—for example, if you have an If...Then statement block without an End If statement—Microsoft Access displays an error when you try to run the code.

Logic errors   If your code runs without errors but doesn't do what you had planned, you've probably made an error in the logic of your program. Remember, the computer only does what you tell it—you can't make any assumptions about how things will work! The toughest kind of error to figure out, a logic error requires that you step through code to watch what's happening, and then correct any mistakes you find.

Run-time errors   There are many errors that Microsoft Access can't detect until your application is running. For example, if your code passes an invalid value as the argument to a Visual Basic function, an error occurs and code stops running. A run-time error sometimes indicates that your code needs rethinking—especially if you made incorrect assumptions about how the user interacts with your application. In many cases, however, run-time errors are to be expected—and later in the lesson, you'll see how your code can respond to them before an error message disrupts your application.

You'll see examples of all these types of errors in this lesson—and you're guaranteed to keep seeing them, just about every time you program. However, as you gain experience with Visual Basic programming, you'll become better at avoiding errors or handling them as they come up.

Telling Microsoft Access to Check Your Code

You've already seen how Microsoft Access checks each line of code you enter to make sure that it doesn't contain any errors. But many errors aren't obvious in a single line. To see them, you have to look at the line of code in the context of the rest of the procedure or application. Although it doesn't do so automatically while you enter code, Microsoft Access does check your procedures thoroughly before it runs them. It checks for various types of consistency—for example, whether the variables you've used in your code are all declared, and whether the procedures you call exist in your application. This process is called *compiling*, because it involves putting together information from various sources in your application, preparing to run the code.

One way to compile a procedure is to try running it. But you won't always want to wait until you run your code to make sure it's all right—that would be like checking to see if you have air in your tires only *after* leaving on a long trip. Fortunately, you can ask Microsoft Access to compile your procedures at any time.

Compile your event procedure and resolve errors

Believe it or not, there are a couple of errors in the PostalCode_AfterUpdate procedure. If you try to run the procedure as it is, it won't work. To find out what they are, you'll ask Microsoft Access to compile your code.

Compile Loaded Modules button

1   Click the Compile Loaded Modules button.

Microsoft Access displays the error message "Variable not defined." This message means, more or less, that Microsoft Access isn't familiar with an expression in your code. The expression it can't figure out is highlighted in the Module window. In this case, the "variable" that Microsoft Access doesn't recognize is *State*.

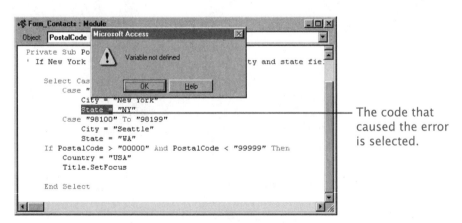

The code that caused the error is selected.

In this line of code, you're not actually referring to a variable at all—you're trying to refer to the State field on the Contacts form. The reason for this error? The field is actually called *StateOrProvince*—a simple mistake, but one we'll need to correct before going on. In cases like this one where you've misspelled something, you'll notice that Microsoft Access isn't always as helpful as it could be. At least it isn't judgmental—just matter-of-fact.

2   In the message box, click OK.

3   Click the end of the word *State* and type **OrProvince**

4   Two lines down, at the other reference to *State,* click the end of the word and type **OrProvince**

Now that you've fixed the error, you should compile again to make sure that everything's just right.

5   Click the Compile Loaded Modules button again.

It's not just right. This time, the message Microsoft Access displays is "Block If without End If." This message indicates that you used the If...Then statement, included a block of code after it, but didn't include the End If statement to indicate the end of the block.

The statement that's selected is the one immediately *after* the point where Microsoft Access expects to see the End If statement.

6   Click OK.

7   Click the blank line above the End Select statement and type **End If**

8   Click the Compile Loaded Modules button once again.

No surprises this time; your house is in order.

 TIP   In any Visual Basic error message, you can click the Help button to see a Help topic giving you more information about the error and how to fix it.

139

Run the event procedure from the Contacts form

Now that the code compiles fine, you can test the procedure to see if it works correctly. You'll want to step through the code, so you should set a breakpoint in the event procedure.

1 With the right mouse button, click the Select Case line in the event procedure, and then click Toggle Breakpoint.

2 Switch to the Contacts form.

New Record button

3 Click the New Record button on the toolbar.

4 Fill in the fields in the record as follows:

Field Name	Value
First Name	Katherine
Last Name	Ransel
Address	102 W. 86th St.
Postal Code	10024

5 Press TAB to leave the PostalCode field.

When you leave the field, your event procedure runs. When Microsoft Access reaches the breakpoint, it suspends the running code and brings the Module window to the front.

Before you step through the code, check to see what the PostalCode value is.

6 With the right mouse button, click the word PostalCode, and then click Instant Watch on the shortcut menu.

The Instant Watch dialog box appears, showing the value you entered for the PostalCode field: 10024.

The Instant Watch dialog box shows the current value of an expression.

7 Click Cancel—this time, you don't want to add the watch expression to the Debug window.

Now that you've verified that the value of the Select Case expression is 10024, step through the code and watch what happens.

Step Into button

8 Click the Step Into button on the toolbar.

The current statement indicator moves to the Case statement for the first block of code, where it will check whether the value 10024 falls in the range of 10000 to 10200.

9 Click the Step Into button again.

As expected, the current statement indicator moves into the first block of code, because the value 10024 does fall in the range of 10000 to 10200. When you allow it to continue, Microsoft Access will run the two lines underneath the Case statement, which set the City and State values for New York.

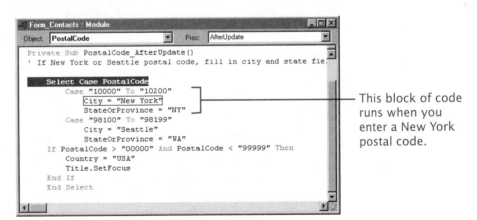

This block of code runs when you enter a New York postal code.

Continue button

10 Click the Continue button on the toolbar.

11 Switch to the Contacts form.

The City and State fields are filled in as you'd planned. However, look at the Country field. Your code was supposed to set it for you, but it doesn't have a value. Something in the event procedure isn't working correctly.

141

Fix a bug in your code

To figure out the problem, you need to run the event procedure again. This time, you'll try a different postal code, and see what happens in the code.

1 Click the PostalCode field and type **02134**

2 Press TAB.

The PostalCode_AfterUpdate event procedure runs and stops at the breakpoint.

3 Click the Step Into button twice.

Microsoft Access steps over the Case statements, because the postal code you entered doesn't fall in the range.

4 Click the Step Into button a third time.

Step Into button

As you expected, the two lines underneath the second case statement didn't run. But look where the current statement indicator jumped to: it skipped over not only the two lines under the Case statement, but also the entire block of code that sets the Country field, and ended up on the End Select statement at the very end of the procedure.

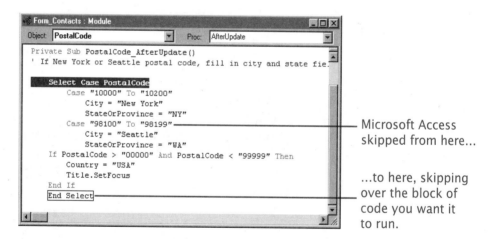

You've found the mistake in the code. Because the block of code is between the Case statement and the End Select statement, Microsoft Access assumes it is part of that "case," and runs it only when the postal code is in that range. To make the If...Then block run independently, you need to move it completely outside the Select Case...End Select structure.

5 Click the left margin of the Module window, to the left of the If...Then statement, and drag down to the End If statement to select the entire block of code.

The four lines appear highlighted.

6 Press CTRL+X to cut the lines to the Clipboard.

7 Press the DOWN ARROW key once to move to the line following the End Select statement.

8   Press CTRL+V to paste the block of code.

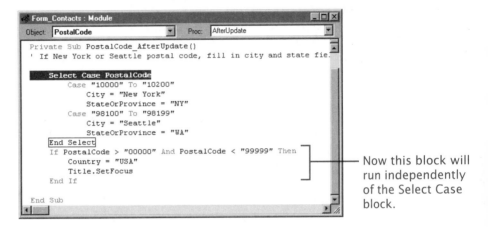

Now this block will run independently of the Select Case block.

Retest the procedure

Debugging your code is all about testing and retesting your procedures—and it's time to test it once more. First, however, you'll need to stop the code that's currently running and clear the breakpoint so the procedure can run without interruption.

Reset button

1   Click the Reset button on the toolbar.

Microsoft Access ends the procedure and resets all variables.

2   On the Run menu, click Clear All Breakpoints.

3   Switch to the Contacts form.

4   Click the PostalCode field, and then type **10024**

5   Press TAB.

This time, the Country field gets filled in with the value "USA," and the focus moves to the Title field. The bug is fixed!

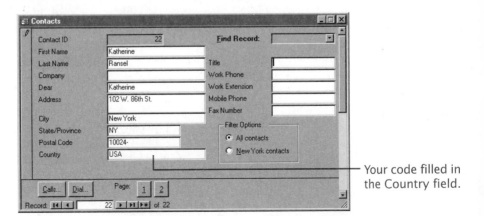

Your code filled in the Country field.

As you continue to program in Visual Basic, you're guaranteed to get all sorts of unexpected results from your code—some because of typos, some because of mistakes in program logic, and still others because of misunderstandings about how Microsoft Access works. But using the tools available in the Debug window—along with a healthy dose of patience and diligence in testing and retesting your procedures—you'll be able to solve these problems and get your application working just right.

Close the form and exit Microsoft Access

1   Close the Contacts form, clicking Yes when Microsoft Access asks if you want to save changes to the form.

2   On the File menu, click Exit.

Lesson Summary

To	Do this	Button
Stop a procedure from running so you can monitor its progress	Set a breakpoint at the line where you want to stop the code from running (click the line in the Module window and then click the Breakpoint button).	
Step through code in a procedure line by line, moving into the procedures that your code calls	Click the Step Into button (or press the F8 key).	
Step through code line by line, skipping over the procedures that your code calls	Click the Step Over button.	
Continue running code after you've stopped it	Click the Continue button.	
View the value of a variable or other expression while code is running	Click the text of the variable or expression in the Module window, and then click Instant Watch. To add the watch expression to the Debug window so you can monitor it continuously, click Add.	
Run one of several different blocks of code based on the value of a single expression	Use the Select...Case statement.	
Check your code to make sure the structure and all the syntax are correct	Compile your code using the Compile Loaded Modules command or the Compile All Modules command.	

For online information about	On the Help menu, click Microsoft Access Help Topics, click the Index tab, and then
Using tools in the Module window	Search for "Module window"
Finding and fixing bugs in your code	Search for "debugging Visual Basic code"
Controlling the flow of code in your application	Search for "control flow"

For more information on	In *Building Applications with Microsoft Access*, see
Using tools in the Module window	Chapter 2, "Introducing Visual Basic"
Finding and fixing bugs in your code	Chapter 8, "Handling Run-Time Errors"
Controlling the flow of code in your application	Chapter 2, "Introducing Visual Basic"

Preview of the Next Lesson

In this lesson, you discovered more about how your procedures work, and learned to find programming errors. In the next lesson, you'll learn about errors that can't be fixed—errors due to unexpected conditions or actions the user takes, that occur while the application runs. Instead of fixing your code, you'll learn how to write code that anticipates such errors and handles them accordingly.

Respond to Errors and Unexpected Conditions

Estimated time
35 min.

In this lesson you will learn how to:

- Replace standard Microsoft Access error messages with your own.
- Write code that responds to errors and unexpected conditions.
- Add a value to a combo box list.

If you've ever been on a trip into the wilderness, you know that there's quite a bit of work involved in preparation. You need to be ready for anything—confusing trails make it easy to get lost, unexpected weather can catch you off guard, and even a minor injury can be a big deal away from civilization. For safety, you bring maps, a compass, first aid supplies, and extra food and clothing in case of a prolonged stay. Most of the time, you won't take advantage of your precautions—but who wants to be stuck in the middle of nowhere without these bases covered? You don't mind the risks, of course—it wouldn't be any fun if it were as safe as sitting in your living room!

Planning for the unexpected has its application in Visual Basic programming as well. The nature of an event-driven system like Microsoft Access is that your application waits around for things to happen. Most of them are what you expect: the user adds data here, clicks a button there. But computer users have a way of trying everything, and sooner or later, someone will try something you didn't anticipate. Although the errors that can occur in your application are less exciting than being stuck in the wilderness, it nevertheless pays to prepare your application for anything before sending it out into the wild world of daily use.

The Visual Basic language provides sophisticated ways to control what happens when errors occur. Normally, errors can interrupt your application, causing it to appear unpolished or even making it unusable. In this lesson, you'll learn to respond to special events that occur when users perform unexpected actions on your forms. Additionally, you'll learn to use Visual Basic statements to intercept errors that occur while your procedures are running. Overall, you'll discover strategies for making your application foolproof—so that whatever comes its way, it can respond gracefully and effectively.

Start the lesson

 Start Microsoft Access and open the 07 Contacts database in the practice files folder.

Replacing Standard Error Messages

There are many errors that can occur when users interact with the forms in your application. Some of these errors will come as a complete surprise, and there may be nothing you can do about them. On the other hand, you occasionally *intend* to have a specific error occur. For example, suppose you set the Required property to Yes for a field in a table, and then the user tries to leave the field blank when entering data. As you would expect, Microsoft Access displays an error message saying that the field can't be blank. In Lesson 4, you did this very thing for the LastName and FirstName fields in the Contacts table.

If you expect that users will commonly encounter a specific error in a form, such as the error for leaving a required field blank, you'll want to ensure that the message they receive makes sense to them, so they can fix the problem and continue with their work. But the standard error messages Microsoft Access displays won't always make sense to your users. In this section, you'll learn to replace the standard error messages that occur on your forms with your own messages. Specifically, you'll respond to the error that occurs when a user leaves a required field blank, creating an event procedure that displays your own message for this situation.

Responding to the Error Event

Each time an error occurs in a form, the form's Error event occurs. You can place code in this event procedure to display a message, or even to fix the problem that's causing the error. But to respond, you'll need to know what error has occurred. For this purpose, the Error event procedure includes an argument called DataErr, which contains the code number of the error that occurred. You'll use this number to determine whether it's the error you're expecting, so you can respond appropriately.

But first, you must do a little detective work. You need to find out what the code number is for the error you want to respond to. To do this, you'll add code to the Error event procedure telling Microsoft Access to display the error number in the Debug window. Then, you'll cause the error to occur so you can discover the number. After you know the code number of the error that occurs when the user leaves a required field blank, you'll change the code to respond to this specific error.

Find out the code number for an error in a form

You'll first open the Contacts form, and then add a line of code to the Error event procedure.

1   In the Database window, click the Forms tab.

2   Click the Contacts form, and then click the Design button.

3   If the property sheet isn't open, click the Properties button on the toolbar.

Properties button

4   Click the Event tab in the property sheet.

5   Select the OnError property, and then click the Build button.

Click the Build Button.

6   Click Code Builder, and then click OK.

Microsoft Access displays the Form_Error event procedure in the Module window.

```
Form_Contacts : Module                                    _□×
Object: Form              ▼   Proc:  Error              ▼
    Private Sub Form_Error(DataErr As Integer, Response As Integer)

    End Sub
```

Note the two arguments in the Sub header for the Form_Error procedure, DataErr and Response.

7   Press TAB and type the following line of code:

```
Debug.Print "DataErr = "; DataErr
```

Debug Window button

8   Click the Debug Window button.

This opens the Debug window so your code will have somewhere to send its message.

Cause the error to occur

Now you'll jump back to the Contacts form and cause the error to occur by trying to save a record without a name.

149

Form View button

1 Switch to the Contacts form.

2 Click the Form View button on the toolbar.

3 Press DELETE to delete the data in the FirstName field.

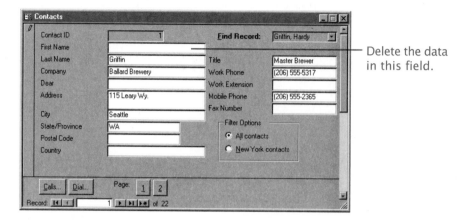

Delete the data in this field.

4 Press TAB.

Because the FirstName field is required, Microsoft Access displays an error message.

As you can see, the error message isn't all that friendly—but you'll replace it with your own message.

5 Click OK.

When you caused the Error event to run the event procedure, your code sent a message to the Debug window.

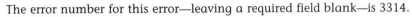

The error number for this error—leaving a required field blank—is 3314.

6 Close the Debug window.

7 Press ESC to undo your change.

Displaying Your Own Message for a Specific Error

Now that you know the error number, you can write code to respond to the error. In the Error event procedure, you'll check to see if the error is due to the user leaving a required field blank. If it is, you'll display an appropriate message; if not, you'll allow Microsoft Access to display the standard error message.

In addition to the DataErr argument that provides you with the number of the error that occurred, the Error event procedure has another argument: the Response argument. You use this argument to tell Microsoft Access how to proceed after your code runs. You have two options: you can tell Microsoft Access to display the standard message for the error, or you can tell it to ignore the error, either because you've solved the problem, or because you've displayed your own custom error message.

Write code that displays a custom error message

You'll replace the Debug.Print code you wrote before with code that displays your own message.

1 Switch to the Contacts form's module.

The Module window still shows the Form_Error event procedure.

2 Enter the following Visual Basic code for the procedure, replacing the line containing Debug.Print with the lines of code shown here:

```
Private Sub Form_Error(DataErr As Integer, Response As Integer)
' If error is because of name, display a custom error message.

    Const conErrFieldRequired = 3314

    If DataErr = conErrFieldRequired Then
        DisplayMessage "You must fill in both First Name and Last Name."
        Response = acDataErrContinue
    Else
        Response = acDataErrDisplay    ' Display standard error message.
    End If
End Sub
```

Let's walk through the procedure line by line:

■ The Const statement declares a constant value for the error code you discovered. This helps to make your code more readable, because it clarifies what the number 3314 means. You can use the constant conErrFieldRequired in place of the number later in the procedure.

■ The condition in the If...Then statement checks whether the DataErr value passed to the event procedure is equal to the error value conErrFieldRequired. If it is, the procedure runs the first block of code, displaying your custom message.

■ The DisplayMessage line of code uses the general procedure you created in Lesson 5 to display a message box. The message tells users what to do to solve the problem: fill in both the first and last name before saving the record.

■ The next line sets the Response argument of the Error event procedure, using the predefined constant acDataErrContinue. Setting the Response argument to this value tells Microsoft Access to skip displaying the standard error message—which is what you want in this case, because you displayed your own message.

■ The Else block of code, which runs if the error is something other than the one you want to respond to, sets the Response argument to acDataErrDisplay. This tells Microsoft Access to display the standard error message for the error, because you don't know what the error is.

Try the new message

If you cause the error again, it should display your new message.

1 Switch to the Contacts form.

2 Click the label of the First Name field to select the data in the field.

3 Press DELETE to delete the data in the field.

4 Press TAB.

Microsoft Access displays the new error message.

5 Click OK.

6 Press ESC.

This simple use of the Error event shows how you can make life easier for users by anticipating problems they may encounter. Of course, this code responds only to a single error. By writing more complex code for the Error event, you can respond to errors in various ways. For example, you might want to use a Select...Case statement to branch to several different blocks of code, providing your own error message for several errors. Or you might write code to help the user solve the problem—for example, your code could enter a required value automatically so that the record could be saved. The possibilities are endless; the main thing to remember is that when an error occurring in a form causes confusion, the Error event procedure is there as a resource to help you solve the problem.

Responding to a Combo Box Error

While the Error event helps you respond to many errors, there's one error that you respond to using a different event—an error that commonly occurs if you use combo boxes on your application's forms. Combo boxes and list boxes are one of the most powerful features of Microsoft Access, because they provide a way to look up values stored in different tables. In this section, you'll learn how to make them work even better by responding to the NotInList event.

The Contacts form has a lookup field courtesy of the Database Wizard: the Contact Type field. This field displays values from the Contact Types table, so you can easily specify the type of each contact you enter by selecting from the list. For many fields, you'll want to ensure that only certain values are entered in the list. Combo boxes do this automatically if their LimitToList property is set to Yes—if you try to type a value in the Contact Type field that isn't in the list, you get an error.

Try typing a new value in the Contact Type field

Suppose you want to enter the contact type for the first record in the Contacts form.

1 Click the Page 2 button in the Contacts form footer.

2   Click the Contact Type field, and then click the drop-down arrow next to the combo box.

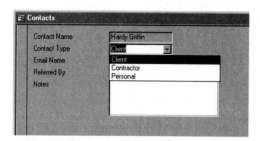

You don't see the contact type you want.

3   Click the drop-down arrow again to close the list, and then type **Dummy** and press ENTER.

Microsoft Access displays an error message, telling you that this value isn't in the list.

4   Click OK.

5   Press ESC.

This error message is a form of validation—Microsoft Access makes sure you don't enter an incorrect value. But what if you want users to be able to add their own contact types? They could do this by opening the Contact Types form, but this would interrupt their task of entering a contact. Ideally, you'd like them to do this easily from within the Contacts form. What you want to do is run an event procedure any time the user enters a value that isn't in the list. You can do this by responding to the NotInList event, which occurs when the user tries to enter the value—but before the error message tells the user the value must be in the list.

Allow users to add a contact type to the list automatically

When a user enters a contact type value that isn't in the list, you want to ask if the user really wants this value to appear in the list permanently. To ask the question, you'll use the Confirm function you wrote in Lesson 5. If the user does want to add the new type, you'll use Visual Basic code to add the value to the Contact Types table behind the scenes.

Design View button

1 Click the Design View button.

2 Scroll down in the form window so you can see the ContactTypeID combo box.

3 Click the ContactTypeID control.

Microsoft Access displays the event properties for the ContactTypeID control.

4 Click the OnNotInList property, and then click the Build button.

5 Select Code Builder, and then click OK.

Microsoft Access opens the form module for the Contacts form and creates the ContactTypeID_NotInList event procedure.

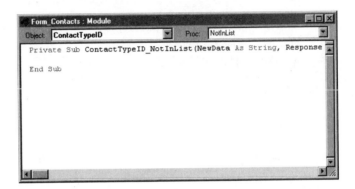

You'll notice that the header for the NotInList procedure includes two arguments: NewData and Response. The NewData argument contains the value the user entered in the field—the value that isn't yet in the list. The Response argument lets you tell Microsoft Access what to do after your procedure ends—just like the Response argument you saw earlier in the Error event procedure.

6 Enter the following Visual Basic code for the procedure:

```
Private Sub ContactTypeID_NotInList(NewData As String, Response As Integer)
' Ask the user whether to add a value to the list.

    Dim strMessage As String
    Dim dbsContacts As Database
    Dim rstTypes As Recordset

    strMessage = "Are you sure you want to add '" & NewData & _
              "' to the list of contact types?"

    If Confirm(strMessage) Then

        ' Open the Contact Types table and add the NewData value.
        Set dbsContacts = CurrentDb()
        Set rstTypes = dbsContacts.OpenRecordset("Contact Types")
        rstTypes.AddNew
        rstTypes!ContactType = NewData
        rstTypes.Update
```

155

```
            Response = acDataErrAdded      ' Requery the list.

      Else
            Response = acDataErrDisplay    ' Display the error.
      End If
End Sub
```

This event procedure uses the same type of code you've seen before to ask the user a question. However, there are several important new elements:

- The procedure has three Dim statements declaring variables you're going to use later in the procedure. The first declares a string variable you'll use to store your message to the user. The other two are *object variables*—so named because they store whole database objects, not just values—which you'll use when you add a record to the Contact Types table. The first of these is dbsContacts, a Database-type variable that will store information about the database; the second is rstTypes, a Recordset-type variable that will represent the Contact Types table when you add records.

- The line that sets the value of the strMessage variable concatenates string values with the ampersand (&) operator. In this case, the line of code combines your message text with the value of the NewData variable, so the message can include the new value in the question it asks: "Do you want to add *this value* to the list of contact types?"

- The condition in the If...Then statement is actually a call to your own Confirm function, which asks the user a question and returns True or False. If the Confirm function returns True, it means the user chose OK in the message box, and the first block of code runs.

- The key to this procedure is the block of code that runs if the user chooses OK. These five lines are known as *data access object* (DAO) code, because they utilize methods and statements belonging to the DAO code library, which you use when working directly with databases. For example, the first line uses the Set statement to assign an object to the dbsContacts variable—in this case it assigns the current database object, which is returned by the CurrentDb function. Before you can work with data in Visual Basic, you have to open a database in this way.

- The next line uses the OpenRecordset method of the new database object to open the Contact Types table. To add or edit records using Visual Basic, you need to open a recordset object, either a table or a query. The Set statement assigns the recordset object to the rstTypes variable. As with other methods, you type the method after the object, separated by a period.

- The next line uses the AddNew method of the rstTypes recordset to add a record to the end of the table.

- The next line assigns the value of the NewData argument, which is the value the user wants in the list, to the ContactType field in the table. To refer to the value of a field in a recordset, you follow the recordset name with the field name, separated by an exclamation point (!).

- The final line of DAO code uses the Update method to save the change to the recordset, adding the new record to the Contact Types table.

- After your procedure adds the record to the table, the last task is to tell Microsoft Access how to proceed. Setting the Response argument to the constant acDataErrAdded tells Microsoft Access that you've added the value, and you want it to requery the list box so that the value will show up in the list.

- The line after the Else keyword runs if the condition is False, in which case it sets the Response argument to acDataErrDisplay. This setting tells Microsoft Access that you didn't add the value, and that you want it to display the standard error message and require the user to enter a value in the list.

The NotInList procedure gives a simple example of DAO code for manipulating a database—in later lessons, you'll learn advanced techniques for working with databases in Visual Basic. But this procedure does the trick for now: it adds a new record to the list. Perhaps most importantly, it allows your users to avoid a potentially annoying error message every time they try to type something in this box.

Try the NotInList event procedure

Form View button

1 Close the Module window.

2 Click the Form View button on the toolbar.

3 Click the Page 2 button in the form footer.

4 Click the Contact Type field, and then type **Dummy** and press ENTER.

The NotInList event occurs, and your event procedure displays the message box, asking if you want to add your entry to the list.

5 Click OK.

Your code opens the Contact Types table, adds the new record, and then tells Microsoft Access to requery the list to include your new value.

6 Click the drop-down arrow next to the Contact Type box.

The list now includes your new entry.

Adding a record to the list behind the scenes is just one possible strategy for responding to the NotInList event; you may need to choose another based on your application's needs. For example, if the records shown in a combo box list are just part of a complete set of records that includes other values—a list of contacts names, perhaps, taken from a complete table with addresses and phone numbers—you couldn't add records automatically. In a case like this, your NotInList event procedure might display another form where users could enter contact information.

157

Creating Error-Handling Routines

Up to this point, you've learned how to respond to errors that occur due to users' actions on a form, particularly when they enter data that isn't allowed. These errors are easy to respond to, because form events occur whenever they happen. When you program in Visual Basic, there's an even more important class of errors: those that happen as a result of actions your code performs, rather than as a result of users' actions. Some errors occur because of mistakes in the code you've written; these you should fix. But others happen not because of an error in your code, but just because your code can't anticipate every possible condition that might be in place when it runs.

For example, suppose your code works with a database on a network, and the network suddenly goes down. Obviously, this would cause an error. Or what if your code makes changes to a database, but the user opens the database using the read-only option so that changes can't be made? These unexpected conditions will cause run-time errors, and would normally cause your application to stop abruptly, showing a message that would mean very little to a user who doesn't know about programming.

Fortunately, Visual Basic provides a mechanism with which you can respond to any type of error that occurs while your code is running. It's called *error handling*. Error handling allows you to avoid abrupt interruptions of your application whenever unexpected things happen. By handling errors, you can either solve problems that come up and move on with your business, or give the user appropriate feedback about the problem and bow out gracefully. In this section, you'll learn how to use the On Error GoTo statement along with other Visual Basic statements to respond to run-time errors.

Handling Errors That Occur When Your Application Is Read-Only

When testing your application, it's a good idea to think of all the different conditions that might arise when users run it. One situation is that the user might open the application database in read-only mode. This isn't a common case, but it is certainly possible, and you want your application to be able to cope with it gracefully. Fortunately, when users open an application as read-only, Microsoft Access automatically forbids them to change data in forms—you don't have to do anything special to make it work. You only have to worry if your code itself makes changes to data.

But guess what? In Lesson 4, you wrote code that sets the value of controls on the form. It's the Form_KeyDown procedure, which sets city, state, and country values on the form for New York whenever a user presses CTRL+1. If the data can't be updated—for example, if the database is read-only—this code will cause a run-time error.

Set up a run-time error in your code

Before you write code to handle this error, let's see what happens if you don't handle it at all. Rather than closing the database and reopening it in read-only mode, you'll simulate this condition by making just the data in the Contacts form read-only. To do this, you can set the RecordsetType property for the form to Snapshot.

Design View button

Form View button

1 Click the Design View button on the toolbar.

2 On the Edit menu, click Select Form.

3 Click the Data tab in the property sheet.

4 Click the RecordsetType property, and select Snapshot from the list of values.

5 Click the Form View button on the toolbar.

6 Press CTRL+1.

An error occurs—and not one you'd like your users to see.

As with all run-time errors, you have two choices: Debug or End (you can also get Help on the message, but you still have to choose one of the other two options). If you click Debug, Microsoft Access opens the Module window and displays the procedure that caused the error, highlighting the specific line of code that caused it. If you click End, the procedure that caused the error stops running.

Note the code number of the error; you'll use it in your error-handling code: 3326.

7 Click Debug.

The Module window shows the existing Form_KeyDown event procedure, which you wrote in Lesson 4.

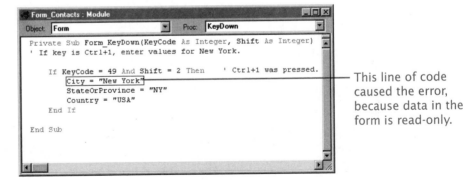

This line of code caused the error, because data in the form is read-only.

NOTE When you click the Debug button in a run-time error message, the procedure stops running temporarily, but doesn't end. It's just as if you'd set a breakpoint on the statement that caused the error—except that you can't keep stepping through this code unless you first take care of the error. If you want to end the procedure that caused an error, rather than stop and view it, click the End button in the run-time error message.

Add error-handling code to the form's KeyDown event procedure

Because you want to avoid having users see an error message like this—especially one that lets them dive right into your code—you'll add error-handling code to the procedure. But first you'll want to reset the code that you left running when the error occurred.

Reset button

1 Click the Reset button on the toolbar.

2 Edit the existing KeyDown event procedure to appear as follows:

```
Private Sub Form_KeyDown(KeyCode As Integer, Shift As Integer)
' If key is CTRL+1, enter values for New York.

On Error GoTo Err_Form_KeyDown

    Const conErrNotUpdatable = 3326

    If KeyCode = 49 And Shift = 2 Then   ' CTRL+1 was pressed.
        City = "New York"
        StateOrProvince = "NY"
        Country = "USA"
    End If

Exit_Form_KeyDown:
    Exit Sub

Err_Form_KeyDown:
    If Err.Number = conErrNotUpdatable Then
        DisplayMessage "Can't edit record; data is read-only."
    Else
        DisplayMessage Err.Description
    End If
    Resume Exit_Form_KeyDown
End Sub
```

Here's what the code does:

- The On Error GoTo statement says that if an error occurs while the procedure is running, Microsoft Access should jump to the line labeled Err_Form_KeyDown, rather than halting the code and displaying an error message.

- The Const statement declares a constant value for the error code you saw earlier (3326), which signifies the "Recordset not updatable" error.

- The Exit_Form_KeyDown line is a *label*, a name followed by a colon that you can use to identify a line of code you want Microsoft Access to jump to. The Exit Sub statement below the label makes sure that if the procedure runs normally without error, it will exit after running the main code, rather than continuing with the error-handling code below. You should always add the Exit Sub or Exit Function statement before error-handling code, so the error-handling code won't run unless an error actually occurs.

- The Err_Form_KeyDown label introduces the error-handling code, and provides a place for Microsoft Access to jump to if an error does occur.

- The If...Then statement on the next line checks to see if the error is in fact the one you expected. It uses the Number property of the Err object, which always contains the number of the last error that occurred in your application.

- If the error is caused by read-only data, the following line displays your custom message using the DisplayMessage Sub procedure you created in Lesson 5. If the error is caused by something else you didn't expect, the line under the Else statement displays the standard Microsoft Access error message, which you can find using the Description property of the Err object.

- Finally, the Resume statement in the last line tells Microsoft Access that your error-handling code is finished, and that you want to continue running your procedure at the line labeled Exit_Form_KeyDown. Resuming at this line runs the Exit Sub line, causing the procedure to end.

Now, if this procedure can't set values in the form for any reason, the user will receive a message explaining the problem, but your application will continue running instead of ending abruptly with an error message.

Step through the error-handling code

To try out the new error-handling code, you'll cause the error to happen again. However, before you start, you'll set a breakpoint in the procedure so you can step through and see how it works.

1 With the right mouse button, click the sixth line of the procedure—the line that sets the City field to "New York"—and then click Toggle Breakpoint on the shortcut menu.

Now the procedure will stop at this line, regardless of whether an error occurs.

2 Switch to the Contacts form.

3 Press CTRL+1.

The KeyDown event procedure runs, reaches your breakpoint, and appears again in the Module window. The next statement to run will try to set a value in the form. Because data in the form is still read-only, you can expect that this statement will cause an error.

4 Click the Step Over button.

Step Over button

Instead of moving to the next statement, the current statement indicator jumps all the way down to the line below the label Err_Form_KeyDown—the line you specified in the On Error GoTo statement at the beginning of the procedure.

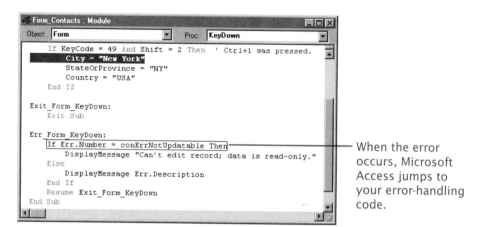

When the error occurs, Microsoft Access jumps to your error-handling code.

In effect, the error-handling code you wrote is now interrupting the normal flow of code—you might say your procedure is in "error-handling mode."

5 Click the Step Over button twice.

Your code displays the error message.

6 Click OK.

7 Click the Step Over button two more times.

When your error-handling code finishes running, the Resume statement sends the current statement indicator up to the line under the Exit_Form_KeyDown label: the Exit Sub line.

The Resume statement ends your error-handling code...

...and jumps up to this line.

8   Click the Step Over button a final time.

9   Close the Module window.

Stepping through your error-handling code helped to show you how this technique works. For your users, this is all hidden—but the important difference is that now they won't see the run-time error message that appeared before your error-handling code was in place.

Anticipating Other Problems That Cause Errors

Having data turn out to be read-only is just one of many unexpected conditions that can occur in your application—the possibilities for errors are endless. And there are plenty of other procedures in the application that don't yet have error-handling code in them. To be thorough, you would want to provide error-handling code in every proce-dure you write, so that users will never see your application halt abruptly with an error message. However, most procedures you write won't perform any actions that are likely to cause errors. To save time and effort, you can concentrate on providing error han-dling only where errors are likely to occur.

Although by no means complete, the following list shows a few actions for which you should be sure to provide error handling. You should anticipate that errors could occur any time your code attempts to:

- Access any file on disk, directly or indirectly
- Run queries or change data in a database
- Set properties of objects
- Perform mathematical calculations

163

Additional Error-Handling Techniques

You've seen one simple way to handle errors using the On Error GoTo statement. But there are several other techniques you can use to handle errors. Here's a sampling:

Resume code at the statement that caused the error. If your code can diagnose and solve the problem that occurred, you'll want to allow your code to continue running with the statement that caused the error. By using the Resume statement on a line by itself at the end of your error-handling code, you can tell Microsoft Access to return to the line that caused the error and try it over again.

For example, if your code tries to access a file on a floppy disk drive and an error occurs because the disk isn't in the drive, your code could display a message telling the user to insert the correct disk. At the end of the error-handling code, you'd use the Resume statement so that the statement that tried to access the disk could run again.

Skip over the statement that caused the error. If the statement that causes an error is not critical to your application, you can use the Resume Next statement to tell Microsoft Access to continue running code at the statement *after* the one that caused the error. In this type of situation, you might even *expect* the error to occur on a regular basis, and you want the statement to run only if it doesn't result in an error.

For example, suppose you have a procedure that sets a value on a form that may or may not be open. If the form is open, the line of code that sets the value runs as expected. If it's not, the line causes an error—but because you don't want to set the value unless the form is open, you're content to simply skip the statement altogether using Resume Next.

Tell Microsoft Access to ignore errors temporarily. If you know that an error is likely to occur on a particular statement and you don't want to suspend the running code at all, you can use the On Error GoTo Next statement to suspend error handling altogether. This causes Microsoft Access to skip over a line that causes an error as if the error didn't occur. For example, if you want to set a property for a control only if the control has the property, you could use On Error GoTo Next before setting the property so that an error won't occur if the property doesn't exist.

If you use this strategy, you'll usually want to check the Err.Number value immediately following the statement to determine what error occurred, if any. Additionally, be sure to turn error handling back on by including another On Error GoTo statement, or additional errors could occur without your knowledge, causing problems in your application.

The technique you choose will depend on the types of errors you anticipate and what you want to do with them. If you don't know how you want to handle an error, the best fallback position is the strategy you used in this lesson: display the description of the error in a message box, and then exit the procedure.

Close the form and exit Microsoft Access

1 Close the Contacts form, clicking Yes when Microsoft Access asks if you want to save changes to the form.

2 On the File menu, click Exit.

Lesson Summary

To	Do this
Respond when an error occurs in a form	Write an event procedure for the form's Error event, using the DataErr argument to determine which error occurred.
Respond when the user enters a value in a combo box that isn't in the list	Write an event procedure for the control's NotInList event. To add the value to the combo box list automatically, use DAO code to add a new record to the table that the list comes from.
Specify the action Microsoft Access should perform after the Error or NotInList event procedure finishes	Set the Response argument to one of the following constants: acDataErrContinue, acDataErrDisplay, or acDataErrAdded.
Specify error-handling code to run if an error occurs in your code	Include the On Error GoTo statement at the beginning of your procedure, followed by a line label where error-handling code begins.
Determine the last run-time error that occurred in your code	Include Err.Number in your procedure. For a description of the error, use Err.Description.
Continue running your procedure after error-handling code finishes	Include the Resume statement at the end of your error-handling code.

For online information about	On the Help menu, click Microsoft Access Help Topics, click the Index tab, and then
Handling errors in forms and code	Search for "error handling"
Using combo boxes	Search for "combo boxes"
Using list boxes	Search for "list boxes"
Using data access object (DAO) code to work directly with databases	Search for "recordsets"

For more information on	In *Building Applications with Microsoft Access*, see
Handling errors in forms and code	Chapter 8, "Handling Run-Time Errors"
Using combo boxes and list boxes	Chapter 3, "Using Forms to Collect, Display, and Filter Information"
Using data access object (DAO) code to work directly with databases	Chapter 9, "Working with Sets of Records"

Preview of the Next Lesson

Throughout Part 2, you learned Visual Basic programming techniques for writing, debugging, and polishing your code, while working with the Contacts database created by the Database Wizard. With these techniques at your disposal, you're ready to move forward to create an application from scratch. In Part 3, you'll learn to put together all the pieces of a complete user interface, working with a custom application rather than one created by the Database Wizard. In Lessons 8 and 9, you'll start by working with your own dialog boxes and pop-up forms, both powerful tools for interacting with users of your applications.

Creating a Custom Application

Gather Information in a Dialog Box

Estimated time
45 min.

In this lesson you will learn how to:

■ Create an unbound form to act as a dialog box.

■ Find a record in a form's recordset.

■ Filter records in a report using criteria the user selects.

Have you noticed that every other phone number you call these days has some sort of automated answering system? "Welcome to our automated information center. If you're using a touch-tone phone, please press 1 now." It's becoming rare to talk to an actual person, unless of course you first jump through all the required hoops: "To wait to talk to an actual human being, please stay on the line...." If you're like me, you've chosen to wait for the good old human representative more than a few times!

These systems save companies lots of money, and often provide just the information callers need. But even as we become more accustomed to them, it's clear that they're much less flexible than most human beings. Automated answering systems are limited—for now, anyway—by the keypad provided on your telephone. They don't always have the options you need at a given time, and you have to answer several questions to get where you want to be.

Like a telephone answering system, your database applications need to help users get to information. Fortunately, your computer's interface is much more flexible than a telephone—but you'll still need to consider the same types of challenges and pitfalls. You need to ask users questions about what they want to do—establish a dialogue with them—and respond to their input. Of course, the conversations you have can exchange quite a bit more information than pressing 0 through 9 on a telephone keypad.

One of the tools you have for conversing with the user is the *dialog box*, a form you can present on the screen to provide information and ask questions. In this lesson, you'll learn to communicate with your application's users by creating dialog boxes and accessing the information the users provide in them.

Start the lesson

> Start Microsoft Access and open the 08 Subscription database in the practice files folder.

Creating an Application on Your Own

In Parts 1 and 2 of this book, you enhanced a database that you created with the Database Wizard. But as a Microsoft Access developer, you're likely to need databases that the wizard doesn't create. Your applications may need to store a type of data that the wizard doesn't handle, or you may just want to communicate with users in your own way. In Part 3, you'll create an application user interface on your own.

When you create an application from scratch, you need to plan in advance the features you want it to have. First, you create the tables that will store all the information you need. Then, you begin creating forms, reports, and other objects that make up the interface for your application. Finally, you'll tie all the objects together by writing Visual Basic code. Along the way, you might use many different wizards and builders to help you—even if you bypass the Database Wizard, you can get help creating parts of your application by relying on other wizards, such as the Table Wizard and the Command Button Wizard.

View the tables in the Subscription database

Starting in this lesson, you'll work with an application that stores subscriptions to a journal. The Subscription sample database already has tables full of subscriber data, and even some of the forms and reports you'll need—but you'll create additional objects and the Visual Basic code that makes it work. First, however, you should take a look at what's already in the Subscription database.

1   In the Database window, click the Tables tab.

The Subscription database contains two tables, Subscribers and Payments. If you'd designed this database from scratch, you would have created these tables and chosen their fields either by running the Table Wizard or by using Table Design view.

2   Click the Relationships button on the toolbar.

*Relationships
button*

Microsoft Access displays the Relationships window, showing the fields in the Subscribers and Payments tables and the relationship between the two tables.

This line indicates that the two tables are related based on values in the SubscriberID field.

As you can see, the Subscribers table includes fields for name and address information—everything you'll need to send mailings to journal subscribers. The Payments table includes fields that store each payment received from a subscriber. There is a *one-to-many* relationship between the tables, because for each subscriber, there can be many related payment records.

3 Close the Relationships window.

These two tables are all that's required for this database. But for a more complex application, you may need many tables that relate in different ways.

Open the Subscribers form

Most applications have a *main form*—the place where users spend most of their time viewing and entering data. In the Subscription database, the main form is the Subscribers form, which is already provided for you in the practice database.

1 In the Database window, click the Forms tab.

2 Double-click the Subscribers form.

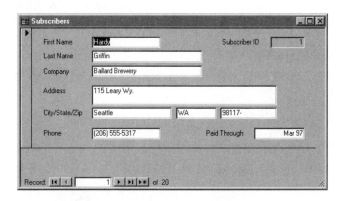

To create a form like this for your own application, you can use the Form Wizard. After you create a form and let the wizard lay out the fields for you, you may want to open the form in Design view to rearrange and resize fields, or perhaps to add formatting or pictures to give the form a custom look. Then, you may want to add additional capabilities to the form; for example, in the next section, you'll add a useful command button to the form.

Using Dialog Boxes in Your Applications

So far, the only interaction you've learned to have with the user is through message boxes, which are a simple type of dialog box. You've displayed a message, and the user has responded by clicking a button. But message boxes all look the same, and are limited to one, two, or three buttons. By creating a custom dialog box form, you can include any combination of controls and buttons you want. What all dialog boxes have in common, however, is that they pop up on top of the user's work and wait for a response.

Dialog boxes are especially useful for:

Presenting users with a custom message box   If you want to display a message that has a custom appearance or special command buttons—with text other than Yes, No, OK, or Cancel—you can't just rely on the MsgBox function. For example, you might want a dialog box to allow four or more actions, or to include command buttons with icons on them.

Asking questions before opening a form or report   When you provide a way for users to open a form or report, you may want to allow them to specify options. For example, you might want to ask users which records they want to view or in which order to display them.

Allowing users to specify general options for your application   A dialog box can have many controls for entering diverse types of information in one place. For example, you might want to allow users to customize the appearance or behavior of your application by collecting their preferences in a dialog box called Options and then saving them in a table.

Gathering additional information for a menu command   If your application uses custom menu bars, you may want one of the commands to open a dialog box to get details on how to proceed. Microsoft Access itself, like most Windows applications, has several dialog boxes accessible from menus and toolbars. In Lesson 10, you'll learn to create custom menu bars and toolbars that perform actions such as opening a dialog box.

There are as many uses for dialog boxes as there are types of applications. In this lesson, you'll create two common kinds of dialog boxes, and learn all the basic techniques you need to create a dialog box for any purpose.

Creating a Dialog Box to Go to a Specific Record

In this section, you'll create a dialog box that helps users jump to a specific record in the Subscribers form. In the dialog box you'll add a list box to display the available records, and you'll write code for a new button to display the record that the user selects.

You've already written code to help users locate a record: in Lesson 3, you created a combo box to do this. But by using a dialog box, you can keep this tool out of the way of users, giving you more room on the form—and more flexibility in how users select the records they're looking for. When a user clicks a button, your dialog box will pop up.

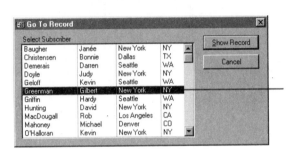

Users can select the record they want from a list in the dialog box.

Create the GoToRecord dialog box form

A dialog box is a special type of form—instead of displaying data in its controls, it allows the user to set the control values so you can collect information. A form that doesn't display data is called an *unbound* form, because it isn't bound to a table or query—its RecordSource property is blank. You create unbound forms from scratch in Design view, because there's no wizard to create them for you.

Database Window button

1   Click the Database Window button on the toolbar.

2   Click the New button.

Microsoft Access displays the New Form dialog box. Design view is selected by default, so you don't have to choose a method for designing the form. And because you want the form to be unbound, you won't select a table or query either.

3   Click OK.

Microsoft Access creates a blank form and displays it in Design view. As you can see by the Design view rulers, the new form's Detail section is 5 inches wide and 2 inches long.

173

4   Click the right side of the Detail section of the form and drag to resize it to 4½ by 2 inches.

Drag the side of the section to resize it.

Save button

5   Click the Save button on the toolbar.

6   Type **GoToRecordDialog** and then click OK.

Microsoft Access saves the form in the database.

Use a wizard to create the Select Subscriber list box

Now you're ready to add controls to the dialog box to get the user's input. The primary control for the dialog box is a list box from which the user can select a subscriber's record. You'll create this control using the List Box Wizard.

Control Wizards tool

1   In the toolbox, make sure the Control Wizards tool is selected, and then click the List Box tool.

2   Click near the top of the form.

List Box tool

Click here to create the list box.

The List Box Wizard starts, asking how you want the list box to get the values it displays.

3 Select the first option, I Want The List Box To Look Up The Values In A Table Or Query, and then click Next.

The wizard asks which table you want the list box to get values from.

4 Click Subscribers, and then click Next.

The wizard asks which fields you want to include in the list box.

5 Double-click the LastName field to add it to the Selected Fields list, followed by the FirstName, City, and State fields (in that order), and then click Next.

Add these fields to the list.

The wizard displays the list of subscribers as it will appear in the list box.

6 Resize the columns of data:

- Double-click the right side of the FirstName column selector to have it fit the data.

- Drag the right side of the City column selector to make it slightly wider than the data shown.

- Double-click the right side of the State column selector to have it fit the data.

Use the column selectors to resize columns as shown.

7 Click Next.

The wizard asks what label you want for your combo box.

8 Type **Select Subscriber** and then click Finish.

The wizard creates the list box and places it on your form. Behind the scenes, the wizard sets properties for the list box so it will display the data you specified. It also automatically includes the SubscriberID field—the primary key field in the Subscribers table—as a hidden field in the list box. Users won't see this field, but the list box will be based on it, and you'll use its value to set the current record in the Subscribers form.

Notice that the wizard gave the list box the default name List0. You'll use this name in code when referring to the value of the list box.

Position the list box on the dialog box form

The list box isn't quite right yet. Before you test it, you'll want to make a few adjustments.

1 Point to the upper left corner of the list box's label and drag it just above the upper left corner of the list box.

2 Double-click the right side of the label, resizing it to fit the text.

3 Click and drag the list box to move it near the upper left corner of the form.

4 Drag the bottom right corner of the list box to make it slightly wider (about ¼ inch) and nearly as long as the Detail section of the form.

The form should look like this:

To test your list box, you can switch to Form view.

*Form View
button*

5 Click the Form View button on the toolbar.

The list box shows records from the Subscribers table.

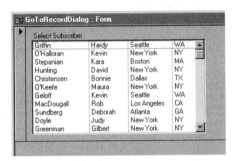

Modify the list box to sort by last name

You may have noticed that the records in the form aren't sorted alphabetically—unfortunately, the List Box Wizard doesn't do this for you. It would be quite a bit easier for users to find the records they want if the subscribers were in order. To sort the records, you'll need to modify the RowSource query that the wizard created for your list box.

*Design View
button*

*Properties
button*

1 Click the Design View button on the toolbar.

2 If the property sheet isn't open, click the Properties button to display it.

3 Click the Data tab in the property sheet.

4 Click the RowSource property, and then click the Build button.

Click the Build button.

Microsoft Access displays the query for the list box in a Query Builder window.

5 Select the Sort row underneath the LastName field, and then click the drop-down arrow and select Ascending from the list.

Set the sort order for the LastName field to Ascending.

6 Close the Query Builder window, clicking Yes when Microsoft Access asks if you want to save changes to the RowSource property.

Now records in the list box will be sorted by last name. The list box is ready to go!

7 Close the property sheet.

Add a button that changes records in the Subscribers form

You'll try out the list box soon enough—first, you need to add buttons and Visual Basic code to the dialog box to make it work. The most important item to add is the button that actually finds the selected record in the Subscribers form.

Control Wizards tool

1 In the toolbox, click the Control Wizards tool to deselect it, and then click the Command Button tool.

Command Button tool

2 Click near the top of the form, just to the right of the list box.

Click here to create the button.

Microsoft Access creates the button, giving it a default caption such as Command2.

*Properties
button*

3 Click the Properties button on the toolbar, and then click the All tab in the property sheet.

4 Click the Name property and type **ShowRecord**

5 Click the Caption property and type **&Show Record**

6 Set the Default property to Yes.

With the Default property set to Yes, the button will be selected automatically if the user presses ENTER while in the dialog box.

7 Set the Enabled property to No.

Setting the button's Enabled property to No disables it, so the user can't click it when the dialog box first opens. You wouldn't normally want to disable a button, but in this case, there's a good reason to do so. When you first open a form that has a list box, the list box doesn't have a value—nothing is selected. Until the user selects a subscriber in this list box, you don't want the ShowRecord button to be available. Later, you'll add code that enables the button as soon as the user selects something in the list.

8 Close the property sheet.

9 With the right mouse button, click the ShowRecord button, and then click Build Event.

10 Double-click Code Builder.

Microsoft Access displays the event procedure for the button's Click event.

11 Add the following code to the procedure (except the Sub and End Sub lines, which are already there):

```
Private Sub ShowRecord_Click()
' Find the selected record, then close the dialog box.

    Dim rst As Recordset

    ' Store the recordset for the Subscribers form.
    Set rst = Forms!Subscribers.RecordsetClone

    ' Locate the record for the selected subscriber.
    rst.FindFirst "SubscriberID = " & List0

    ' Set the form's Bookmark property to move to the record.
    Forms!Subscribers.Bookmark = rst.Bookmark

    ' Close the dialog box.
    DoCmd.Close acForm, "GoToRecordDialog"
End Sub
```

This code changes the current record in the Subscribers form to the one the user has selected in your list box. Let's look at this code more closely:

■ The Dim statement creates a recordset-type variable called *rst*. You'll use this variable to represent the set of subscriber records in the Subscribers form.

■ The second line of code begins with the Set statement. This line contains an expression—*Forms!Subscribers.RecordsetClone*—that refers to the records shown in the Subscribers form. Every form has a RecordsetClone property that you can use to get a copy of the form's underlying recordset. As you've seen before, you refer to a form other than the current form by preceding the form name with the Forms keyword, followed by an exclamation point. And to refer to a property, you separate the object and its property with a period.

A recordset-type variable is an *object* variable—it stores an object rather than a simple value—which means you must use the Set statement to assign an object to it. In plain English, the whole line says: "Create a copy of the set of records in the Subscribers form and assign it to the rst variable so I can refer to it later."

■ Recordset objects have many methods that help you work with them. In Lesson 7, you learned how to add a record to a recordset by using the AddNew method. The third code line uses a new method, FindFirst, to move to a specific record in the recordset. To use a method, you follow the object variable with its method, separated by a period, as in rst.FindFirst.

The FindFirst method takes an argument that specifies the criteria you want to use to find the record. As you recall, when you created the List0 list box, you specified that its value should be based on the SubscriberID for the selected subscriber. Now, you want this argument to specify that the value you're looking for in the recordset is the one that's selected in the list box. Using the ampersand (&) operator, this line combines the string *SubscriberID =* with the list box value.

All put together, this line of code says, "In the recordset stored in the rst variable, find the first record where the Subscriber ID field contains the same value as the List0 list box."

■ Normally, your next step would be to check whether Microsoft Access found the record you were looking for. In this case, however, you know that the record is there, because the list box contains the same records as the Subscribers form. So the current record in the rst recordset is now the one the user selected in the list box.

It's important to note that finding the record doesn't automatically change the record shown in the Subscribers form. This is because you're actually working with a *copy* of the recordset, which you stored in the rst variable using the RecordsetClone property. To actually move to the record you want, the next line of code sets the Bookmark property of the Subscribers form. Forms and recordsets both have a Bookmark property, which is a special value Microsoft Access uses to keep track of which record is current— just as if the record were the page you had reached in a book. When two recordsets contain the same records, you can synchronize one recordset with another by setting its Bookmark to the same value as the other's.

At the risk of oversimplification, you can read the Bookmark line as saying, "In the Subscribers form's set of records, move to the same record that's current in the rst recordset object."

■ Now that you've moved to the record the user specified, the work of the dialog box is complete. The next line of code uses the Close method of the DoCmd object to close the dialog box. The arguments for the Close method specify which object to close. Using the predefined constant acForm, you tell Microsoft Access that the object to close is a form; with the second argument, you give the name of the form to close, GoToRecordDialog.

Add code that enables the ShowRecords button

As you recall, you made sure the ShowRecords button is disabled by default, because no item is selected in the list when the dialog box first appears. As soon as the user selects a value in the list, you want to enable the button. You can do this by responding to the list box's AfterUpdate event, which occurs whenever the user changes the value of the list box.

1 Switch back to the GoToRecordDialog form.

2 Click the list box control to select it.

3 Click the Properties button on the toolbar, and then click the Event tab in the property sheet.

4 Click the AfterUpdate property, and then click the Build button.

— Click the Build button.

5 Double-click Code Builder.

Microsoft Access displays the List0_AfterUpdate event procedure.

6 Add the following code to the procedure:

```
Private Sub List0_AfterUpdate()
' Once a record is chosen in the list, enable the ShowRecord button.

    ShowRecord.Enabled = True

End Sub
```

The line of code in this procedure sets the Enabled property for the ShowRecord button to True—just as if you'd set the property to Yes in the property sheet—so the button appears enabled and the user can click it.

Add code that responds when the user double-clicks an entry in the list

To make your dialog box easier to use, there's one other event that you can respond to. When the user double-clicks a value in the list box, you want to respond as if the ShowRecord button had been clicked immediately afterward. This way, a user can avoid the added step of clicking the button after selecting a subscriber.

1   In the Module window's Proc box, select DblClick.

Microsoft Access displays the List0_DblClick procedure in the Module window.

2   Add the following code to the procedure:

```
Private Sub List0_DblClick(Cancel As Integer)
' When the user double-clicks, act as though
' the ShowRecord button was chosen.

    If Not IsNull(List0) Then
        ShowRecord_Click
    End If

End Sub
```

The line in the middle of this procedure tells Microsoft Access to run the ShowRecord_Click event procedure. You can run a procedure in the current module by simply entering the name of the procedure on a line by itself. When Microsoft Access encounters this line, it jumps to the ShowRecord_Click procedure, running it just as it would have if the ShowRecord button had actually been clicked.

The If...Then statement in this procedure is a safety measure. It checks to make sure the List0 list box has a value; if it doesn't, the button shouldn't be enabled, so you wouldn't want to run its event procedure. Normally, when the user double-clicks the list box, this action sets a value for the list box. However, by double-clicking the list box label, it is possible to make the DblClick event occur when the list box has no value. If the List0 control doesn't have a subscriber selected, the value of the expression *Not IsNull(List0)* is False, so the code in the procedure does nothing.

Check your Visual Basic code for errors

You've written quite a bit of code for the dialog box! It's a good idea to get in the habit of compiling your code from time to time—this lets Microsoft Access catch any errors right away and saves you from being interrupted when you run your code.

Compile Loaded Modules button

1 Click the Compile Loaded Modules button on the toolbar.

If Microsoft Access encounters any errors, it identifies them for you—otherwise, it does nothing (other than preparing your code to run). Of course, if there are errors, you should fix them and compile your code again.

Save button

2 Click the Save button on the toolbar.

3 Close the Module window.

4 Close the property sheet.

Add a Cancel button that closes the form

Your dialog box is almost complete! But in addition to a button that performs an action, such as the ShowRecord button you created, every dialog box should have a Cancel or Close button, in case the user has a change of heart and doesn't really want to do anything. In this case, you just need a button to close the GoToRecordDialog form, performing no action at all. The easiest way to create this button is by using the Command Button Wizard.

Control Wizards tool

1 In the toolbox, click the Control Wizards tool to select it, and then click the Command Button tool.

2 Click the right side of the form, just underneath the left side of the ShowRecord button.

Click here to create the command button.

The Command Button Wizard starts, asking what action you want the button to perform.

3 Select Form Operations from the Categories list, select Close Form from the Actions list, and then click Next.

The wizard asks whether you want a picture or text on your button.

4   Select the Close Form text from the Text box, type **Cancel** to replace the text, and then click Next.

The wizard asks what you want to name the button.

5   Type **Cancel** and then click Finish.

The wizard creates the Cancel button.

6   Drag the bottom right corner of the Cancel button to make it the same size as the ShowRecord button.

Now that the button is complete, there's one more step. With most any Cancel or Close button on a dialog box, you want users to be able to press ESC in lieu of clicking the button. To make this possible, you just set the button's Cancel property to Yes—identifying it to Microsoft Access as the Cancel button for the form.

Properties button

7   Click the Properties button on the toolbar, and then click the Other tab in the property sheet.

8   Set the Cancel property to Yes.

The button is finished—and you're ready to put the final touches on your dialog box.

Set properties for the dialog box

Although a dialog box is a form like any other, you want it to look and behave differently in many ways. First, you'll take a look at the form as it stands now, with its default property settings. Then, you'll change several properties to make it work the way you want.

Form View button

1 Click the Form View button on the toolbar.

The list box shows records in alphabetical order, and everything seems to be in its place. Notice, however, that like any ordinary Microsoft Access form, this form has several features used for moving around in a set of records—navigation buttons, scroll bars, and a record selector—all things that dialog boxes *don't* customarily have.

A dialog box shouldn't have these navigation features.

Each of these features has a corresponding form property you can set to remove it from your form.

Design View button

2 Click the Design View button on the toolbar.

3 On the Edit menu, click Select Form.

4 In the property sheet, click the Format tab.

5 Set the following properties to the values shown:

Property	Value
Caption	Go To Record
ScrollBars	Neither
RecordSelectors	No
NavigationButtons	No
AutoCenter	Yes
BorderStyle	Dialog

These settings will make your dialog box look much like any other Windows 95 dialog box—a thin border, a simple title, and no extra navigation tools. However, there are two additional properties you'll want to set so that your dialog box *works* the way a dialog box should.

6 In the property sheet, click the Other tab.

7 Set the Popup property to Yes.

This setting makes your dialog box into a pop-up form: it will appear on top of all other windows, including Microsoft Access itself.

8 Set the Modal property to Yes.

This setting makes your dialog box *modal*, which means that users won't be able to click outside of the dialog box while it's open. Most dialog boxes are modal: you intend that the user will complete the action—such as locating a record—and then close the dialog box to move on to the next task.

9 Close the property sheet.

10 Close the GoToRecordDialog form, clicking Yes when Microsoft Access asks if you want to save changes to the form.

Add a button to the Subscribers form that opens the dialog box

Now that your dialog box is complete, the only thing left is to hook it up to the Subscribers form. To do this, you'll add a button using the Command Button Wizard.

1 Switch to the Subscribers form, which is still open behind the Database Window.

2 Click the Design View button on the toolbar

3 Scroll down in the form to display the Form Footer section.

4 In the toolbox, click the Command Button tool.

5 Click the left side of the form footer.

Design View button

Command Button tool

Click here to create the command button.

The Command Button Wizard starts, asking what action you want the button to perform.

6 Select Form Operations from the Categories list, select Open Form from the Actions list, and then click Next.

The wizard asks which form you want to open. Because the GoToRecordDialog form is already selected, you don't have to click it.

7 Click Next.

The wizard asks whether you want a picture or text on your button.

8 Select the Open Form text in the Text box, type **&Go To Record** to replace the text, and then click Next.

187

The wizard asks what you want to name the button.

9   Type **GoToRecord** and then click Finish.

The wizard creates the button, including an event procedure that automatically opens your dialog box whenever the button is clicked.

Save button

10   Click the Save button on the toolbar.

Try the new dialog box

No more waiting—you're finally ready to click that button and try out the dialog box!

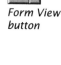

Form View button

1   Click the Form View button on the toolbar.

2   Click the Go To Record button.

The Go To Record dialog box appears.

As you can see, the form no longer looks like an ordinary Microsoft Access form—it has a thin border, and no navigation tools. Because the form is modal, if you try to click on a Microsoft Access menu or on the Subscribers form behind it, your computer beeps and nothing happens. The only actions you can take are to move or close the dialog box, or to select a record in the list box and click a button.

And notice that the Show Record button is disabled because you haven't yet selected a subscriber in the dialog box.

3   In the Select Subscriber list box, click the entry for Judy Doyle.

The Show Record button is now enabled—when you set the value of the list box, the AfterUpdate event procedure ran, and your code set the Enabled property.

4   Click the Show Record button.

Your event procedure for the button changes the current record in the Subscribers form's recordset to the record for Judy Doyle, and then closes the dialog box. It works!

5   Click the Go To Record button again.

This time, you can test the double-clicking feature you added.

6   In the Select Subscriber list box, double-click the entry for Gilbert Greenman.

The Subscribers form now shows this record—your event procedure for the list box's DblClick event took care of it.

Finally, you should test the Cancel button in the dialog box.

7 Click the Go To Record button again, and then click any entry in the list box.

8 Click the Cancel button.

The Subscribers form still shows the same record—as expected, the dialog box has no effect if you click Cancel.

9 Close the Subscribers form.

As you've seen, quite a bit of work goes into creating a custom dialog box. (As you practice, you'll learn ways to make it easier.) It's worthwhile, though, when you consider how polished your applications can look by using custom dialog boxes to meet users' needs.

 TIP To save time when creating a dialog box for your own application, you may want to copy or import an existing dialog box form and start work from there. Because many dialog boxes have similar controls and property settings, you'll be well on your way—and much happier than if you'd started from scratch.

Hiding a Dialog Box and Referring to Its Controls

When you click the ShowRecord button on the GoToRecordDialog form, it's the code behind the button that performs an action using the information you enter. After it changes records in the Subscribers form, the same event procedure then closes the dialog box.

However, there's another possible strategy that you could use for this dialog box, one that might prove easier to implement for some dialog boxes. Rather than close a dialog box when the user finishes with it, your code can instead simply hide the dialog box, making it look like it's closed. To do this, you set the dialog box's Visible property to False. The advantage to this strategy is that you can still refer to values on the dialog box from code you've written in other forms. In this case, for example, you could hide the GoToRecordDialog form—set its Visible property to False—and then add code to the Subscribers form that would move to the specified record. From that code, you could refer to the list box value in the dialog box, even though it would no longer be in view.

The strategy you did use—performing actions from code in the dialog box form itself—usually results in code that's easier to follow. On the other hand, in cases where you want to continue referring to values the user entered long after the dialog box is "gone," it might make more sense to simply hide the dialog box form. However, if you do hide a dialog box and leave it open, you'll usually want to close that form later in your application. What's more, you'll need to watch out for code that assumes the dialog box form is open behind the scenes—unless you make sure that it stays open.

Filtering Data in a Report

Because the task of selecting a subset of data is so important in database applications, one common use for a dialog box is to specify criteria for filtering records. Microsoft Access provides a powerful interface for filtering records in forms, so your applications can rely on standard filtering tools in many cases. In other cases, however, you'll want to provide a custom method for selecting records. This is especially true for selecting records to include in reports, because filtering records for reports is much less straightforward than it is for forms. In this section, you'll add code to a dialog box that helps users select which records to include in a report.

As you might imagine, the most critical report in a database of mailing addresses is the report that prints mailing labels. The Subscription database includes a report called MailingLabels, already created for you using the Label Wizard, which lays out and prints subscriber names and addresses on standard mailing label paper. However, users don't want to print a label for every subscriber every time. By providing a custom dialog box, you'll help them select the subset of labels they want.

Try the MailingLabels report

Before working on the dialog box, let's preview the MailingLabels report by itself.

1   In the Database window, click the Reports tab.

2   Double-click the MailingLabels report.

Microsoft Access displays the MailingLabels report in Print Preview, showing several subscribers' names and addresses.

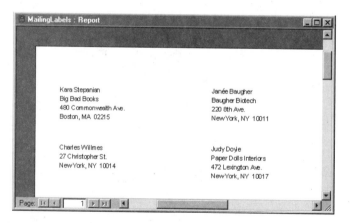

3   Click anywhere on the page of the report to zoom out.

All 20 subscribers' names and addresses are shown. This could be useful if you want to send a mailing to everyone who's ever subscribed—not too many people at this point. But as the database grows and the mailing labels span many pages, users will need a way to print only the labels appropriate for a particular mailing.

4   Close the report window.

Open the MailingLabelsDialog form in Design view

The Subscription database contains a dialog box for filtering records in the report. This form was created for you using many of the same steps you followed to create the GoToRecordDialog form. Now you'll add the Visual Basic code to make it work.

1 In the Database window, click the Forms tab.

2 Click the MailingLabelsDialog form, and then click the Design button.

The form has an option group, created using the Option Group Wizard, that allows the user to select which group of subscribers to include in a mailing. There are three options: the first includes all subscribers who are paid to the current date, the second includes all subscribers who need to make a payment in the next three months in order to stay current, and the third includes subscribers who recently failed to pay and are no longer receiving issues. The form also has three command buttons: one to print labels, one to preview them, and a third that closes the dialog box without doing anything.

Add code for the PrintLabels button

The PrintLabels button doesn't yet have a Click event procedure to do the job. When a user clicks this button, you want the code to open the MailingLabels report—that much will be easy using the OpenReport method of the DoCmd object. But you don't want the report to display all the subscriber records, as it did when you opened it from the Database window. Instead, your code needs to interpret the selected option in the option group, and then filter the subscriber records according to the user's selection.

1 With the right mouse button, click the PrintLabels button, and then click Build Event on the shortcut menu.

2 Double-click Code Builder.

Microsoft Access opens the Module window and displays the PrintLabels_Click event procedure.

3   Add the following code to the procedure:

```
Private Sub PrintLabels_Click()
' Open the MailingLabels report with a filter, then close the dialog.

    Dim strFilter As String

    Select Case MailingType     ' User's selection in option group.

    Case 1      ' Journal mailing -- all current subscribers.
        strFilter = "PaidThrough >= Date()"

    Case 2      ' Subscriptions expiring within 3 months.
        strFilter = "PaidThrough >= Date() And PaidThrough < Date() + 90"

    Case 3       ' Subscriptions that expired in past 3 months.
        strFilter = "PaidThrough < Date() And PaidThrough > Date() - 90"

    End Select

    DoCmd.OpenReport "MailingLabels", acNormal, , strFilter
    DoCmd.Close acForm, "MailingLabelsDialog"

End Sub
```

This code covers mostly familiar territory, but it uses a couple of new techniques. Here's how it works:

- At the end of this procedure, you specify filter criteria—a description of the records you want to see in the report—for Microsoft Access to use when opening the report. The Dim statement at the beginning of the procedure defines a string variable, strFilter, for storing these criteria.

- Each criteria string you specify in this procedure refers to a field in the Subscribers table called PaidThrough. This field stores the last month in which a subscriber should receive an issue (assuming that the subscriber doesn't make another payment). Each time a subscriber makes a payment, the field is updated to reflect the new date.

- Each criteria string also uses the Date function, a Microsoft Access function that returns the current date stored by the computer system. By comparing the value of this function with the values in the PaidThrough field, you can determine whether any given subscriber is "paid up."

- The Select Case...End Select block allows you to specify three different statements to run, depending on which option the user selected in the option group. The statement uses the expression MailingType because that's the name of the option group control on the form.

■ The first Case block, Case 1, runs if the user selected the first option in the group (MailingType is 1). For this option, you want to include all subscribers who have paid through the current date—in other words, subscribers whose PaidThrough date is the same as or later than the current date. The criteria string is:

```
"PaidThrough >= Date()"
```

■ In the second Case block, you want to include all subscribers who need to make a payment within three months if they want their subscriptions to continue. To specify this condition, you make two comparisons, combining them with the And operator— this way, Microsoft Access makes sure both comparisons are true for records it includes in the report. This criteria string includes subscribers whose PaidThrough date the same as or later than the current date *and* whose PaidThrough date is less than the 90 days from now:

```
strFilter = "PaidThrough >= Date() And PaidThrough < Date() + 90"
```

As this expression demonstrates, adding or subtracting an integer value to a date expression changes the date value by that many days.

■ In the third Case block, you want to include all subscribers who've let their subscriptions expire—but only those who have done so in the past three months. The criteria string includes subscribers whose PaidThrough date is earlier than the current date (they're no longer paid up) *and* whose PaidThrough date is within the past 90 days:

```
strFilter = "PaidThrough < Date() And PaidThrough > Date() - 90"
```

■ After your code sets the strFilter variable to the appropriate criteria, it's time to use it to open the report. The line after the End Select statement uses the OpenReport method of the DoCmd object, specifying the MailingLabels report as the report name.

The second argument to the OpenReport method lets you specify whether to open and print the report (specified using the acNormal constant) or preview the report (specified using the acPreview constant). The fourth argument—you skip the third argument by including two commas in a row—is the WhereCondition argument, with which you specify the criteria string Microsoft Access will use to filter records in the report. This is where you put your variable, strFilter, which contains the filter string you set in the Select...Case block.

■ The last statement in the procedure uses the Close method of the DoCmd object to close the dialog box form.

When you click the Print Labels button, your code will select a filter string, open the report to print the set of labels the user wants, and close the dialog box.

Copy the code for the PreviewLabels button

Print Preview is a powerful Microsoft Access feature that you can easily take advantage of in your applications—and Windows users have come to expect it. Whenever you provide the option to print a report, it's also a good idea to allow previewing. Fortunately, the code you'll use for the PreviewLabels button is nearly identical to the code for printing a report. In fact, you'll just copy the code to the other button's event procedure, and then make a small modification to allow previewing.

1   Select all the code between the Sub and End Sub lines in the PrintLabels event procedure (click at the beginning of the second line and drag to just before the last line).

2   Press CTRL+C.

3   In the Module window's Object box, select PreviewLabels.

    Microsoft Access displays the PreviewLabels_Click event procedure.

4   Press CTRL+V.

5   Edit the line that contains the OpenReport method (toward the end of the procedure) to use the acPreview constant instead of the acNormal constant:

```
DoCmd.OpenReport "MailingLabels", acPreview, , strFilter
```

Using this constant for the View argument of the OpenReport method tells Microsoft Access to display the form in Print Preview rather than printing it directly.

6   Close the Module window.

7   Close the MailingLabelsDialog form, clicking Yes when Microsoft Access asks if you want to save changes.

Try the dialog box

Now that the dialog box is finished, you can use it to open the report.

1   In the Database window, double-click the MailingLabelsDialog form.

    The dialog box appears, allowing you to select an option for your mailing labels.

2 Select the second option, Invoice Mailing.

3 Click Preview Labels.

Your event procedure runs, opening the report in Print Preview.

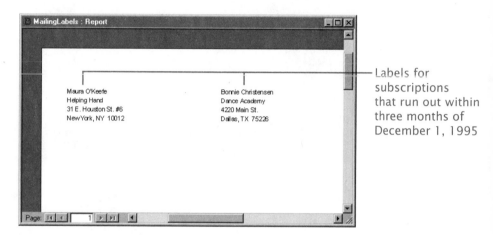

Labels for subscriptions that run out within three months of December 1, 1995

Because your code opens the report using the filter string *PaidThrough >= Date()
And PaidThrough < Date() + 90* it includes just a few of the subscribers—those
whose subscriptions haven't yet expired as of today's date, but that will expire
within three months. (Note that depending on the current date setting on your
computer, you might see different subscribers in the report or even no subscribers
at all. To include subscribers, change their PaidThrough date in the table to
within three months of the current date.)

4 Close the report.

If you want to try out the other filters on the report, repeat this procedure, selecting the
first and third options in the dialog box.

Other Ways to Change the Records in a Form or Report

The code you wrote uses a straightforward way of filtering the records in a report: specifying an OpenReport WhereCondition argument when opening the report. However, there are other ways you can change the records that appear in a report.

Base the report on a query. If you always want to display the same subset of records in a report, or if you want the records to appear in a specific order, create a query that displays records as you want them, and then set the report's RecordSource property to the query. This way, you don't have to write any code to filter records.

Set the report's Filter and FilterOn properties. If you want to change records that are displayed in a report that's already open in Print Preview, you can use Visual Basic code to set the report's Filter property to a criteria string. Then, set its FilterOn property to True to apply the filter.

Set the report's OrderBy and OrderByOn properties. If you want to change the sort order of a report that's already open in Print Preview, you can set the report's OrderBy property to the name of the field you want to sort, and then set its OrderByOn property to True to apply the sort.

All these techniques work for forms as well as reports—in fact, in the next lesson you'll learn how to use the Filter property in forms.

Exit Microsoft Access

 On the File menu, click Exit.

Lesson Summary

To	Do this
Create a dialog box form	Create a blank form in Design view, add controls, and then set properties on the Format and Other tabs to make the dialog box appear and work as you want it to. Add buttons that perform desired actions.
Create a list box	Use the List Box Wizard in Form Design view, specifying the fields you want the list box to display.
Move to a specific record in a form	Get a copy of the form's underlying recordset using the RecordsetClone property, and then move to the record using the FindFirst method. Finally, set the form's Bookmark property to the Bookmark value for the copy of the recordset.
Open a report to print specific records	Use the OpenReport method of the DoCmd object, specifying a filter string for the WhereCondition argument. In the filter string, specify criteria for one or more fields in the underlying table or query for the report.

For online information about	**On the Help menu, click Microsoft Access Help Topics, click the Index tab, and then**
Creating dialog boxes	Search for "dialog boxes"
Filtering records in forms and reports	Search for "filters"
Using data access object (DAO) code to work with recordsets, or finding records in a recordset	Search for "recordsets"
Using bookmarks	Search for "Bookmark property"
Using the Date function	Search for "date"

For more information on	**In _Building Applications with Microsoft Access_, see**
Creating dialog boxes, or filtering records in forms and reports	Chapter 3, "Using Forms to Collect, Display, and Filter Information"
Using data access object (DAO) code to work with recordsets, finding records in a recordset, or using bookmarks	Chapter 9, "Working with Sets of Records"
Using the Date function	Chapter 2, "Introducing Visual Basic"

Preview of the Next Lesson

In this lesson, you began adding features to the Subscription database, a custom application created from scratch. In Lesson 9, you'll learn to link the forms of an application together, helping users jump from one task to another and putting the information they need at their fingertips. As Part 3 progresses, you'll complete the custom user interface for the Subscription database, learning techniques you can use to create your own custom database applications.

Navigate Through Your Application

Estimated time
35 min.

In this lesson you will learn how to:

■ Display records in a pop-up form.

■ Synchronize the records in one form with records the user selects in another form.

■ Requery a form to display current data.

In a relay race, the performance of each individual team member is important, but the transitions are critical. When a runner hands off the baton to a teammate, that's the moment when seconds are gained or lost. Relay teams train extensively to make transitions as efficient as possible, and arrange each of the runners in the position that is most beneficial to the team.

No matter how well your forms and reports work on their own, it's the way they work together that makes your database applications powerful and easy to use. As when planning for a relay race, you'll need to consider the ways your objects "hand off" from one to another. To make the transitions seamless, you can use Visual Basic code to customize the way a new object starts and how it works with other objects. Of course, the structure of an application is much more flexible than the structure of a relay race, so there are even more variables to consider—because of the flexibility of event-driven applications, users can take any number of paths through your application, and you'll need to anticipate all of them.

In this lesson, you'll learn techniques for handing off control from one form or report to another—passing the baton, so to speak. You'll write event procedures that check which other forms are currently open, copy values and set properties from one form or report to another, and update objects at appropriate times. By anticipating how users will run the course, you'll see how to make your application work smoothly.

Start the lesson

 Start Microsoft Access and open the 09 Subscription database in the practice files folder.

Making Forms Work Together

In an ideal world, everything computer users need to do their work would be in one place—in a database application, for example, it would be nice if all the data you needed were on a single form. In all but the simplest applications, however, you'll need several objects to handle the different types of information required, and the tasks the user needs to complete. For example, you'll have forms for entering information, forms for summarizing information, and still other forms that help users accomplish a specific task. How you organize these objects depends on what information and tasks are most important to users. In planning your application, you'll want to prioritize these items and decide how to best serve everyone's needs.

Most relational database applications store information in separate but related tables. For example, in the Subscription database, the Subscribers and Payments tables contain related information. In presenting this information on the screen, you can take several different approaches—some approaches work on their own, while others require Visual Basic code to make them work. Here are some of the ways you can organize data in an application, and factors you'll need to consider when using them:

Place subforms on forms to display related records. The subform control provides a powerful way to display related records in a single form without writing any code. For example, you could use a subform to display a list of subscriber payments—on the same form that displays subscriber information. You can set up this type of subform using the Subform Wizard, or create form and subform at once using the Form Wizard. However, in many cases there won't be enough room on the screen to display all the information you need on the main form as well as all the related information contained in a subform. Additionally, subforms can be less intuitive for entering data, especially when space is limited. Still, because Microsoft Access handles the relationships between form and subform automatically, you may want to use this approach when you want all related information to appear in one place.

Build forms and reports based on multiple-table queries. By designing queries that combine information from two or more tables, you can easily present data from several tables on a single form or report. Whenever possible, Microsoft Access allows users to update all the information in a query, automatically making changes in the underlying tables—but beware: some fields in multiple-table queries aren't updatable, so users can sometimes encounter unintelligible error messages when trying to make changes. And as with subforms, you won't always have room on a single form for all the fields you need to display. For forms and reports in which you summarize information, however, queries are indispensable tools for combining data from multiple tables.

Create a separate form for each table. By making separate forms for data in related tables, you present a very straightforward model to users: "Here is where you view and enter information about this; for other types of information, click these buttons." This approach requires users to switch from one place to another more frequently—between a main form and a pop-up form, for example—but it gives you the most screen space and flexibility for each form. When you do have several forms, however, users will expect them to work together intelligently—for example, if you've chosen a value in one form, you shouldn't have to choose it again in another form. As you'll see, it's important to link objects together using Visual Basic event procedures.

Separate data entry and data display. In some cases, you'll want to provide more than one form for the same information, each of which is used for a different task. Forms that allow you to enter new data often need different controls and features than those for finding or summarizing data. But as you increase the number of forms that make up your user interface, your application becomes much more complex. In some cases, you'll want to limit what users can do in a given form, making some forms or controls read-only and carefully controlling the paths users can take through your application.

In this lesson, we'll focus on the last two techniques, connecting separate forms in the Subscription database to display and enter related information. In the process, you'll learn to write Visual Basic code that links objects together in custom ways. In your own applications, you'll most likely draw from all these approaches—using subforms and queries to combine some of your application's data, while linking together a series of forms when it makes sense to keep information separated into different chunks.

Displaying Related Records in a Pop-Up Form

In any database that contains more than one table, you'll commonly have records in one table that are related to records in another. For example, in the Subscription database, each subscriber has one or more related payment records documenting the payments that that subscriber has made. When users are viewing records in a main form, such as the Subscriber form, they'll commonly want to see related records on the screen. One way to show related records is in a *pop-up* form, a special type of form that always remains on top of other windows. In this section, you'll add a pop-up form that displays the payment history for the current subscriber (the subscriber currently selected in the Subscribers form).

Open the PaymentHistory form

The practice database already includes the PaymentHistory form, which displays payment records. By default, the form shows payments for all subscribers together in one list.

1 In the Database window, click the Forms tab.

2 Double-click the PaymentHistory form.

Date	Yearly Rate	Years Paid	Total Amount
8/2/94	$24.00	0.5	$12.00
8/29/94	$24.00	1	$24.00
9/16/94	$24.00	1	$24.00
11/2/94	$18.00	1	$18.00
11/16/94	$24.00	1	$24.00

Record: 1 of 25

This simple form has the Payments table as its record source, and has four fields. The TotalAmount field is not actually in the Payments table—it's a calculated field, which means that its ControlSource property is set to an expression. The expression multiplies the YearlyRate value by the YearsPaid value to show the total.

Display the PaymentHistory form as a pop-up form

When users view the PaymentHistory form, they'll want it to remain on top of other windows so they can see it while they work in the Subscribers form. To make it work this way, you'll set its Popup property to Yes. You'll also set properties to make the form read-only, so that users can view payments in the form, but not change them.

Design View button

Properties button

1 Click the Design View button on the toolbar.

2 If the property sheet isn't displayed, click the Properties button on the toolbar.

3 Click the Other tab in the property sheet.

4 Set the Popup property to Yes.

5 Click the Data tab in the property sheet.

6 Set the AllowEdits, AllowDeletions, and AllowAdditions properties to No.

7 Close the PaymentHistory form, clicking Yes when Microsoft Access asks if you want to save changes.

Add a button to the Subscribers form that opens the PaymentHistory form

The PaymentHistory form is designed to work hand in hand with the Subscribers form. To make the pop-up form accessible, you'll add a button that opens it, displaying the payment records for the current subscriber. You can use the Command Button Wizard to create the button and its event procedure.

1 In the Database window, select the Subscribers form, and then click the Design button.

The form opens in Design view. (If the property sheet is in the way, drag it to the lower right corner of the screen.)

2 Scroll down in the form to display the Form Footer section.

3 In the toolbox, make sure the Control Wizards tool is selected, and then click the Command Button tool.

Control Wizards tool

Command Button tool

4 Click the form footer just to the right of the Go To Record button.

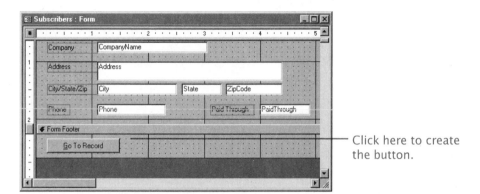

Click here to create the button.

The Command Button Wizard starts, asking what action you want the button to perform.

5 Select Form Operations from the Categories list, select Open Form from the Actions list, and then click Next.

The wizard asks which form you want to open.

6 Select PaymentHistory, and then click Next.

The wizard asks whether you want to display specific information in the form. This gives you the chance to filter records in the pop-up form to include only the payments for the current subscriber.

7 Select Open The Form And Find Specific Data To Display, and then click Next.

The wizard asks which field in the Subscribers form contains matching data in the PaymentHistory form. Because the Subscribers and Payments tables are related based on the SubscriberID values in each record, you'll specify this field.

8 Select SubscriberID in both list boxes, click the button between the lists to create a link between them, and then click Next.

Select fields in both lists...

...and then click here to link them.

The wizard asks whether you want a picture or text on your button.

9   Select the Open Form text in the Text box, type **&Payment History** to replace the text, and then click Next.

The wizard asks what you want to name the button.

10 Type **PaymentHistory** and then click Finish.

The wizard creates the button.

11 Click and drag the bottom right corner of the button to make it the same size as the Go To Record button.

Try the new button

Now you can use your new button to open the pop-up form.

Form View button

1   Click the Form View button on the toolbar.

2   Click the Payment History button.

The button's Click event procedure runs, opening the PaymentHistory pop-up form.

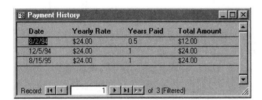

The form shows only three records: the past payments made by Hardy Griffin, whose subscriber record is displayed in the Subscriber form.

Change records in the Subscriber form

When the PaymentHistory pop-up form is open, you can still work in the Subscribers form—the pop-up form isn't modal like a dialog box. Let's see what happens when you change subscriber records.

1   Click anywhere on the Subscribers form. (If necessary, you can first drag the PaymentHistory form out of the way so that you can see the name of the current subscriber.)

2   Press the PAGE DOWN key several times to change records.

The same three records are displayed in the PaymentHistory form, regardless of which subscriber record you're viewing. When the user changes records in the Subscribers form, you'd like the PaymentHistory form to display payment records for the currently selected subscriber—in other words, you'd like the pop-up form to stay *synchronized* with the main form.

3   Close the PaymentHistory pop-up form.

Add code that keeps the pop-up form synchronized

To make the pop-up form stay synchronized, you need to update the records it displays each time the user changes records in the main form. To do this, you'll add an event procedure to the Subscribers form that makes sure the pop-up form displays related payment records as you move from one subscriber to another.

Design View button

1 Click the Design View button on the toolbar.

2 On the Edit menu, click Select Form.

3 In the property sheet, click the Event tab.

4 Click the OnCurrent property, and then click the Build button.

Click the Build button.

Microsoft Access displays the Choose Builder dialog box.

5 Double-click Code Builder.

Microsoft Access opens the Module window and displays the form's Current event procedure. The code you add to this procedure will run any time the user changes from one record to another in the Subscribers form.

6 Enter the following code for the procedure:

```
Private Sub Form_Current()
' Synchronize the PaymentHistory form if it's open.

    If IsOpen("PaymentHistory") Then
        Forms!PaymentHistory.Filter = "SubscriberID = " & _
            Nz(SubscriberID, 0)
    End If

End Sub
```

The If...Then statement in this code uses a special function called IsOpen to check whether the PaymentHistory form is open. This is an important step, because unless the user has opened the pop-up form, attempting to change the records it displays would cause an error. The IsOpen function returns True if the form is open, causing the line of code in the If...Then block to run. The IsOpen function is included in the practice database in the Miscellaneous module; for more information, see "Looking Into the IsOpen Function," later in this section.

205

If the PaymentHistory form is open, the next line actually synchronizes the form. To do this, it sets the pop-up form's Filter property, referring to the property by using the expression *Forms!PaymentHistory.Filter*. For the property setting, the code combines the text *SubscriberID =* with the actual SubscriberID value currently on the Subscribers form. For example, if the current subscriber's ID is 4, it sets the Filter property to *SubscriberID = 4* and the pop-up form displays only the payment records for that subscriber.

The line also uses the Nz function ("Nz" stands for Null-Zero), which converts the SubscriberID value to zero in the unlikely event that it is null (has no value). This is necessary because if the value is Null—which occurs if the user moves to the new (blank) record in the Subscriber form—the Filter would get set to *SubscriberID = * and an error would occur. This way, if the SubscriberID value is Null, the Filter gets set to *SubscriberID = 0* and the pop-up form displays no records (because no subscriber is number 0).

Add code that closes the pop-up form automatically

The PaymentHistory pop-up form only works as an auxiliary tool for the Subscribers form. If the user closes the Subscribers form while the pop-up form is still open, you may as well close the pop-up form. To do this, you can add code to the Subscribers form's Close event procedure.

1 In the Proc box at the top of the Module window, select the Close event.

The Module window shows the blank Form_Close event procedure.

2 Enter the following code for the procedure:

```
Private Sub Form_Close()
' Close the PaymentHistory pop-up form if it's open.

    If IsOpen("PaymentHistory") Then
        DoCmd.Close acForm, "PaymentHistory"
    End If

End Sub
```

Like the code you wrote to synchronize the two forms, this procedure uses the IsOpen function to check whether the PaymentHistory form is open. If it is, the Close method of the DoCmd object closes the form.

3 Close the Module window.

4 Click the Save button on the toolbar.

Save button

Test the synchronized form

The pop-up form should now work properly, even if you change records. When you close the Subscribers form, the pop-up form should close as well.

Form View button

1 Click the Form View button on the toolbar.

2 Click the Payment History button in the form footer.

The PaymentHistory pop-up form appears, again showing the three payments for the current subscriber.

3 Click anywhere on the Subscribers form, and then press the PAGE DOWN key several times to change subscriber records.

Each time you change records, your event procedure runs, setting the pop-up form's Filter property and causing it to display a different set of payments—those related by the SubscriberID value to the current subscriber. As you can see, most subscribers have made only one or two payments.

As you change subscribers...

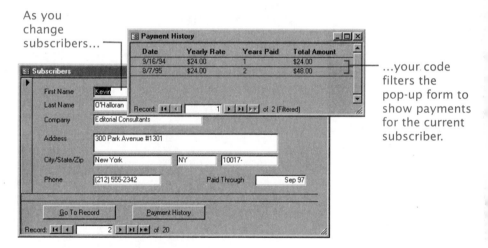

...your code filters the pop-up form to show payments for the current subscriber.

4 Close the Subscribers form.

Your Close event procedure runs, closing the pop-up form automatically.

Looking into the IsOpen Function

The Subscription database includes a standard module called Miscellaneous, which contains three general procedures. The first two are the procedures you wrote in Lesson 5 to display message boxes. The third is the IsOpen function, which you just used in the Subscribers form's Current event procedure to check whether the PaymentHistory form is open. Because it's so useful, you'll want to include the IsOpen function in other applications you create.

Here's the code, which you can also view by opening the Miscellaneous module in the Subscription database:

```
Public Function IsOpen(ByVal strFormName As String) As Boolean
' Returns True if the specified form is open in Form view.

    Const conDesignView = 0
    Const conObjStateClosed = 0

    IsOpen = False
    If SysCmd(acSysCmdGetObjectState, acForm, strFormName) <> _
            conObjStateClosed Then

        If Forms(strFormName).CurrentView <> conDesignView Then
            IsOpen = True
        End If
    End If
End Function
```

As its function declaration states, the IsOpen function accepts as an argument the name of a form and returns a *Boolean* value—either True or False, depending on whether the specified form is open or not. Early in the function, a line of code sets the return value to False—assuming the form is *not* open—and then the function goes on to check whether to change this value to True.

The procedure uses If...Then statements to check two conditions:

Whether the form is in Microsoft Access' list of open objects

Microsoft Access keeps an internal list of all the objects that are open. The SysCmd (pronounced "SIS-command") function is a built-in function that lets you ask for information about the system and its status. By calling this function, you can find out whether a form is open.

You pass three arguments to the SysCmd function: a constant that specifies the type of information you want, in this case the state of an object; the type of object you're interested in, in this case a form; and a string containing the name of the object, in this case the string variable that was passed to the IsOpen function. The SysCmd function returns a number that indicates the status of the form, and this code compares the return value with a constant value indicating that the object is closed. If the return value doesn't equal (<>) the value for a closed object, the code continues; otherwise, the IsOpen function returns False.

Looking into the IsOpen Function, *continued*

Whether the form is in Design view If the form is in Design view, you want the IsOpen function to return False, because most code that refers to a form in Design view would cause errors. Forms have a property called CurrentView, which stores a number representing the current view of the form. This code compares the current view to the constant value that indicates Design view, and then sets the function's return value to True if the property doesn't equal that value.

The expression that refers to the CurrentView property uses a technique you haven't seen yet. So far, you've used the exclamation point operator to refer to a form in the Forms collection of the database, as in *Forms!Subscribers*. An alternative method for referring to a member of a collection—and the method you must use when the form name is contained in a variable—is to say *Forms("Subscribers")*. To refer to the form that was passed to the function, this code uses the expression *Forms(strFormName)*.

Because this function is provided for you in the practice database, you don't need to concern yourself too much with how it works—you can simply call it whenever you want to check whether a form is open. As you've seen, the expression *IsOpen("NameOfForm")* gives you the information you need. To take advantage of the techniques you learn in this lesson, simply copy or import this function into any application that needs to refer to one form from another.

Opening a Form to Add Related Records

A pop-up form is useful for showing a small amount of information that you want to keep on top of other forms. However, most forms you present to users won't be pop-up forms, because you'll want users to be able to switch from one form to another, bringing the current form to the front. Any time you provide the user with ways to switch between forms, you'll want to consider how the forms work together. As was the case with the PaymentHistory pop-up form, you'll often need to create event procedures to get the results you want.

In this section, you'll work with a form designed for entering new payments into the Subscription database. The form is called EnterPayment, and is already in the practice database, ready for you to use. Anticipating that users will jump to this form from the PaymentHistory form, you'll add code that makes the two forms work together well.

Add a button that opens the EnterPayment form

Because users will often want to enter a payment for a subscriber while viewing data in the Subscribers form, your first step is to add another button to the Subscribers form. As before, you'll use the Command Button Wizard.

1 In the Database window, select the Subscribers form, and then click the Design button.

The form opens in Design view.

*Command
Button tool*

2 Scroll down in the form to display the Form Footer section.

3 In the toolbox, click the Command Button tool.

4 Click the form footer just to the right of the Payment History button.

Click here to create the button.

The Command Button Wizard starts, asking what action you want the button to perform.

5 Select Form Operations from the Categories list, select Open Form from the Actions list, and then click Next.

The wizard asks which form you want to open. Because the EnterPayment form is already selected, you don't have to select it.

6 Click Next.

The wizard asks whether you want to display specific information in the form. This time, you'll go with the default option, Open The Form And Show All The Records.

7 Click Next again.

The wizard asks whether you want a picture or text on your button.

8 Select the Open Form text in the Text box, type &**Enter Payment** to replace the text, and then click Next.

The wizard asks what you want to name the button.

9 Type **EnterPayment** and then click Finish.

The wizard creates the button.

10 Click and drag the bottom right corner of the button to make it the same size as the other buttons in the footer.

*Form View
button*

11   Click the Form View button on the toolbar.

12   Click the Enter Payment button.

The button's Click event procedure runs, opening the EnterPayment form.

The EnterPayment form is specially designed for entering new payments into the Payments table. For example, the form's DataEntry property is set to Yes, so it opens without any existing payment records displayed, ready for a new payment. It also has the AllowEdits and AllowDeletions properties set to No, so that only new payments can be edited in the form.

Note that the Subscriber field on the form is blank, even though you came from the Subscribers form where you're viewing a specific subscriber. It would be nice if the subscriber record were automatically set when opening this form, so the user wouldn't have to select one. In the next procedure, you'll add code to make this happen.

Features of the EnterPayment Form

The EnterPayment form has several features already implemented in the practice file. Although they aren't directly related to the subject you're learning about in this lesson, you may want to take a look at the Visual Basic code for these features to see how the form works. Here's what you'll find behind the form:

- Three command buttons created using the Command Button Wizard: Save Payment, Add New Payment, and Close.

- Code that enables the credit card text boxes in the PaymentMethod option group when a user selects the Credit Card option. To view this code, open the AfterUpdate event procedure for the PaymentMethod option group.

- Code that runs when the user tries to save a record, in response to the form's BeforeUpdate event. The first half of this procedure checks to make sure the user entered a value for the PaymentMethod field, and cancels the update if its value is 0. If the record is valid, the second half of the procedure updates the PaidThrough field to add the number of months the subscriber paid for. The PaidThrough field is actually stored in the Payments table, but is included in the underlying query of this form to make it easier to update. Here's the code:

```
Private Sub Form_BeforeUpdate(Cancel As Integer)
' Check to make sure a payment method is selected.
' Then update the PaidThrough field (in the Subscribers table)
' to reflect additional time due to this payment.

    Dim bytMonths As Byte

    If PaymentMethod = 0 Then
        DisplayMessage "You must select a payment method."
        Cancel = True
        Exit Sub
    End If

    bytMonths = YearsPaid * 12

    If IsNull(PaidThrough) Or PaidThrough < Date Then
        ' If this is the first payment, set PaidThrough from current date.
        PaidThrough = DateSerial(Year(Date), Month(Date) + bytMonths, 1)
    Else
        ' Otherwise, add additional months to the PaidThrough value.
        PaidThrough = DateSerial(Year(PaidThrough), Month(PaidThrough) + _
            bytMonths, 1)
    End If
End Sub
```

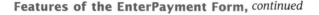

Features of the EnterPayment Form, *continued*

The second part of this procedure uses an If...Then statement to check whether the PaidThrough field is already set. If it isn't, or if the subscription has expired, it adds additional months to the PaidThrough value beginning at today's date. If the PaidThrough field is set and the subscription is current, it adds the additional months to the current PaidThrough value.

Both these statements use Microsoft Access date functions to calculate the new PaidThrough date value. Date values are stored as numbers by Microsoft Access, so you can't work with them directly—except to add or subtract days from them. But using date functions as shown in this procedure makes it possible to add *months* to the date value rather than days, and also makes it easy to set the PaidThrough value to the first day of the month. The Year and Month functions, as their names suggest, return the year and month for a given date value; the DateSerial function lets you build a date value from individual date parts. So the second line that includes these functions in effect says, "Create a date where the year is the same as the PaidThrough date, the month is so many months later than the PaidThrough month, and the day is the first of the month—and set the new PaidThrough value to that date."

Add code that sets the subscriber automatically

When users click the Enter Payment command button on the Subscribers form, they most likely want to add a payment record for the subscriber they were looking at. In order to help users enter data more easily, you can set the default value for the SubscriberID control on the data entry form.

*Design View
button*

1   Click the Design View button on the toolbar.

2   Click the OnOpen property in the property sheet, and then click the Build button.

Microsoft Access displays the Choose Builder dialog box.

3   Double-click Code Builder.

Microsoft Access opens the Module window and displays the Form_Open event procedure for the EnterPayment form. Whenever a user opens the form, the code in this procedure will run—which makes it a great place to initialize controls on the form such as the SubscriberID combo box.

4   Add the following code to the event procedure:

```
Private Sub Form_Open(Cancel As Integer)
' Set the default to the current subscriber on the Subscribers form.

    If IsOpen("Subscribers") Then
        SubscriberID.DefaultValue = Forms!Subscribers!SubscriberID
    End If

End Sub
```

This code first checks whether the Subscribers form is open using the IsOpen function, which you used before. Users might open the EnterPayment form by itself, in which case trying to match it up with the Subscriber form would cause an error.

If the Subscribers form is open, the line of code in the middle sets the DefaultValue property of the SubscriberID combo box to the value of the SubscriberID field on the Subscribers form. As you've seen before, you can refer to a field on another open form using the Forms collection—and separating the collection name, form name, and field name with exclamation points. This line of code says, "Set the default value for the SubscriberID field (on this form) to the current value of the SubscriberID field on the form called Subscribers."

5 Close the Module window.

6 Click the Form View button on the toolbar.

Form View button

Your event procedure runs, using the current subscriber on the Subscribers form as the default value for the field. Note that although the combo box displays the name of the subscriber, your code actually set it to the appropriate SubscriberID value, because this is the field the combo box is actually bound to.

The current subscriber...

...becomes the default for a new payment.

Add code to update other open forms after the user enters a payment

When a user enters a payment, the status of that subscriber changes—the PaidThrough field gets changed to reflect the new payment, for example. If you open another form to display data after the change is made, that form would reflect the changes; but forms that are already open don't automatically show the new data. If forms that show changed data are open, you should update them. You can do this by adding code to the AfterUpdate event procedure for the form, which runs whenever a change gets saved in the form.

*Design View
button*

1   Click the Design View button on the toolbar.

2   Click the AfterUpdate property in the property sheet, and then click the Build button.

Microsoft Access displays the Choose Builder dialog box.

3   Double-click Code Builder.

Microsoft Access opens the Module window and displays the Form_AfterUpdate event procedure for the EnterPayment form. Whenever a user saves a new payment, this event procedure will run.

4   Add the following code to the event procedure:

```
Private Sub Form_AfterUpdate()
' Update other forms if they are open.

    If IsOpen("Subscribers") Then
        ' Refresh the Subscribers form to show
        ' the PaidThrough value.
        Forms!Subscribers.Refresh
    End If

    If IsOpen("PaymentHistory") Then
        ' Requery the PaymentHistory pop-up form
        ' to show the new payment.
        Forms!PaymentHistory.Requery
    End If

End Sub
```

The first If...Then statement in this procedure checks whether the Subscribers form is open. If it is, the code uses the Refresh method for the form, which tells Microsoft Access to update the data displayed on the form with the current values from the underlying table. Note that using the Refresh method doesn't cause the query to run again, so new records aren't added, deleted records aren't removed, and the sort order remains the same. You don't need to make these types of changes now, because adding a payment doesn't affect the number of subscribers in the database.

The second part of the procedure checks whether the PaymentHistory pop-up form is displayed. If it is, the code uses the Requery method of the form, which tells Microsoft Access to requery records in the form as if you'd closed and re-opened it. Unlike refreshing, requerying a form does add new records, which is necessary in this case so that the pop-up form will show the new payment record. Note, however, that this has the sometimes undesirable side effect of resetting the current record—when you requery a form, the first record in the recordset becomes the current one. In an informational pop-up form like this one, you don't mind, because it doesn't matter which record is current.

5   Close the Module window.

6   Close the EnterPayment form, clicking Yes when Microsoft Access asks if you want to save changes.

Try the new features

If the Subscribers form and the PaymentHistory form are open, adding a new payment should now be reflected in these two forms. Let's see if it works.

1 On the Subscribers form, click the Payment History button.

Code behind the button opens the PaymentHistory pop-up form, showing the payments for the current subscriber. Next, you'll enter a new payment for this subscriber.

2 Click the Enter Payment button.

Code behind this button opens the EnterPayment form, ready for you to add a payment for the current subscriber. If the PaymentHistory form is in the way, you may need to move it down to the bottom right corner of the screen.

3 In the Payment Method option group, select Check.

Changing a field in this form adds a new record to the Payments table, and causes it to display the subscriber's current PaidThrough date. You could go on to specify values for other fields, but because the other fields all have default values, you don't have to enter anything in them (assuming you want the default payment of one year at $24).

4 Click the Save Payment button.

Clicking this button saves the payment record. The PaidThrough field is now a year later than before. When the record was saved, your AfterUpdate event procedure also updated both the Subscribers form and the PaymentHistory form. In the pop-up form, you'll notice the new payment is listed—your code requeried that form.

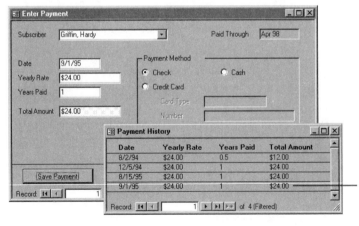

When you save a payment, your event procedure requeries the pop-up form so it displays the new record.

5 Close the PaymentHistory form.

6 In the EnterPayment form footer, click the Close button.

The PaidThrough field in the Subscribers form shows the new date—your code refreshed it.

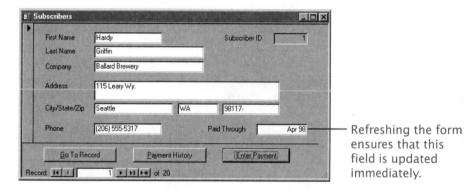

Refreshing the form ensures that this field is updated immediately.

It's tough to anticipate when you'll need to refresh or requery the data in a form. When you test your application, look out for changes you make that aren't reflected as you expect. If they aren't, add a line of code that uses the Refresh or Requery method.

 TIP You can also use the Requery method on a combo box or list box to update the records that are displayed in the list. For example, if you add a new subscriber in the Subscribers form, the combo box on the EnterPayment form won't automatically include that subscriber (until the next time the form is opened). To take care of this detail, you could requery the list each time a record is saved in the Subscribers form.

Close the form and exit Microsoft Access

1   Close the Subscribers form, clicking Yes when Microsoft Access asks if you want to save changes to the form.

2   On the File menu, click Exit.

Lesson Summary

To	Do this
Make a form stay on top of other forms at all times	Set the form's Popup property to Yes.
Create a button that opens another form and displays only records that are related to the currently displayed record	Use the Command Button Wizard, selecting the Open The Form And Find Specific Data To Display option. Specify the key fields that link data in the two forms.
Keep a form synchronized to display related records as you move between records in a main form	In the Current event procedure for the main form, write code that sets the Filter property of the other form. In the property setting, concatenate the key fields that you want to match in the two forms.
Check whether a form is open before you refer to it in code	Call the IsOpen function, which is included in the Miscellaneous module in the practice database.
Automatically set the value of a field on a form designed to add new records	In the Open event procedure for the form, set the DefaultValue property of the control.
Update data currently displayed on a separate form, showing new values but not adding, deleting, or reordering records	In the AfterUpdate event procedure, use the Refresh method on the form you want to update.
Update all data displayed in a separate form when the user adds or deletes a record	In the AfterUpdate event procedure, use the Requery method on the form you want to update.

For online information about	On the Help menu, click Microsoft Access Help Topics, click the Index tab, and then
Creating pop-up forms	Search for "pop-up forms"
Synchronizing forms to display related data	Search for "synchronizing forms"
Using date functions	Search for "date"
Referring to objects and their properties	Search for "objects"
Using methods	Search for "methods"

For more information on	In *Building Applications with Microsoft Access*, see
Creating pop-up forms, or synchronizing forms to display related data	Chapter 3, "Using Forms to Collect, Display, and Filter Information"
Using date functions	Chapter 2, "Introducing Visual Basic"
Referring to objects and their properties, or using methods	Chapter 5, "Working with Objects and Collections"

Preview of the Next Lesson

So far, you've used primarily command buttons to help users tell you what they want to do. But like most Windows applications, yours can allow users to select menu items and click toolbar buttons to access common application commands. In the next lesson, you'll learn to customize the menus and toolbars that are displayed with your application's forms.

10

Display Custom Menus and Toolbars

Estimated time
30 min.

In this lesson you will learn how to:

■ Use the Menu Builder to create and customize menu bars.

■ Customize your application's toolbars.

■ Display and hide toolbars.

When you work in a well-organized kitchen, cooking can be a joy. The cookware and utensils you need are at hand but not in the way, your ingredients are all within easy reach in the cabinets, and the counter space is clear and ready for action. If you're like me, on the other hand, you don't always plan ahead for creating your culinary master-pieces, and you end up searching for tools and ingredients—and running out of space. "Next time," you say, "I'll get the kitchen in shape before I start...."

In some ways, using a database application is like working in the kitchen. It's much easier to get your work done if you have all the tools you need within reach—but space on the screen is limited, so you want features to stay hidden away until you're ready to use them. In order to prepare the "data kitchen" for your users, you'll want to organize your application's commands and objects in the cleanest possible way.

In this lesson, you'll learn two important elements of an organized user interface: menus and toolbars. By hiding commands away on menus and using compact toolbar buttons to provide access to forms and reports, you'll make the Subscription application less cluttered, while at the same time making sure everything users need is easy to find.

221

Start the lesson

 Start Microsoft Access and open the 10 Subscription database in the practice files folder.

Using Menus and Toolbars in Your User Interface

So far, you've used command buttons on forms to make commands available to users—for example, you created three buttons on the Subscribers form that allowed users to jump to a specific record, view payment history, or enter payments. Although some common actions are important enough to warrant a command button on a form, most of the commands users need can be organized on your application's menus and toolbars, where they take less space. Like other Windows applications, your application can include *both* a menu command and a toolbar button to perform a given action, making it even more accessible. In this lesson, you'll create menus and a toolbar for the Subscribers form, replacing the command button strategy you used before.

You can design menus and toolbars to be used with a single form, or to work with several forms. You can even design a global menu or toolbar that's available throughout your application. However, because many commands apply only to certain places in your application, you're likely to need separate menus and toolbars for individual forms. Of course, you can always display the standard Microsoft Access menu or toolbar for some of the forms and reports in your application if they don't need custom commands.

When creating either menus or toolbars, you also have the option of using existing Microsoft Access commands. In most cases, you'll want to make most standard commands available to users, especially if they already know how to use Microsoft Access or other Windows applications. On the other hand, if you want to limit the options users have in your application, you can create menus and toolbars that contain just the commands you want to make available. To plan for your menus and toolbars, take a look at the other Windows applications you use to see how their interfaces are structured. Then, when you've planned your interface, you'll use the techniques shown in this lesson to put it into place.

Open the Subscribers form

1   In the Database window, click the Forms tab.

2 Double-click the Subscribers form.

As you can see, the Subscribers form in the practice database no longer has command buttons in its footer—you're going to replace them with menu commands and toolbar buttons.

Creating a Custom Menu Bar

The menus in Microsoft Access—File, Edit, View, and so on—are grouped into one object called a *menu bar*. You create and edit menu bars using the Menu Builder. Although the Menu Builder does allow you to create menus from scratch, you'll most likely want to start with an existing Microsoft Access menu bar and customize from there. For example, you might want to add a menu command—available when users are in the Subscribers form—that allows users to print mailing labels. Or, considering that your application has its own dialog box for jumping to a specific subscriber's record, you might want to make the dialog box available to users by way of a menu command.

To make these commands appear on a menu of the Subscribers form menu bar, you'll create a copy of the standard Form view menu bar, add these menu commands, and then specify that the Subscribers form should use the new custom menu bar. Microsoft Access will take it from there, displaying your additional menu items whenever the Subscribers form is active.

Creating a custom menu bar for the Subscribers form

To specify a menu bar for a form, you set the form's MenuBar property. Because you don't already have a custom menu bar, the Menu Builder helps you "build" the menu bar for the setting. With the help of the Menu Builder, you'll create a custom menu bar called SubscribersMenuBar, adding a command to the File menu, replacing a command on the Edit menu with your own version, and deleting unnecessary commands from the Tools menu.

Add a command to the File menu

*Design View
button*

*Properties
button*

1 Click the Design View button on the toolbar.

2 If the property sheet isn't displayed, click the Properties button on the toolbar.

3 Click the Other tab in the property sheet.

4 Click the MenuBar property, and then click the Build button.

Click the Build button.

Microsoft Access asks whether you want to create an empty menu bar—starting from scratch—or base your menu bar on a standard menu bar. You want to base your custom menu bar on the standard Form view menus.

5 Select Form from the list box, and then click OK.

The Menu Builder appears, ready for you to add or change items on the menu bar. The box in the bottom half of the window displays all the menu entries for the Form view menus, for you to modify. Starting with an existing menu bar as a template makes creating a menu bar quite a bit easier than starting from scratch.

Menu entries for the standard
Form view menu bar

The menu entries are organized in a hierarchy—each actual menu (such as File, Edit, or View) is shown at the left of the list box, while the individual menu commands on a menu are indented underneath it. To modify a menu or menu command, you select it and then change its settings in the top part of the dialog box. To add or remove menu entries, you use the Insert and Delete buttons. Your first change will be adding a command to the File menu—a custom menu command for printing mailing labels.

6   Scroll down in the menu entries list box until you see the entry for the Print command, shown under the File menu, and then click the entry directly underneath it—three dots followed by a dash.

Select this menu entry, above which you'll insert a new menu command.

A dash as a menu entry indicates that the menu will display a *separator*—a horizontal line between menu commands—at this point in the menu. A separator menu item doesn't do anything, but it helps group commands on a menu logically.

7   Click the Insert button.

A new line appears underneath the entry for the Print command, making room for you to insert a menu entry on the File menu.

8   In the Caption box, type **P&rint Mailing Labels...**

As with command button captions, you can include an ampersand in a menu entry caption to provide an accelerator key for users who prefer the keyboard. Also, it's customary to include an ellipsis (three dots) after any menu command that displays a dialog box rather than immediately carrying out an action.

9   In the Action box, select RunCode.

Selecting RunCode allows you to run any general function procedure in your database when a user clicks the menu command. After you finish modifying the menu bar, you'll write the code that the new menu commands will run.

225

10 In the Argument(s) box, type **OpenMailingLabelsDialog()**

The argument you provide for the RunCode action is the name of the Visual Basic function you want to run, followed by open and close parentheses.

11 In the Status Bar Text box, type **Print or preview mailing labels with subscriber addresses**

Microsoft Access will display this informational text in the status bar whenever this menu command is highlighted.

Now that you've filled in all the fields, your new menu command is complete.

Replace a command on the Edit menu

Next, you'll move down to the Edit menu and substitute your own command for the existing Go To menu commands. Because the existing item has a submenu showing several commands, you'll first have to delete the submenu entries, and then change the main menu entry into a command.

1 Scroll down in the list box to find the Go To menu item entry, and then select the First menu item entry directly underneath it.

2 Click the Delete button five times to delete the submenu items.

3 Click the Go To menu item entry.

4 Enter the following settings for this menu item:

Property	Setting
Caption	&Go To Record...
Action	RunCode
Argument(s)	OpenGoToRecordDialog()
Status Bar Text	Jump to a specific subscriber's record

Like the previous menu command you created, this command will run a Visual Basic function—which you'll create after you've finished customizing your menu bar. Now that you've added your two new menu items, the last thing you'll do is delete some advanced menu commands that you don't want to make available to users.

Delete unnecessary commands on the Tools menu

There are many commands on the Tools menu that are exclusively for power users and developers—you don't want your users to be messing around with them. By deleting them from the Tools menu altogether, you'll make the menu much simpler, and you won't have to worry about users selecting them.

1 Scroll down in the list to find the Relationships menu item entry under the Tools menu, and then click to select it.

2 Click the Delete button 23 times, until the Options menu item entry is selected.

Now the Tools menu will contain only the four menu items that users need.

Build the new menu bar

You've finished customizing the menu bar—now you just need to tell the Menu Builder to create it!

1 Click OK.

Microsoft Access displays the Save As dialog box.

2 In the Menu Bar Name box, type **SubscribersMenuBar**

3 Click OK.

The Menu Builder creates your custom menu bar (this may take some time) and saves it in the Subscription database. When the Menu Builder finishes, it also sets the MenuBar property for the Subscribers form to the menu bar name you typed, so the form will now use the custom menu bar automatically.

4 Click the Save button on the toolbar.

Save button

In reality, a menu bar is just a collection of several macros—one for the menu bar itself, and one for each menu and submenu—that Microsoft Access interprets to create menus and display them whenever your form is active. If you now go view macros in the Database window, you'll see several macros that have names starting with SubscribersMenuBar.

Write code for your custom menu items to run

All the standard menu items you leave on a custom menu will carry out actions just as they do normally. But for the custom menu items you added, you need to write functions to carry out the commands. You'll write two functions, OpenMailingLabelsDialog and OpenGoToRecordDialog, placing them in a new module called MenuCommands.

Database Window button

1 Click the Database Window button on the toolbar.

2 Click the Modules tab.

3 Click the New button.

Insert Procedure button

4 Click the Insert Procedure button on the toolbar.

Microsoft Access displays the Insert Procedure dialog box.

5 In the Name box, type **OpenMailingLabelsDialog** and then click OK.

Microsoft Access creates the procedure and displays it in the Module window.

6 Enter the following code for the procedure (except the Function and End Function lines, which are already there):

```
Public Function OpenMailingLabelsDialog()
' Open MailingLabelsDialog form.

    DoCmd.OpenForm "MailingLabelsDialog"

End Function
```

This code opens the MailingLabelsDialog form—it will run whenever a user clicks the Print Mailing Labels menu item on your custom menu bar.

7 Click the Insert Procedure button again.

8 In the Name box, type **OpenGoToRecordDialog** and then click OK.

9 Enter the following code for the procedure:

```
Public Function OpenGoToRecordDialog()
' Open GoToRecordDialog form.

    DoCmd.OpenForm "GoToRecordDialog"

End Function
```

10 Close the Module window, clicking Yes when Microsoft Access asks if you want to save changes to the module.

Microsoft Access displays the Save As dialog box.

11 In the Module Name box, type **MenuCommands** and then click OK.

Microsoft Access saves the module in the database, making the code available to your menus. The name you give the module doesn't matter, but giving it this name will help you remember what the functions are used for.

Try your custom menu bar

You're ready to test your menu bar. Because you've set the MenuBar property for the Subscribers form, your custom menus should appear automatically when you switch the form into Form view.

1 Switch to the Subscribers form, still in Design view.

2 Click the Form View button on the toolbar.

*Form View
button*

Microsoft Access changes the menus that are displayed to show your custom menu bar—of course, to see them, you'll have to pull down the menus you customized.

3 Click the File menu.

The Print Mailing Labels item you added to the menu is there! When you point to the menu item, you'll see your description of the menu item in the status bar at the bottom of the Microsoft Access window.

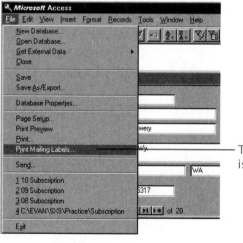

The File menu has a command that isn't usually there!

4   Click the Print Mailing Labels menu command.

The menu macro runs, which in turn runs the OpenMailingLabelsDialog function you wrote, and the dialog box appears.

5   Click Cancel.

Now, try out the other menu item you added.

6   On the Edit menu, click Go To Record.

Your function runs and opens the dialog box, which you created in Lesson 8.

7   Double-click an entry in the list box.

You jump to the specified record in the Subscribers form. Finally, you might as well check the Tools menu to make sure your changes are there.

8   Click the Tools menu.

There are only four commands on the menu—the items you deleted are gone.

9   Click the Subscribers form to close the menu.

Note that this custom menu bar only appears when the Subscribers form is active—that's the form you created it for. However, if you create a menu bar that's appropriate for more than one form, the forms can share it—just set the MenuBar property in each form to the same menu name. You can also create a single menu bar that applies to all forms in your application (unless they each have their own menu bar). To specify a "global" menu, you use the Startup command on the Tools menu.

Creating Custom Shortcut Menus

When you click the right mouse button nearly anywhere in Windows 95 or Microsoft Access, a shortcut menu appears with commands that are appropriate to the current context you're in or the place you've just clicked. For example, when you click with the right mouse button in a field on a form, a shortcut menu appears with options for filtering, copying, and pasting. By default, these shortcut menus appear in your application just as any other menu does.

In most cases, the default shortcut menus will work fine for your applications. If you want, however, you can replace shortcut menus with your own—using steps similar to those for regular menu bars. To replace the shortcut menu bar for a form, set the form's ShortcutMenuBar property to the name of another menu bar— or use the Menu Builder to create a new one. You can also specify different shortcut menus for individual controls on your forms by setting the ShortcutMenuBar property for each control (regular menu bars don't allow this).

Creating Custom Shortcut Menus, *continued*

When you use the Menu Builder to create a shortcut menu bar, the procedure is more or less the same as for a regular menu bar. However, there are a few key differences:

- You'll always create a shortcut menu bar from scratch, rather than basing it on an existing menu bar. This is because the existing menus you can start with are all regular menu bars, and aren't appropriate as shortcut menus.

- A shortcut menu bar has only one menu. When adding menu items for a shortcut menu bar, you must include a single menu name and then create the items you want indented underneath it.

- Even though you must give a name to the one menu in a shortcut menu bar, the menu name doesn't appear anywhere when you use the shortcut menu, because shortcut menus don't have a title.

As with a standard menu bar, you can add items to a shortcut menu that perform Microsoft Access menu commands or run macros or Visual Basic functions.

Customizing Toolbars

For better or worse, software today uses graphical interface elements more and more to interact with users. In your Microsoft Access applications, one way you can follow this graphical trend is by making use of toolbars. Toolbars are a handy way to make commands available to users—many buttons can fit on a toolbar, and once users learn what they are, the commands they need are always just a click away. And when you want to add new buttons to a toolbar, Microsoft Access provides many icons to choose from—or, if you're an aspiring artist, you can create your own.

There are several basic strategies for creating toolbars. The simplest strategy is to customize an existing toolbar, such as the Form View toolbar, adding and deleting buttons as desired. However, the standard toolbars are stored with your Microsoft Access installation, so other users who open your databases won't see your toolbar changes.

To make special toolbars available on other computers, you'll want to create your own custom toolbars, either supplementing or replacing the standard ones. Custom toolbars are stored with your application's database, so they're available to all users. When you customize toolbars, you choose which buttons they have and whether the buttons have icons or text on them. You can even customize the ToolTip text that appears when users hold the mouse pointer over a button.

In this section, you'll create simple a toolbar designed to be used in addition to the standard Form View toolbar. Using this strategy, you keep the buttons that apply to a specific form, such as the Subscribers form, grouped in one place.

In your own applications, you may want to create toolbars that replace standard toolbars. If you do, you'll probably want to include some of the buttons users are accustomed to seeing there—such as the Print, Cut, Copy, and Paste buttons—and then add your own selection of buttons in place of those you don't expect users to need.

Creating a Custom Toolbar for the Subscribers Form

The toolbar you'll create will help users of the Subscribers form to open other forms quickly and easily. Fortunately, the easiest type of toolbar button to create is one that opens a form or report in your database. You'll start by creating a new, empty toolbar, and then you'll add four buttons to it.

Create a new toolbar

1   On the View menu, click Toolbars.

2   Click the New button.

Microsoft Access displays the New Toolbar dialog box.

3   In the Toolbar Name box, type **Subscribers** and then click OK.

An empty floating toolbar appears near the upper left corner of the screen.

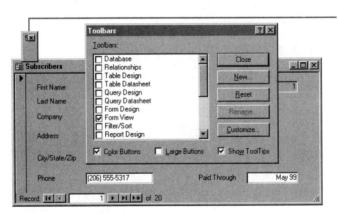

The new toolbar is ready for you to add buttons.

Add a standard button to the toolbar

On any toolbar you create, you can add as many standard buttons as you like, and they work just as they do on the built-in Microsoft Access toolbars. Here you want to make the Save Record command more accessible to users.

1   In the Toolbars dialog box, click Customize.

The Customize Toolbars dialog box appears, showing all the button categories and buttons available for your toolbars. Note that holding the mouse pointer over any button in the button well causes a ToolTip to pop up, telling you the name of the button.

Buttons you can add to your toolbars

2 Click the Save Record button in the button well and drag it over to the new toolbar.

The button appears on the toolbar. You don't have to do anything to make the button work—it's a standard toolbar button.

Add three custom buttons

Now you'll add three custom buttons—one to open the GoToRecord dialog form, one to open the MailingLabels dialog form, and one to open the EnterPayment form. These toolbar buttons will function just like the menu commands you created earlier. But first, because toolbars are slightly easier to customize when they're *docked*—stuck at the top or side of the screen—you'll dock this toolbar before adding the new buttons.

1 Drag the new toolbar to the top of the screen, dropping it just under the existing toolbar.

The toolbar sticks at the upper left corner of the screen, underneath the standard Form toolbar (or, if you have enough screen space, at the right side of the existing toolbar).

2 Select All Forms from the Categories list.

Instead of toolbar buttons, the right half of the Customize Toolbars dialog box now shows all the forms available in the database, so you can create custom buttons to open them.

3 Select GoToRecordDialog from the Objects list, and drag from the text up to the new toolbar, dropping it just to the right of the existing button.

The new button appears on the toolbar, showing a form icon as its button image.

The new toolbar button will open the GoToRecordDialog form when users click it.

In order to tell your toolbar buttons apart, you'll want to select a different icon for each button. To do this, you use the Choose Button Image command.

4 With the right mouse button, click the button that opens the GoToRecordDialog form, and then click Choose Button Image on the shortcut menu.

In the Choose Button Image dialog box, you can select a button image from many predesigned buttons. Although you can design your own toolbar buttons, it's easiest to choose from these, even though they don't always have just the image you want.

5 Click the image of a blue arrow pointing to the right (depending on your screen resolution, it's probably the third image in the second row).

Click here to select the button image.

You'll use this button image to indicate the Go To Record command.

6 Select the existing text in the Description box, and type **Go To Record** to replace it.

This changes the ToolTip text that appears when users hold the mouse pointer over the button.

7 Click OK.

The button image on your toolbar changes.

8 Select MailingLabelsDialog from the Objects list and drag it to the toolbar.

9 With the right mouse button, click the new toolbar button, and then click Choose Button Image on the shortcut menu.

10   Click the image of an envelope (usually the second image from the right in the fourth row).

11   Select the existing text in the Description box, type **Print Mailing Labels**, and then click OK.

12   Select EnterPayment from the Objects list, and drag it to the toolbar.

13   With the right mouse button, click the new toolbar button, and then click Choose Button Image on the shortcut menu.

14   Click the image of a pencil on top of two lists (usually the first image in the second row).

15   Select the existing text in the Description box, type **Enter Payment**, and then click OK.

Your toolbar now has four buttons ready for action! If you want, you can re-arrange buttons by dragging them around on the toolbar. Or, you can drag any button a bit to the right to make separations between groups of buttons—for example, you might want to move the Enter Payment button a bit to the right because it will be used for a very distinct task.

16   In the Customize Toolbars dialog box, click Close.

Try out the new toolbar

It's time to take your new toolbar for a spin! Try hovering over each of the buttons to view the ToolTip. Then follow these steps to see the toolbar buttons in action.

1   Click the Go To Record button on the toolbar.

THe button opens the Go To Record dialog box.

2   Double-click a subscriber in the list.

3   Click the Print Mailing Labels button on the toolbar.

The button opens the Print Mailing Labels dialog box.

4   Click Cancel.

Next, you'll add one more button to the toolbar before calling it complete—a button that lets users view payment histories. When you're finished, you will have replaced all the command buttons that used to be in the Subscribers form footer.

Creating Toolbar Buttons to Run Macros or Visual Basic Code

The toolbar buttons you've created so far have simply opened forms—they haven't done anything special beyond this. If opening an object is all you want to do, this technique is very straightforward. But you may want a toolbar button to do more—for example, you may want to run a Visual Basic procedure when users click the button. Unfortunately, toolbar buttons can't run code directly. If you want a button to do something other than open an object, you must create a Microsoft Access macro, which a toolbar button *can* run. The macro you create can either perform the actions you want itself, or it can in turn run a Visual Basic procedure—using the RunCode macro action—allowing you in effect to run code when the button is clicked.

In this section, you'll create a toolbar button that runs a macro. In this case, you want a toolbar button to open the PaymentHistory pop-up form, which shows a subscriber's payment history. However, you don't just want to open the form—you also need to set a filter so that the form displays only payments for the current subscriber. Although a toolbar button can't do this by itself, you can use a simple macro that does the job.

Add a toolbar button that runs a macro

The last button you'll add to the toolbar will use a macro to open the PaymentHistory form. The macro, called OpenPaymentHistory, is already included in the practice database. It has just one macro action: the OpenForm action—with the WhereCondition argument set so that the form will display only payments for the current subscriber. Of course, you could run a much more complex macro when a toolbar button is clicked; in this case, however, all you need to do is open the form.

1 With the right mouse button, click the toolbar, and then click Customize on the shortcut menu.

2 Select All Macros from the Categories list.

3 Select OpenPaymentHistory from the Objects list and drag from the text up to the new toolbar, dropping it just to the right of the Enter Payment button.

 — Drop the button here.

When users click this button, the macro will run, opening the pop-up form and setting its filter.

4 With the right mouse button, click the new toolbar button, and then click Choose Button Image on the shortcut menu.

5 Click the image that looks like a pop-up list on top of another form (usually the fourth image from the right in the third row).

6 Select the existing text in the Description box, type **View Payment History**, and then click OK.

7 In the Customize Toolbars dialog box, click Close.

Undock and test the toolbar

Your application's users can always dock or undock a toolbar they're using, including a custom toolbar you create. However, you decide the toolbar's default position—simply by leaving it there. For example, if you want the Subscribers toolbar to be undocked when it appears, you can undock it now and drag it where you want it to appear.

1 Click the edge of the toolbar around any of the buttons, and drag the toolbar down near the top of the Subscribers form.

The toolbar is floating again. If you like, you can resize the toolbar to another shape by dragging its border—for example, you can make it vertical, like the Microsoft Access toolbox, or horizontal.

2 Click the View Payment History button on the floating toolbar.

The toolbar button runs the OpenPaymentHistory macro, which in turn opens the pop-up form.

3 Close the Payment History pop-up form.

Your custom toolbar is complete!

Add code that shows and hides the toolbar

A custom toolbar doesn't appear automatically. What's more, after you open a custom toolbar, it stays open even after you leave the form it applies to. But you want this toolbar to appear only when the Subscribers form is active. To achieve this, you need to write two simple event procedures—one to hide the toolbar when the user changes to another object, and one to show it when the Subscribers form becomes active.

DesignView button

1 Click the Design View button on the toolbar.

2 Click the Event tab in the property sheet.

3 Select the OnActivate property, and then click the Build button.

4 Double-click Code Builder.

Microsoft Access opens the Module window and displays the form's Activate event procedure. This procedure runs whenever the form becomes active—whenever you switch to it from another window.

5   Enter the following code for the procedure:

```
Private Sub Form_Activate()
' Show the Subscribers toolbar.

    DoCmd.ShowToolbar "Subscribers", acToolbarYes

End Sub
```

This code uses the ShowToolbar method of the DoCmd object to display your custom toolbar. This method takes two arguments—the name of the toolbar you want to show or hide, and a predefined constant that states whether you want the toolbar to show or not. Next, you'll copy this code to the Deactivate event procedure.

6   Select the two lines of code after the Sub header (click the left edge of the comment mark and drag down until the lines are highlighted), and press CTRL+C.

7   Select Deactivate from the Proc box at the top of the Module window, and press CTRL+V.

8   Edit the DoCmd line to change the constant from acToolbarYes to acToolbarNo.

This code will turn the toolbar off whenever you leave the Subscribers form.

9   In the comment line, replace the word Show with the word **Hide**

10   Close the Module window.

Note that you can use the ShowToolbar method to show and hide standard Microsoft Access toolbars as well. For example, if you created a toolbar designed to replace the standard Form View toolbar in a given form, you could use an Activate event procedure that runs two ShowToolbar methods—one to hide the standard toolbar and one to show your custom one—and then reverse the process in the Deactivate event procedure. In this case, however, you want the standard toolbar to remain available to users.

Test the code that shows and hides your toolbar

Now when you switch to and from the Subscribers form, the Subscribers toolbar should come and go as well.

Form View button

1   Click the Form View button on the toolbar.

2   Switch to the Database window.

The form's Deactivate event occurs, running your code—and your toolbar disappears.

3   Switch back to the Subscribers form.

Your toolbar appears again—it now belongs to the Subscribers form.

Providing Pop-up Tips for Controls on Your Forms

In this section, you saw how to customize the ToolTips on toolbar buttons so users can figure out what your buttons are called. Like toolbar buttons, controls on your forms can have tips that pop up when users hold the mouse pointer over them. They're called *control tips*, providing a very simple but effective way for you to display help for your application's users. Control tips are perhaps most effective on command buttons and option groups—these are controls that users click with the mouse, so they'll see the tip text when they point the mouse at the control.

To create a control tip for a control, set its ControlTip property to the Help text you want to provide—up to 255 characters. When users hold the mouse pointer over the control, the text you typed will pop up in a small yellow box.

Close the form and exit Microsoft Access

1   Close the Subscribers form, clicking Yes when Microsoft Access asks if you want to save changes.

2   On the File menu, click Exit.

Lesson Summary

To	Do this
Create a custom menu bar for a form	Set the form's MenuBar property, clicking the Build button to start the Menu Builder. Start from a copy of the standard menu bar, adding and deleting menu items as desired.
Add a menu item that runs a procedure	In the Menu Builder, insert a line where you want the menu item to appear. Set the action for the item to RunCode, and then set the argument to the name of the standard function you want to run, followed by open and close parentheses.
Create a custom toolbar	On the View menu, click Toolbars, and then click New and type a name for the toolbar. Click Customize to add buttons, and then drag the buttons you want from the Customize dialog box to the toolbar.
Add custom toolbar buttons that open a form or report or run a macro	In the Customize dialog box, select the All Forms, All Report, or All Macros category, select the object you want the button to open, and then drag it to the toolbar. To change the image on the button, click it with the right mouse button, and then click Choose Button Image.
Show and hide toolbars with a form	In the form's Activate and Deactivate event procedures, write code that uses the ShowToolbar method of the DoCmd object.

For online information about	On the Help menu, click Microsoft Access Help Topics, click the Index tab, and then
Creating custom menu bars	Search for "menus"
Creating custom toolbars	Search for "toolbars"
Responding to the Activate and Deactivate events	Search for "Activate" and "Deactivate"
Using methods of the DoCmd object	Search for "DoCmd" or the method name, such as "OpenForm" or "ShowToolbar"

For more information on	In *Building Applications with Microsoft Access*, see
Creating custom menus and toolbars	Chapter 1, "Creating an Application"
Responding to the Activate and Deactivate events	Chapter 6, "Responding to Events"
Using methods of the DoCmd object	Chapter 2, "Introducing Visual Basic"

Preview of the Next Lesson

Now that you've created dialog boxes, menus, and toolbars, you know how to create almost every part of a custom user interface. All that's left is to package all the parts of your application into a coherent whole. In the next lesson, you'll learn ways to customize your application's general appearance and behavior, such as giving it its own title bar and icon. What's more, you'll learn how to control what happens when your application starts—and how to provide a startup form that leads users through their tasks.

Put Final Touches on an Application

Estimated time
20 min.

In this lesson you will learn how to:

- Create an application startup form.
- Control how your application starts.
- Customize the title bar and appearance of your application.
- Separate your application's data from its other objects.

The first impression is the most important, goes the common wisdom. Of course, it's important that when you order a fancy cake it tastes good, but it's the "icing on the cake" that catches people's attention—and their first look at that delicious cake will affect their overall opinion more than any other factor. As in other areas of life, this maxim holds true for computer software—the appearance and first impression of a product is as important as its capabilities. As Microsoft itself has learned, a polished, graphical product inspires excitement that might cause users to excuse a missing feature or two.

In previous lessons, you've learned how to put most of the substance into your applications—creating and customizing forms, adding menus and toolbars, linking everything together in a logical way. Before your application is ready for public consumption, however, it needs a few final touches—the icing on the cake. After all, the application will represent *you* to the users who start it up, and you want their first experience with your application to be a good one.

In this lesson, you'll learn techniques for making your applications look professional and polished. You'll work with the Subscription application, making it easier for users to get started—and helping the application make a great first impression. Finally, you'll learn tips and tricks for distributing an application to users so that it will be easier to maintain down the road.

Start the lesson

 Start Microsoft Access and open the 11 Subscription database in the practice files folder.

Controlling How Your Application Starts

After you've created the tables, forms, and reports for your application and added all the code to make them work together well, it's time to prepare your application for delivery. You want to make your application look like a unique, finished product rather than simply a Microsoft Access database with a few frills. Additionally, if users are to have a good experience with the application, you'll need to make sure it's easy for them to get started.

Here are some of the final preparations you'll want to consider:

Designate a startup form. You can select a form in your database that Microsoft Access opens automatically each time a user starts the application. For example, you might want to jump directly to your application's main data entry or display form, such as the Subscribers form you've been working with. Or, in many applications, you'll want to provide a switchboard-type form—similar to the Switchboard form the Database Wizard creates—that acts as a main menu for users' tasks. In either case, you'll most likely want to hide the standard Database window, because your forms will provide users with easy access to all your application's capabilities.

Customize the startup appearance of your application. In addition to providing a startup form, you can customize several other startup details, such as what the title bar displays. And if you create general application menu bars, shortcut menus, and toolbars, you'll want them to be hooked up when your application starts.

Prepare your application for network use and easy maintenance. Before you deliver your application, you should consider how it will be used and maintained. To make things easier down the road, you may want to split your application into two separate files: one for tables, and another for other objects. Additionally, you'll decide whether the application will be located on a network, and whether you need to protect your data by setting a password.

Test, test, test! Of course, the final step before you distribute your application is to make sure everything is foolproof. Try all the possible paths through the forms and reports, and make any necessary fixes before you deliver it. The work you put in up front will pay off in reducing the updates you'll need to provide down the road!

In this lesson, you'll use several of these techniques to customize the Subscription application. When you're finished, the Subscription application will be ready to deliver—making its debut to users as a stand-alone product rather than just another database, and helping users get started with their work right away.

Providing a Startup Form for Your Application

Any form in your application can act as the startup form, opening automatically for users. However, the most common strategy for starting an application—and the one you'll use with the Subscription application—is to provide a separate switchboard form that acts as a main menu for users. The Subscription practice database already includes a preliminary version of such a startup form, designed to introduce the application to users at an imaginary publication called *Dance Journal*.

In this section you'll add the final elements to the design of the Switchboard form. In the practice database, the form already contains the picture, text in several labels, and two simple buttons created using the Command Button Wizard. You'll add the third button, and then get the form ready for use as the application's startup form. In your own database, you would create a switchboard form from scratch, adding whatever text, pictures, and buttons you'd like. A startup form is a great place to show your creativity and put your personal touch on your application.

Completing the Switchboard Form for the Subscription Database

To finish up the Switchboard form in the practice database, you'll open it in Design view, add a command button using the Command Button Wizard, and then add a label for the button. You'll also set several form properties that make the form look like a switchboard—similar to properties you set for dialog boxes and pop-up forms in previous lessons.

Add a command button

In the Database window, click the Forms tab.

1 Select the Switchboard form, and then click Design.

The Switchboard form opens in Design view. The two command buttons on this form open the Subscribers form and the PrintMailingLabelsDialog form. You'll create one additional button at the bottom of the form, providing an easy way for users to exit the Subscription application when they're finished with their work.

2 Scroll down a bit in the form to display the blank area underneath the two buttons.

3 In the toolbox, make sure the Control Wizards tool is selected, and then click the Command Button tool.

Control Wizards tool

4 Click to create the new button just underneath the left side of the OpenMailingDialog button (the one that has an envelope icon on it).

Command Button tool

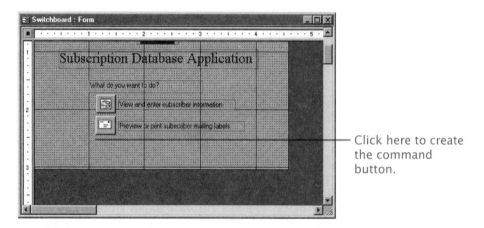

Click here to create the command button.

The Command Button Wizard starts, asking what action you want the button to perform.

5 Select Application from the Categories list.

Quit Application is already selected in the Actions list, so you can continue.

6 Click Next.

The wizard asks whether you want a picture or text on your button. Unlike the command buttons you've created in earlier lessons, for which you typed text, you'll put a picture on this button. You can choose from one of two pictures the wizard suggests for the button.

7 In the Picture list box, select Exit, and then click Next.

The wizard asks what you want to name the button.

8 Type **QuitApplication** and then click Finish.

The wizard creates the button, including an event procedure that automatically closes your application—and Microsoft Access—whenever the button is clicked.

9 Drag the bottom right corner of the button to make it the same size as the buttons above it.

Label the command button

Next, you'll add text next to the button to clarify what the button is for.

Label tool

1   In the toolbox, click the Label tool.

2   Click just to the right of the new button.

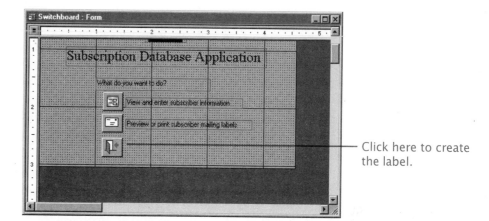

Click here to create the label.

An empty label appears on the form, ready for you to enter the text you want to display. You could use this same technique to add other text to the form, just like the labels that display the title of the application at the top of this form.

3   Type **Exit the Subscription application**

Set the Switchboard form's properties

To make the form look and work like a switchboard, all that's left is to set form properties.

Properties button

1   On the Edit menu, click Select Form.

2   If the property sheet isn't displayed, click the Properties button on the toolbar.

3   Click the Format tab in the property sheet.

4   Set the following properties to the values shown:

Property	Value
Caption	Switchboard
ViewsAllowed	Form
ScrollBars	Neither
RecordSelectors	No
NavigationButtons	No
AutoCenter	Yes
BorderStyle	Thin

These settings will make the Switchboard form look much like a dialog box, with a thin border and no extra navigation tools.

5   Close the Switchboard form, clicking Yes when Microsoft Access asks whether you want to save changes to the form.

Try out the Switchboard form

The Switchboard form will act as the control center of your application—users will think of it as their "home base," from which they'll navigate to their various tasks. Let's try it out.

1   In the Database window, double-click the Switchboard form.

The form appears in the center of the screen, announcing your application and showing the three buttons available for navigation.

2   Click the first button, View And Enter Subscriber Information.

The button's event procedure opens the Subscribers form. The toolbar and menus you created in Lesson 10 appear as well, providing a way to navigate through the other parts of your application. When you close the Subscribers form, you'll return to the application's switchboard.

3   Close the Subscribers form.

When users finish working in the Subscription application, they would normally click your new button to exit Microsoft Access. However, we have some more work to do, so you should just close the form.

4   Close the Switchboard form.

 NOTE   When you deliver your application to users, you may not want to allow them to close the Switchboard form without closing the whole application. To prevent the application from staying open, you could add a simple line of code to the form's Close event procedure that either closes the application or exits Microsoft Access. Use the CloseCurrentDatabase method to close the application; to exit Microsoft Access, use the Quit method of the DoCmd object.

Make your switchboard form open automatically

Now that the switchboard form is ready to go, the next step is to tell Microsoft Access to open the form automatically when users start your application, making it the startup form for the application. You do this with the Startup command.

1   On the Tools menu, click Startup.

Microsoft Access displays the Startup dialog box, where you can specify options for how your application starts.

2   In the Display Form box, click the drop-down arrow, and then select Switchboard from the list of forms.

Select the form you want to open when your application starts.

Next time you open the database, the Switchboard form will open automatically.

Customizing Your Application's Appearance

While you're in the Startup dialog box, you can set other options for your application. One nice detail to customize is the application's title bar. Instead of "Microsoft Access" you can specify the title of your application. Additionally, now is the time to tell Microsoft Access to hide the standard Database window from users, and to make sure users don't change the toolbars you've provided in your application.

Set startup options to control how your application looks

1   In the Startup dialog box, click the Application Title box, and then type **Subscription Database Application**

This text will appear in the title bar of the application window in place of "Microsoft Access," making your custom application look less like a Microsoft Access database and more like your own creation.

2   Clear the Display Database Window check box.

Now, when users open the Subscription database, the Database window won't appear. They won't need it—your switchboard form replaces it as the navigation tool for the application.

3   Clear the Allow Toolbar Changes check box.

Clearing this option ensures that users can't change your custom Subscribers toolbar—or the built-in toolbars—so they'll always be available.

Complete startup settings for the Subscription application

4   Click OK.

Although the Subscription database doesn't require any other startup options, you may want to use some of the other options in your own applications. Here are some additional changes you can make by setting options with the Startup command:

Provide your own application icon.   By setting the Application Icon option to an icon or bitmap image file, you can change the icon that's displayed in the upper left corner of the title bar (and in the taskbar button when your application is minimized).

Hide the status bar.   If you clear the Display Status Bar check box, the status bar won't appear at the bottom of the application window.

Change standard menus.   In Lesson 10, you learned how to change menus on a single form. However, you can also specify menu behavior for your entire application by setting startup options. To display a menu bar for forms and reports that don't have their own custom menu bar, set the Menu Bar and Shortcut Menu Bar options. To make built-in menus unavailable, clear the Allow Full Menus and Allow Default Shortcut Menus check boxes.

Hide built-in toolbars.   By clearing the Allow Built-in Toolbars check box, you can tell Microsoft Access not to display the toolbars that are normally available, so that only your custom toolbars appear.

Secure your application from tampering.   If you click the Advanced button in the Startup dialog box, you'll see two more options: Allow Viewing Code After Error and Use Access Special Keys. By clearing these check boxes, you can make it impossible for users to break into your application's code. Be careful, though—you'll be locking *yourself* out as well.

NOTE   After you've set startup options, they take effect the next time you open your application. Having these options in effect is great for your users—but while your application is still under development, you may not want the startup options to apply. For example, you'll probably want to open the Database window rather than the startup form, so you'll have access to all objects in the application.

To bypass the startup options for an application, hold down the SHIFT key when you open the database, either as you double-click the database file's icon or as you click the Open button. Microsoft Access will ignore all options you've set using the Startup command.

Replacing the Microsoft Access Splash Screen

Each time you start Microsoft Access, it displays a *splash screen*, a bitmap that announces the name and version number of Microsoft Access. For your applications, you may want to replace this screen with your own, so that opening your application will display your application's name.

You can provide a custom splash screen that appears while Microsoft Access starts.

To replace the standard splash screen, all you have to do is place a bitmap image (.bmp) file in the same folder as your application's database (.mdb) file, giving it the same name as the database file. To create a custom splash screen, you can use the Windows Paint application or any other application that creates bitmap image files.

Rename the splash screen file so Microsoft Access will display it

The practice folder includes a bitmap file called 11 Splash Screen, which provides the splash screen bitmap for the Subscription database. To cause Microsoft Access to display this bitmap, you'll simply rename it to match the name of the Subscription database.

1 Minimize Microsoft Access (and any other open applications).

2 On the Windows desktop, double-click the shortcut icon for the Access VBA Practice folder. (Or, if the practice files folder isn't there, locate it in the Windows Explorer.)

3 Select the 11 Splash Screen file, and then click its name to select the text.

4 Type **11 Subscription** to rename the file, and then press ENTER.

Microsoft Access will automatically use this bitmap file as the splash screen whenever you start your application by double-clicking its Windows icon. Note, however, that the splash screen doesn't appear if you open the application from within Microsoft Access.

5 Click the Subscription Database Application button on the taskbar to restore Microsoft Access.

Soon, you'll try out your application with its new startup options and splash screen. First, however, there are a few more details to take care of.

Protecting Your Application by Setting a Password

Many databases contain sensitive or confidential information, which you may want to protect by requiring that users enter a password before they begin working in the application. The simplest way to do this is by setting a password for the database. To do this, on the Tools menu point to Security, and then click Set Database Password. Each time the database opens, Microsoft Access will ask for the password.

Although setting a database password is a simple method of securing your database, it isn't very flexible. For example, what if you want to provide access only to certain objects, or data in your application only to specific users and not to others? Or what if you want to provide various levels of access, such as allowing users to view data, but not to change it? You can customize access to your application in these ways by setting up user and group security. And if you do create this more advanced type of security, you can protect your application itself from any design changes—making yourself the only user who has permission to view code and change objects.

To set up advanced security, you start by running the User-Level Security Wizard. You then use the other Security commands on the Tools menu to create user and group accounts, and to grant permissions to each account for the various objects in your application. Beware, however: advanced security is not for the faint of heart. Although Microsoft Access provides all the tools you need for setting up security, it is a time-consuming and challenging process. If a single password for your application will suffice, consider sticking with the database password strategy.

Preparing to Distribute Your Application to Users

Your application is ready to go to work—all you need to do is make it available to users. In the simplest case, this just involves copying the database application file to the user's system or to a network location where users can access it. However, before you send out your application, it's a good idea to give some thought to how you'll distribute and maintain it. How will you distribute updates to the application? How will users back up and compact the database? Are there any additional files you need to deliver along with your application?

If your application is designed for many users or for users on a network, or if it's a large application, these questions will become important to you. Here are some ideas for addressing the challenges of distributing and maintaining a Microsoft Access application:

Split your application into two database files. By default, all the data and objects for an application are stored in a single database file. This file can become very large and difficult to handle. With a large application, it's a good idea to have one Microsoft Access file for the queries, forms, and other objects that make your application work, and a separate file for its tables. The main application file is often referred to as the *front-end* database, because this is what users open and use; the data file containing your tables is referred to as the *back-end* database.

Place your application or its data file on a network drive.   Microsoft Access is a *multiuser* database system, which means that more than one user can view and change data in the same database at the same time. To make your application available to multiple users, you can simply place the file on a network. Or, if you split the application into two separate databases, you can place only the data file on a network drive, while distributing copies of the application file to each user—which may make your application run faster.

Create Windows shortcuts to run your application or perform other tasks.   In Windows 95, you can provide shortcut icons that make your application easier to run, especially if it's located on a network or stored in a folder along with many other files. You may want to provide other miscellaneous shortcuts for users as well—for example, you might create a shortcut for compacting or backing up a database file. For information on creating shortcuts, see your Windows documentation or search Help for "shortcuts."

Make sure users have all the files they need.   Most everything your application needs is included in your database file or installed with Microsoft Access. If your application uses more than one file, be sure to distribute all the files users need. For example, if you split your application into two files, users must have access to both. If your application has a splash screen or other external files, these files must be available as well. Finally, if your application uses special features of Microsoft Access, such as data access drivers or custom controls, users must have installed them with Microsoft Access.

In this section, you'll implement the first of these strategies for the Subscription application, splitting it into two separate database files for easier maintenance.

Split the Subscription database into two files

As you'll see, splitting an application into two database files is easy: you just run the Database Splitter.

1   On the Tools menu, point to Add-Ins, and then click Database Splitter.

The Database Splitter starts.

2   Click the Split Database button.

The Database Splitter displays the Create Back-End Database dialog box, where you specify the name and location of the database file that will contain your application's tables.

3   In the dialog box, move to the practice files folder on your computer's hard disk (if you're not already there).

Note that if you were planning to make this data available to users on a network, you would move instead to a folder on a network drive. That way, the Database Splitter would put the data on the network for you. For your current purpose, however, having both databases on your hard disk is fine.

4   Click the Split button.

The Database Splitter creates a new database file called 11 Subscription_be (the "be" stands for "back end"), exports the two tables in the Subscription database to the new file, creates linked tables to them in the current database, and then displays a message saying that the database was successfully split.

5   Click OK.

6   On the File menu, click Exit.

When Microsoft Access closes, you can see files in the practice folder, which is still displayed on your desktop. The folder now contains three files belonging to the Subscription database for this lesson: the application itself, the data file, and the splash screen bitmap file.

Even though you've split it into two database files, your application will work exactly as before. Now, however, the database is much more flexible. First, you can back up the data file—a very important task—without backing up the entire application, which doesn't often change. What's more, you can replace the application file—to update forms and reports, for example—without any effect on the existing data. Finally, if users work on a network, they can run your application from their individual systems while accessing the data on a network drive.

 NOTE   After you've split a database, the linked tables in the application file refer to the folder they're in on your computer's hard disk at the time you perform the split. If you rename folders or move the data file to another location—for example, if you place it on a network drive—you'll have to refresh the linked tables, or else Microsoft Access won't be able to find them.

To refresh linked tables easily, use the Linked Table Manager (on the Add-Ins submenu of the Tools menu). The Linked Table Manager locates the data file—wherever it has been moved to—and relinks the tables so the database works again.

Try out the final Subscription application

1   In the practice files folder on the Windows desktop, double-click the 11 Subscription database file (be sure to double-click the Microsoft Access database file, not the bitmap image file).

Microsoft Access starts up behind the scenes. What you see, however, is a custom splash screen announcing the Subscription Database Application—the bitmap you renamed earlier in the lesson. After a few seconds, the splash screen disappears, and Microsoft Access displays your startup form: the Switchboard form.

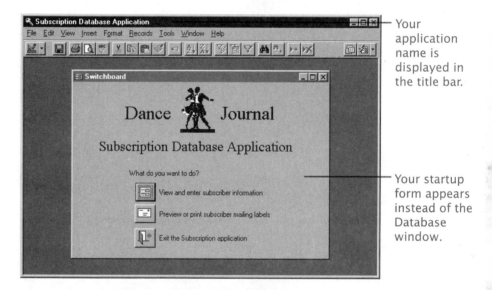

Your application name is displayed in the title bar.

Your startup form appears instead of the Database window.

The Subscription database is now a complete, stand-alone application—it has its own splash screen, its own title bar, and a customized user interface to help users navigate while performing their work. And when they're finished, it even has a custom way for them to quit!

2   On the Switchboard form, click the Exit The Subscription Application button.

The button's event procedure runs the Quit method of the DoCmd object, and Microsoft Access shuts down.

253

Additional Tools in the Microsoft Access Developer's Toolkit

In order to run your Microsoft Access application, users must have Microsoft Access installed on their computers. However, now that you've customized an application so it looks like it could stand on its own, you may be wondering if there's a way to distribute it to users who *don't* have Microsoft Access. You can do this—if you have the Microsoft Access Developer's Toolkit (ADT) for Windows 95. This add-on product contains several tools for developers, including the *run-time* version of Microsoft Access—a version that runs applications but doesn't allow you to change or create them. You can distribute the run-time version of Microsoft Access to an unlimited number of users, so they can run your application regardless of whether they have Microsoft Access.

One other important tool in the ADT is the Setup Wizard, which allows you to create a full-featured custom Setup program for your application. In addition to installing your application's files on users' systems, the Setup program can install the Microsoft Access run-time files, create Windows shortcuts, and customize users' systems in other ways.

If you're distributing applications to many different users, you'd probably benefit from purchasing this product. In addition to these tools, the ADT includes additional custom controls, tools for using replicated databases, the Windows Help compiler for creating your own Help files, and useful informational resources for developers, such as a hard-copy language reference manual and a sampler CD.

Lesson Summary

To	Do this
Create a custom switchboard form	Create a new blank form, add text and pictures that introduce your application, and then add command buttons that navigate to common user tasks. Set Format properties to make the form look like a switchboard.
Cause a form to open automatically when your application starts	On the Tools menu, click Startup, and then select the form in the Display Form box. Set other startup options as desired, and then click OK.
Ignore startup options for an application	Hold down the SHIFT key as you open the application.
Provide a custom splash screen that appears when you start an application from Windows	Create a bitmap image file of the screen you want to display, giving the file the same name as your application file and placing it in the same directory.
Split an application into two database files for easier maintenance	On the Tools menu, point to Add-ins, and then click Database Splitter.
Protect data by setting a password	Using commands on the Security submenu of the Tools menu, specify a database password or set up user and group security.

For online information about	On the Help menu, click Microsoft Access Help Topics, click the Index tab, and then
Creating a startup form or setting startup options	Search for "startup options"
Splitting an application into two database files	Search for "Database Splitter Wizard"
Using security features to protect your databases	Search for "security"
Creating multiuser applications	Search for "multiuser environment"

For more information on	In *Building Applications with Microsoft Access*, see
Creating a startup form or setting startup options	Chapter 1, "Creating an Application"
Splitting an application into two database files	Chapter 14, "Securing and Delivering Your Application"
Using security features to protect your databases	Chapter 14, "Securing and Delivering Your Application"
Creating multiuser applications	Chapter 10, "Developing Multiuser Applications"

Preview of the Next Lesson

Throughout Part 3, you've learned the key techniques for customizing the user interface of an application. In the final part of the book, you'll delve into more advanced Visual Basic programming topics, learning to work directly with data and objects in powerful new ways. In Lesson 12, you'll learn more about manipulating Microsoft Access objects in Visual Basic code—and how you can achieve impressive results in your forms, subforms, and reports by working directly with objects.

Working with Data and Objects

Explore Objects and Collections

In this lesson you will learn how to:

Estimated time
45 min.

- Understand object references in Visual Basic code.
- Perform the same action on all objects in a collection.
- Create a list box that allows users to select multiple items from the list.
- Open a Recordset object and change data in selected records.
- Create a QueryDef object in code that runs an action query and changes data.

Looking at the packaging, I see that the noodles I'm planning to cook for dinner tonight are made from semolina flour—the only ingredient. Modern science tells me that this flour is itself made up of many distinct bits called molecules. The molecules, in turn, are composed of atoms, and those in turn of still smaller particles. Fortunately, I don't need to understand any of this in order to cook my pasta! On the other hand, if I worked in a food-testing laboratory and wanted to understand precisely how the noodles would behave when cooked, I would need to know what was happening below the surface. I imagine I'd need to consult my chemistry books pretty thoroughly before I could predict how the molecules and atoms would work together.

Like chemistry, Microsoft Access admits of many different levels of understanding. As a Microsoft Access user editing data, for example, you don't usually need to know what's going on behind the scenes. But as an application developer, you'll need a better grasp of the underlying mechanism that makes Microsoft Access tick. Like a periodic table of chemical elements, the object model of Microsoft Access is a complex framework of objects that make it all work—and as you increase your understanding of this foundation, you'll be able to create more powerful applications.

In this lesson, you'll discover the framework of objects and collections underlying every Microsoft Access application. You'll learn how to use objects to control forms and data in powerful new ways—and along the way, you'll uncover many of the fundamental principles on which Microsoft Access is built. Although we'll only scratch the surface of the complexities underlying Microsoft Access, the understanding you'll gain should lay the foundation for any further exploration you do on your own.

Start the lesson

➤ Start Microsoft Access and open the 12 Issues database in the practice files folder.

A dialog box appears, introducing the Issues database application, which you'll work with throughout Part 4 of this book.

Introducing the Issues Application

The practice database file you've opened is a useful Microsoft Access application for tracking issues in a workgroup. The fact that several users can open a database at one time over a network makes Microsoft Access an ideal environment for creating *workgroup applications*—systems designed to help people work together better in a networked office environment. The Issues application is an example of such a system: it allows users to keep track of open business issues interactively, assigning them to the appropriate employees and querying the database to find out which issues need to be followed up on.

Sign in to the Issues application

When you first open the Issues application, a dialog box appears asking you to enter your name. This dialog box is a startup form created using the same technique you used in Lesson 11 for the Subscription application.

The dialog box requires you to "log in" to the Issues application (saving your name for later use), and then opens another form that shows open business issues stored in the database. As the user of the Issues application, your first step is to sign in.

1   In the combo box, select Bonnie Christensen.

The dialog box has two command buttons, both of which open a form called Issues. One of them displays issues for all employees; the other filters issues for employees who want to see only the issues currently assigned to them.

2 Click the Show All Issues button.

The button's Click event procedure opens the Issues form, which displays the first issue in the database. Here, you can browse through current issues, assign them to other employees, or make comments concerning them.

The Issues form lets users track the status of business issues...

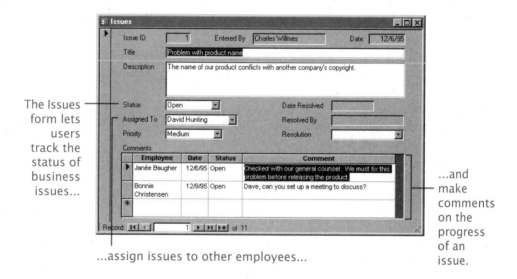

...and make comments on the progress of an issue.

...assign issues to other employees...

The Issues form is nearly complete as it stands—you won't have to add much to it. The form already has several event procedures that make it an effective tool for tracking business problems and items that employees need to act on. In this lesson and the remaining lessons of the book, you'll explore some of these features, and add some of your own capabilities to this custom application.

TIP On your own, you may want to browse the Visual Basic code that makes up the application—it uses many of the techniques you've already learned in previous lessons, combining them in new ways. To do this, open the Issues form in Design view and then explore its form module.

Open the Miscellaneous module

Although you'll be seeing more of the Issues form, you'll put it aside for now to explore some general principles of Microsoft Access. Before getting started, you'll need to open a standard module stored in the Issues database.

Database Window button

1 Click the Database Window button on the toolbar.

2 Click the Modules tab.

3 Double-click the Miscellaneous module.

The module opens and displays its Declarations section.

NOTE You'll notice one Dim statement in the Declarations section of the module—it declares a variable called lngCurrentEmpID. Remember the dialog box that asked for your name in the previous procedure? This variable stores the ID number of the employee name entered in the opening dialog— and because the variable is declared as Public, it is available throughout the application, whenever you need to know who the current user is.

Understanding Objects and Collections

Believe it or not, all the Visual Basic code you've written to this point fits into a logical framework called an *object model*. The object model is a hierarchy of all the items you use in an application—forms and their controls, tables and their fields, controls and their properties. Here, for example, is the graphical representation of the Microsoft Access object model provided in online Help.

Many of the objects in Microsoft Access contain collections of other objects, creating a complex hierarchy.

Application		
Forms		
	Controls	
Reports		
	Controls	
Screen		
DoCmd		

Legend	
▢	Object and collection
▢	Object only

In this section, you'll explore parts of the object model and write some simple Visual Basic code that demonstrates how it works. Then, as the lesson continues, you'll explore some practical uses for powerful objects that you haven't yet worked with.

Try out the Object Browser

So far, you've tried out several of the Module window tools at your disposal. But there's one more handy tool you've yet to try—the Object Browser. The Object Browser is a dialog box that lists all the objects available to your application, shows you how they're related, and allows you to consult online Help about each of them.

Object Browser button

1 Click the Object Browser button on the toolbar.

The Object Browser appears.

2 Click the drop-down arrow next to the Libraries/Databases combo box to display the list.

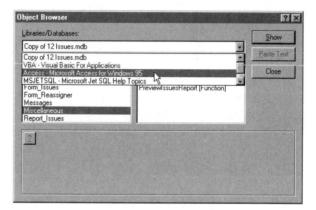

This list includes the object libraries and databases that Microsoft Access is aware of. Just about everything you type in code or refer to in an expression—objects, fields, methods, properties, functions, and other items—belongs to one or another of these groups. The following list describes the four object libraries you'll need to know about:

VBA The Visual Basic for Applications (VBA) object library contains all the Visual Basic functions and constants you're used to seeing, such as the MsgBox and Date functions.

Access The Microsoft Access for Windows 95 object library contains the objects, methods, and constants you use to control the user interface of your application, such as forms, reports, and controls. This library also includes the familiar DoCmd object and its methods.

DAO The Microsoft Data Access Objects (DAO) library contains the objects, methods, and constants you use to work directly with database files, and the data stored in them.

12 Issues.mdb Your application itself is an object library—it contains the forms, reports, and modules of the database, along with their controls, properties, and any procedures they contain. Because Microsoft Access keeps track of your application's objects in the same way it does for its built-in objects, you can refer to them in code—use a function in a module, for example—just as you would refer to those belonging to the Access or VBA libraries.

Using the Object Browser, you can explore each of these object libraries. In this lesson, you'll learn to work with a few important objects in the Access and DAO libraries; most of these techniques will apply to other types of objects as well.

3 In the list, click Access - Microsoft Access For Windows 95.

263

The Object Browser displays the object classes that belong to Microsoft Access. The first class in the Modules/Classes list box, already selected, is Application.

Object classes in the Microsoft Access hierarchy

Methods, properties, and object collection belonging to the selected object class

You'll notice several familiar object classes in the list, corresponding to many of the objects you use throughout Microsoft Access.

Use the Object Browser to get online Help

Next, you'll take a look at the Form class, one of the most fundamental classes in the Microsoft Access hierarchy. You'll then jump directly from the Object Browser to online Help about the object you're viewing.

1   In the Modules/Classes list box, select Form.

The Methods/Properties list on the right displays methods and object collections belonging to forms. If you scroll down in the list, you'll see some form methods you've used in previous lessons, such as GoToPage, Refresh, and Requery.

2   In the Methods/Properties list, select Controls.

Controls is the name of a collection of objects. Every form has this collection, and it contains—you guessed it—the controls included on that form. The lower portion of the Object Browser displays information about the item you've selected—in this case, the text *Controls() As Controls*. In the case of a collection like Controls, this text isn't all that useful, and you might as well ignore it. In many cases, however, the text shown here will give you a clue about how to use the property, function, or method you've selected. Additionally, although the Access object library doesn't provide it, some object libraries—the DAO library, for example—provide an additional line of text for each item you select telling you what the item is for or what it applies to.

The question mark button in the lower portion of the window gives you a handy way to get online help about the selected item. For Microsoft Access objects, as you'll see, using online Help is one of the best ways to explore the object model.

3 Click the question mark (?) button.

The Help topic for the Controls collection appears in a separate window. It provides lots of information about how you can use the collection, and includes jumps to Visual Basic code examples. The topic also displays a graphical representation of the portion of the object model that the collection belongs to, which you can use to navigate to other Help topics.

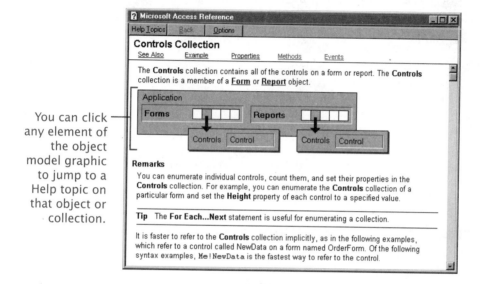

You can click any element of the object model graphic to jump to a Help topic on that object or collection.

As the object model graphic shows, the Application object has a Forms collection and a Reports collection, which contain individual Form and Report objects. Each form and report in turn has a Controls collection containing individual Control objects.

4 In the object model graphic, click the word Forms.

The Help window jumps to the topic for the Forms collection. The Forms collection contains all the forms that are open at any given time. You're already quite familiar with this collection, because you've used the Forms keyword in several lessons to refer to a form by name, as in *Forms!Issues*.

5 Close the Help window.

6 In the Object Browser, click the Close button.

> ## Other Handy Features of the Object Browser
>
> In addition to showing you available objects and allowing you to jump to online Help, the Object Browser has the following features you might want to use:
>
> - When you select a function or method in the Object Browser, the text it displays includes the arguments you use with the function or method. If you want to use this text as a template for code you're entering in a module, you can click the Paste Text button in the Object Browser to paste it into the current module.
>
> - If you're browsing objects in the current database—or in any database that contains Visual Basic procedures—you can use the Object Browser to quickly open the code for any procedure. For example, if you're browsing through the procedures in the Miscellaneous module of the Issues database, you can just double-click a procedure to open it in a Module window.
>
> - All three of the standard object libraries—VBA, Access, and DAO—have a Constants class, which includes all the built-in constants available in that object library. Because you often use constant values in your code, this is a handy place to find out which ones are available—and is especially useful if you can't remember how to spell a constant name.

Referring to Objects and Collections

In earlier lessons, you used plenty of objects—and you learned how to refer to them in your code. For example, you referred to the Contacts form in Part 1 using the expression *Forms!Contacts*, and to the ContactID control on that form using the expression *Forms!Contacts!ContactID*. In fact, most of the object references you'll use in your code will be fairly simple ones like these. Still, because you use them so often, it's important for you to understand more completely how object references work. And as you'll see later in this lesson, not all expressions that include objects are as simple as those you've used up to this point.

When referring to objects in a collection, such as the Forms collection, you can use several alternative forms of reference. One way is to refer to objects by number. Objects in any collection are numbered consecutively starting with zero, so you can refer to an object by placing this number in parentheses. For example, the first form object in the Forms collection is Forms(0), the second is Forms(1), and so on. But there are several other ways to refer to a member of a collection—by name, for example, or by using the exclamation point (!) operator. Each of these methods follows slightly different rules.

Rather than reading about them, perhaps the best way to understand these types of references is to try them out. In this section, you'll experiment with several types of object references using the Debug window.

Try out object references in the Debug window

Debug Window button

1 Click the Debug Window button on the toolbar.

2 In the Debug window, type **?Forms.Count** and press ENTER.

The Debug window displays 1, the number of forms in the Forms collection. The one form that's open is the Issues form.

The first object in a collection is object number 0, and you can refer to it that way. Let's see what the name of the form is by referring to the Name property.

3 Replace the top line in the Debug window with **?Forms(0).Name** and press ENTER. (You don't have to retype the entire line, just edit the existing line of text.)

The Debug window displays Issues, the name of the first form in the Forms collection.

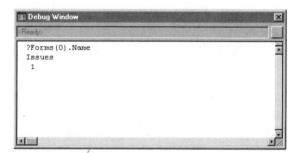

To refer to a member of a collection by name, you can substitute a string value for the object's number—for example, you can use *Forms("Issues")* to refer to the Issues form. Let's use the ActiveControl property of the Forms collection to see which control on the Issues form is currently active.

4 Replace the top line with **?Forms("Issues").ActiveControl.Name** and press ENTER.

The Debug window displays Title, the name of the field that got the focus when you first opened the Issues form.

Note that the technique of placing a string in parentheses after a collection has another important use: if you've stored an object's name in a string variable, you can use this same syntax to refer to it. For example, if the name of the form you wanted to use above had been stored in a variable called *strFormName*, you could use the expression *Forms(strFormName).ActiveControl.Name* to refer to the active control on that form.

Of course, if you know the name of a form, you can just put it after the exclamation point operator as you've done in the past. Next, let's try a reference to the Controls collection—a collection that every form and report object has. To refer to any collection, follow the object that it belongs to—its *parent* object—with a period, and then type the name of the collection. In the next example, *Forms!Issues* is the parent object, while *Controls* is the collection that belongs to it.

5   Replace the top line with **?Forms!Issues.Controls.Count** and press ENTER.

The Debug window displays 24, the number of controls on the Issues form.

Next, you'll refer to the value of the first object in the Controls collection, the IssueID control.

6   Replace the top line with **?Forms!Issues.Controls(0)** and press ENTER.

The Debug window displays 1, the ID number of the issue currently displayed on the Issues form. The reference you used is equivalent to saying *Forms!Issues.Controls("IssueID")*. It's also equivalent to saying *Forms!Issues!IssueID*, the method of reference you're most familiar with. That's because Controls is the default collection for any form object. When you use the exclamation point, Microsoft Access assumes that what follows is a member of the default Controls collection.

Next, you'll refer to the subform on the Issues form. To do this, you refer to the subform control, *Forms!Issues!Comments*. Because you want to refer to properties of the subform that the Issues form is displaying, rather than to the subform control itself, you'll follow the control reference with the Form property—and then follow that with the property whose value you want.

7   Replace the top line with **?Forms!Issues!Comments.Form.Name** and press ENTER.

The Debug window displays CommentsSubform, the name of the actual form stored in the Issues database.

There's one exception to the rule that for subforms you must use the Form property to refer to the form. If you want to refer to a control on a subform, you can leave out the Form keyword—it makes the reference a bit shorter.

8   Replace the top line with **?Forms!Issues!Comments!Comment** and press ENTER.

The Debug window displays the text of the first comment shown in the subform. This expression says, "In the Comments control on the Issues form, what is the value of the Comment field?"

9   Close the Debug window.

Referring to objects and their properties requires some experimentation. Before you write code that uses a new type of expression, it's a good idea to use the Debug window to test out your syntax. If you don't get the value you want, or if Microsoft Access displays an error when you enter the reference, consult online Help for examples of expressions that use the type of object you're interested in.

Now that you've discovered some of the ways you can refer to collections and the objects they contain, you're ready to write some code that uses them. In the next section, you'll see object references in action and learn techniques for storing objects in variables so you can perform actions using the objects.

Using the For Each Statement with a Collection

The objects in a collection share many properties and characteristics, so you'll commonly want to perform the same actions on each object in a collection. For example, you might want to change a specific property, such as the color of text, for every control on a form. When you want to run the same block of code for every object in a collection, you surround the block of code with the For Each and Next statements.

Write a procedure that sets control properties

To see how the For Each statement works, you'll write a procedure that changes the ForeColor property—the color of the text—for every label on the Issues form. You'll create the new procedure, called ChangeLabelColor, in the Miscellaneous module. The Module window still shows the Declarations section, which already contains three lines of code. You'll begin entering code for the new procedure underneath the existing Dim statement.

1 In the Module window, click underneath the Public statement to position the insertion point.

2 Enter the following code, including the Sub header line. (When you enter the Sub statement, the new procedure is displayed in the window by itself—the three existing lines go out of view—and Microsoft Access enters the End Sub line for you automatically.)

```
Sub ChangeLabelColor(lngColorCode As Long)
' Change the color of labels on the Issues form.

    Dim ctl As Control

    For Each ctl In Forms!Issues.Controls
        If TypeOf ctl Is Label Then
            ctl.ForeColor = lngColorCode
        End If
    Next ctl
End Sub
```

Here's what this code does:

■ The Sub procedure head declares an argument, lngColorCode, which stores the code number for the color you want to change labels to. The argument uses the long integer data type, because the ForeColor property accepts this type of value.

■ The Dim line in the procedure declares an object variable. When you want to perform actions on objects, such as tables, forms, or controls, you can store references to them, just as you would store another type of value in a variable. This variable has the data type Control, which can store only a control-type object.

■ The next statement begins a *loop*, a mechanism for repeating a section of code several times. This loop uses the For Each and Next statements—one of several types of loops in Visual Basic—which allow the procedure to perform the same set of actions for every control on the form. At the end of any For Each statement, after the In keyword, is the name of a collection that you want to step through—in this case, the Controls collection on the Issues form. The In keyword is always preceded by a variable—in this case *ctl*—that stores each object in the collection as the code steps through it.

The block of code between the For Each and Next statements will run 24 times, once for each control on the form. Each time it runs, the variable *ctl* will represent a different control on the Issues form.

■ The If...Then block inside the loop checks to see whether the current control is a label. To do this, it uses the special *TypeOf* keyword, which allows you to check the type of control stored in a variable. If the control isn't a label, the code continues on to the Next statement, doing nothing.

■ If the current control is a label, the line in the middle runs, setting the ForeColor property of the control to the value you passed to the procedure by the lngColorCode argument.

■ The Next statement includes *ctl*, the variable that gets incremented each time through the loop. You can think of this statement as saying, "We're finished with that control, move on to the next one please." When Microsoft Access finishes running the block of code for every control in the collection, the procedure ends.

3 Click the Save button on the toolbar.

Save button

Run the procedure from the Debug window

Now you can see your procedure in action, by bringing the Issues form to the front and running your procedure from the Debug window.

Debug Window button

1 Click the Debug Window button on the toolbar.

2 Switch to the Issues form.

The Debug window stays on top of the form.

3 Click the title bar of the Debug window and drag it toward the bottom right corner of the screen (so you can see most of the Issues form behind it).

4 On a new line in the Debug window, type **ChangeLabelColor(16711680)** and press ENTER.

Your procedure runs, changing the foreground color of each label control on the form to blue (the color code for blue is 16711680).

5 Replace the second line in the Debug window with **ChangeLabelColor(0)** and press ENTER.

The labels become black again.

This type of procedure is useful for giving users the capability of customizing forms while your application is running. In the next section, you'll use some of these same tools—object variables and the For Each statement—to add powerful features to the Issues application.

Using a Multiple-Selection List Box

So far, you've used list boxes that allow users to select a single item. As you'll see, you can also create a list box that allows more than one item to be selected at a time. The practice database already includes a form that has a multiple-selection list box. The form, called Reassigner, is a dialog box form designed to allow users to reassign one or more issues to another employee. Unlike a normal list box, a multiple-selection list box requires you to write some extra code to access the selected items. In the rest of this lesson, you'll add code to the Reassigner form to make it work.

To cause a list box to allow multiple selections, you set its MultiSelect property. The property has three settings: None, Simple, and Extended. If the property is set to None, users can select only one item at a time; if Simple, users can select multiple items by clicking them; if Extended, users can select multiple items by holding down the SHIFT and CTRL keys while clicking items. The list box you'll work with on the Reassigner form has its MultiSelect property set to Simple.

Open the Reassigner form

Before you add any code to the Reassigner form, let's see how it works so far. To open it, you'll use a menu command located on the Issues form's custom menu bar.

1 Switch to the Issues form. (Leave the Debug window open—you'll use it again in just a minute.)

2 On the Records menu, click Reassign Issues.

The Reassigner form opens.

3 In the Show Issues Assigned To combo box, select Bonnie Christensen.

The list box on the form shows the four issues currently assigned to that employee.

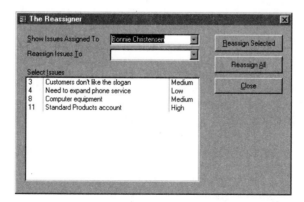

Try out the multiple-selection list box

With any list box you've used before in this book, each time you click an item, the previous item is deselected—the list box has just one value at a time. In this list box, however, you can select more than one value.

1   Click issue number 4 in the list (the second item), and then click issue number 8 (the third item).

Next, you'll learn how to refer to the values you've selected in code. When a list box has just one value, you can just refer to the list box itself to access the value— for example, because the list box control is named IssueList, the expression *Forms!Reassigner!IssueList* would return the ID number of the selected issue. When using a multiple-selection list box, by contrast, you find out which items are selected by referring to a special collection called ItemsSelected. You can see how this works in the Debug window.

2   Switch to the Debug window. (In this case, you must click the title bar at the top of the Debug window to bring it to the front, because the Reassigner form—a modal pop-up dialog box—also wants to stay on top of other forms.)

To refer to the items in the list, you'll have use a pretty complex expression. Don't worry, though, it's really quite similar to references you're already accustomed to.

3   On a new line, type **?Forms!Reassigner!IssueList.ItemsSelected.Count** and press ENTER.

To follow the expression, read it from right to left—it asks for the number of items in the ItemSelected collection of the IssueList control on the Reassigner form. The Debug window displays 2, the number of items you selected in the list box.

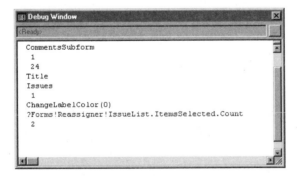

Next, you'll try out expressions that tell you what the selected items are. The ItemsSelected collection actually stores numbers corresponding to the position of the selected item in the list. Like items in the collection, the positions in the list are numbered starting with zero, so the first item has position 0, the second position 1, and so on. Therefore, the first item number is stored in ItemsSelected(0), the second item number in ItemsSelected(1), and so on.

4 Replace the line with **?Forms!Reassigner!IssueList.ItemsSelected(0)** and press ENTER.

The Debug window displays 1, the position of the first item you selected. (You selected the second item in the list, which is position number 1.) You might expect the ItemsSelected collection to contain the actual values of the selected items, but it doesn't—it contains only their positions in the list. To find out the value of each selected item—in this case, the IssueID for each issue—you have to use the ItemData method, supplying the item position number you just found out.

5 Replace the line with **?Forms!Reassigner!IssueList.ItemData(1)** and press ENTER.

The Debug window displays 4, which is, at long last, the IssueID of the first issue you selected.

6 Close the Debug window.

Although the process of finding out what's selected in a list box is complicated, it's worth the effort to tap into the power of a multiple-selection list box. In the next section, you'll add code that makes this list box work, using the list box concepts you just learned to change data in the issues the user has selected.

Working with Data Access Objects

When users change data in a form that's bound to a query or table—the Issues form, for example—Microsoft Access automatically makes the changes in the underlying tables. So far, you've allowed Microsoft Access to do most of this work behind the scenes. However, when you need to take more control over what gets changed in your database, you can work directly with data by writing code that uses data access objects (DAO). In this section, you'll learn two powerful techniques for changing data using DAO code. You'll use these techniques to make the Reassigner form do its work.

The Reassigner form has two command buttons whose event procedures aren't yet complete: Reassign Selected and Reassign All. When a user clicks the Reassign Selected button, you want to open the Issues table and update only the records the user has selected in the list box. To do this, you'll use a Recordset object. When a user clicks the Reassign All button, you want to update every record in the Issues table that has a certain AssignedTo value. To do this you'll run an action query. To perform these two operations in code, you'll need to learn new techniques for working with objects.

What Do Data Access Objects Look Like?

The Data Access Objects library has a complex hierarchy (some might even call it ugly) containing many more objects and collections than even the Microsoft Access hierarchy has. And unlike Microsoft Access objects, which you're used to seeing on your screen, objects in the DAO hierarchy are difficult to visualize— they're really no more than a bunch of abstract structures for storing information.

The DAO hierarchy's huge first layer starts with the DBEngine object, which represents the underlying Microsoft Access database engine (also known as the "Jet" database engine). The DBEngine object has a Workspaces collection, which in turn has a Databases collection, which has many other collections, and so on down the line. Here's a graphical representation of part of the DAO object model— it shows the three objects you'll work with in the rest of this lesson: the Database object, the Recordset object, and the QueryDef object.

 Most of the work you do in DAO will involve these three objects.

After you become familiar with DAO basics, you may want to delve deeper— especially if you want a finer degree of control over the way your applications handle databases. As with Microsoft Access objects, you can use the Object Browser in combination with online Help to learn more about DAO objects and the capabilities they provide.

Finding and Changing Data in a Recordset

Your first task is to add code for the Reassign Selected button. Whenever a user clicks this button, you need to open the Issues table, move to each selected record, and change the value of the AssignedTo field for that issue to another employee's ID number: the one the user chooses in the NewAssignee combo box.

When you want to change a record in a table directly, you first open a Recordset object. Next, you move to the record you want to change. If the recordset is based on a table in a Microsoft Access database, such as the Issues table, the fastest way to do this is to use the Seek method. Then you actually make the change, using the Edit and Update methods to set the values of the fields you want to change. In this section, you'll add code that will go through this process for each record the user selects in the IssueList list box.

Edit the Click event procedure for the Reassign Selected button

The Reassign Selected button already has an event procedure—it's just missing the code that actually reassigns the issues to other employees. To open the event procedure, you'll first need to close the dialog box and open the form in Design view.

*Database
Window button*

1 In the Reassigner dialog box, click the Close button.

2 Click the Database Window button on the toolbar.

3 Click the Forms tab.

4 Click the Reassigner form, and then click the Design button.

As you saw before, the Reassigner form is nearly complete. It even has code that keeps the IssuesList control synchronized with the currently selected employee. Now it's time to add the final touches to the Click event procedure for the Reassign Selected button.

5 With the right mouse button, click the Reassign Selected button, and then click Build Event on the shortcut menu.

The Module window appears, displaying the ReassignSelected_Click procedure. As you can see, the procedure already contains several lines of code.

The code that's already present does several things:

■ The Dim statement declares a variable used later in the procedure to store the text of a message.

■ The first block of code checks that the NewAssignee combo box has a value in it—otherwise, you wouldn't know which user to reassign issues to. If the combo box is blank, the procedure displays a message and exits.

- The second block of code makes sure that at least one issue is selected in the list—to do this, it checks the Count property of the ItemsSelected collection for the list box, just as you did earlier in the lesson.

- Next, the procedure confirms that the user wants to reassign the selected issues. To do this, the procedure calls the Confirm function you wrote in Lesson 5—that function is included in this database as well.

- If the user does confirm the operation, the next line of code uses the Hourglass method of the DoCmd object to display the hourglass cursor while your code changes records. Whenever you run code that might cause a delay, you can use this technique to let the user know your code is working.

- The last block of code is designed to run after your code finishes reassigning issues, to update what's displayed in the dialog box before the procedure ends. For example, the first line sets the value of the AssignedTo combo box to the ID of the employee you just assigned issues to, and the third line requeries the list box to show the new set of issues. This way, the user can easily see that all changes have taken place.

To complete the procedure, you'll add code in two places: near the top of the procedure you'll declare three variables that your code will use, and near the bottom you'll add the code that changes selected records.

6 Click underneath the Dim statement in the procedure, and then enter the following lines of code:

```
Dim dbs As Database, rstIssues As Recordset
Dim varPosition As Variant
```

These Dim statements declare three variables:

- The dbs variable will represent the current database.

- The rstIssues variable will store a reference to the Issues table so that you can change data in it.

- The varPosition variable will store the position of each item selected in the list, so you can get hold of the actual ID value for each selected issue. This variable has the Variant data type, because this is the type of value used to store the position number in the ItemsSelected collection.

 NOTE When you enter the first line of code above, Microsoft Access changes the word Database to all capital letters. If this seems strange, it is—and it probably wasn't really intended by the designers of Microsoft Access. This capitalization occurs with any keyword you type that happens to be part of the SQL language, even if it isn't used in an SQL statement (SQL is described later in this lesson).

---

7 Click the blank area underneath the *DoCmd.Hourglass True* statement and enter the following code:

```
' Open a recordset object in the current database.
Set dbs = CurrentDb()
Set rstIssues = dbs.OpenRecordset("Issues", dbOpenTable)

' Begin a transaction before changing data.
DBEngine.BeginTrans

' Set the Index property to search on the primary key.
rstIssues.Index = "IssueID"

' Loop through each issue selected in the list.
For Each varPosition In IssueList.ItemsSelected

    ' Find the record in the Issues table.
    rstIssues.Seek "=", IssueList.ItemData(varPosition)

    ' Change the AssignedTo value in the table.
    rstIssues.Edit
    rstIssues!AssignedTo = NewAssignee
    rstIssues.Update

Next varPosition

' Save all changes for this transaction.
DBEngine.CommitTrans
```

Let's walk through this code line by line—it introduces several new concepts:

■ The first line of code uses the CurrentDb function to store a reference to the current database, which is required in order to open a table in code. Remember, whenever you set the value of an object variable—as opposed to an ordinary variable, such as a string—you must precede the assignment with the Set statement.

■ The second line uses the OpenRecordset method of the database to open the Issues table, and stores the recordset in the variable rstIssues. Providing the dbOpenTable constant as the second argument to OpenRecordset tells Microsoft Access that you want a table-type recordset. It's important that you open a table-type recordset, because later code in the procedure uses the Seek method, which is allowed only on tables.

■ The next line uses the BeginTrans method of the DBEngine object to open a *transaction*. A transaction is a group of changes that you want Microsoft Access to treat as a single operation. Opening a transaction tells Microsoft Access to keep track of changes you make, but to wait until you close the transaction to save them on disk. You use this method with the DBEngine object, a special object representing the underlying database engine for Microsoft Access. Later, you'll close the transaction using the CommitTrans method.

Using a transaction for multiple changes to data has two advantages: first, it speeds up your code, because you access the disk drive or network only once, rather than each time you change a record; second, you'll never end up with partially changed records—if an error occurs before all the changes have been made, you don't have to save the transaction. (To cancel changes made in a transaction, you use the Rollback method.)

■ Before you can use the Seek method to locate records in a table, you have to set the Index property for the recordset, which tells Microsoft Access which field you want to search. The next line sets the Index property to the IssueID field, the primary key of the Issues table. The field or fields you designate for searching must either be the primary key of the table or else have an index. Because the field has an index, the search will be very fast.

■ The next line uses the For Each statement you learned about in the previous section. In this procedure, you want to update every issue that's selected in the list. Because you'll locate and change records one at a time, you need to run the block of code once for each item in the ItemsSelected collection of the list box. This statement says, "Run the following block of code once for each item in the ItemsSelected collection of the IssueList control, each time storing the position of the selected item in the varPosition variable."

■ The four lines of code you'll loop through for each selected issue must locate the issue in the recordset and then change its AssignedTo value. The first of these lines uses the Seek method to move to the selected record.

■ The Seek method takes two arguments. The first is an operator string, which tells Microsoft Access what type of search you want. Because you want to find only the one record that exactly matches the IssueID value selected in the list, you've used the "=" operator. The second argument tells Microsoft Access what value to look for. As you saw earlier in this lesson, the way to refer to the value of the selected item in a list is to use the ItemData method of the list box control. This argument tells Microsoft Access to search for the IssueID value that's at the current position—stored in the varPosition variable—in the IssueList control. After this line of code runs, the current record in the rstIssues recordset will be the record for one of the issues selected in the list.

■ The next three lines actually reassign the issue by replacing the value in the record's AssignedTo field with the value of the NewAssignee combo box on the form. Before you change data in an existing record, you must use the Edit method of the Recordset object to tell Microsoft Access you want to change data. After you've finished setting values of one or more fields in the recordset, as you do here in the second statement, you complete the change by using the Update method.

■ The Next statement tells Microsoft Access to repeat the For Each block of code for the next item in the list. After the block of code has run for each selected item, the procedure will continue running from this point.

- The final line of code you entered uses the CommitTrans method of the DBEngine object. This method tells the database engine to save all the changes you made since the beginning of the transaction in this procedure.

Compile Loaded Modules button

8 Click the Compile Loaded Modules button on the toolbar.

If the procedure has any typographical errors, compiling will bring them to light so you can fix them before trying to run the code.

Save button

9 Click the Save button on the toolbar.

10 Close the Module window.

Try out the ReassignSelected_Click procedure

Now you're ready to test the procedure by selecting issues and reassigning them.

Form View button

1 Click the Form View button on the toolbar.

2 In the Reassign Issues To combo box, select Charles Willmes.

3 Click issue number 4 in the list (the second item), and then click issue number 8 (the third item).

4 Click the Reassign Selected button, and then click OK when the procedure asks you to confirm that you want to reassign the selected issues.

Your code runs, opening the Issues recordset, and then cycling through the two records you selected and changing their AssignedTo values in the Issues table. When the procedure finishes, the list box displays the issues that changed hands, but now they belong to a different employee, Charles Willmes.

5 Click the Close button.

Handling Errors in DAO Code

For the sake of simplicity, the procedure you worked with in this lesson doesn't contain error-handling code. However, any time *you* use DAO to change records, you should definitely include error-handling code in the procedure. Errors can occur for many reasons when your code changes records, and without error-handling code, your application could end abruptly with a run-time error. For example, suppose another user is changing data at the same time your code is running. The records you're trying to update might be locked, causing an error.

To handle these types of errors, you would add an On Error GoTo statement at the top of the procedure, and then include error-handling code at the end of the procedure—similar to the technique you used in Lesson 7. In the error-handling code, you might want to check which error occurred, and if records are locked, give the user the option to resave them. In any case, if you aren't able to update records as expected, your procedure should exit gracefully, displaying a message telling the user about the problem. If you do decide to exit the procedure, you may want to include the Rollback method of the DBEngine object, which undoes any changes made since you started the transaction using the BeginTrans method—this way, records won't be partially updated, which could confuse the user.

Creating and Running an Action Query

The first command button on the Reassigner dialog box is now complete. The second one, however, still needs some work. This button, labeled Reassign All, is there so that users can reassign all issues, rather than selected issues, from one employee to another. In this section, you'll add the code to do this.

The technique you used to reassign selected issues—opening a recordset, and then locating and changing each record—is perfect for reassigning a few individual issues. On the other hand, when you want to change values in a whole group of records, changing each record individually isn't the most efficient way. To modify a group of records most efficiently, you use an *action query*. With an action query, you can update, add, or delete many records in a single step.

Normally, you use the Microsoft Access query window to create an action query. However, you can also create and run queries in your code by using the DAO QueryDef object. To make the Reassign All button do its work, you'll write code that creates and runs a query. The query you create will change the values in the AssignedTo field for all records in the Issues table from one employee's ID to another.

Using Structured Query Language (SQL)

When defining the action query in this section, you'll use the Microsoft Access query language, called *Structured Query Language*, or SQL. You've probably already noticed examples of SQL statements in the property sheet—SQL is commonly used in the RecordSource and RowSource settings of your forms, combo boxes, and list boxes. When you use wizards to create objects, they frequently set these properties to an appropriate SQL statement. On the Reassigner form, for example, the AssignedTo combo box was created using the Combo Box Wizard. The wizard set the RowSource property for the combo box to the following SQL statement:

```
SELECT DISTINCTROW Employees.EmployeeID, Employees.EmployeeName
FROM Employees
ORDER BY Employees.EmployeeName;
```

This statement tells Microsoft Access to retrieve ("select") the values of two fields—EmployeeID and EmployeeName—from every record in the Employees table, sorting the records by name. In your Microsoft Access applications, you can substitute an SQL statement just about anywhere that the name of a table or query is called for. Additionally, as you'll see in this section, you can build queries in your code using SQL.

To learn SQL, you might want to browse the many SQL topics in online Help. Additionally, there's a handy technique you can use to help you learn SQL. Queries you create using the Query Design window—including action queries—have an SQL view maintained automatically by Microsoft Access. To see the SQL statement corresponding to any query in Design view, just click SQL on the View menu. You can even copy this SQL text into your DAO code.

Edit the Click event procedure for the Reassign All button

Just like the Reassign Selected button, the Reassign All button already has an event procedure—it's just missing the code that actually reassigns issues. You'll add code that creates and runs an action query to update records.

1 In the Database window, click the Reassigner form, and then click the Design button.

2 With the right mouse button, click the Reassign All button, and then click Build Event on the shortcut menu.

The Module window appears and displays the ReassignAll_Click procedure. As you can see, the procedure already contains several lines of code. The code that's there is nearly the same as the code in the ReassignSelected_Click procedure: it makes sure the user has selected employees to assign issues to and from, asks the user to confirm the reassignment, and then displays the hourglass cursor.

To complete the procedure, you'll add a line near the top to declare variables, and then you'll add the code that actually runs the query to change data.

3   Click underneath the Dim statement in the procedure, and then enter the following line of code:

```
Dim dbs As Database, qdfReassign As QueryDef
```

You'll use the *dbs* variable to represent the current database. You'll use the *qdfReassign* variable—an object variable with the QueryDef data type—to store the query object you define and run it in the procedure.

4   Click the blank area underneath the DoCmd.Hourglass statement and enter the following code:

```
' Open a temporary query object in the current database.
Set dbs = CurrentDb()
Set qdfReassign = dbs.CreateQueryDef("")

' Define the SQL update query to reassign issues.
qdfReassign.SQL = "UPDATE Issues " & _
    "SET AssignedTo = " & NewAssignee & _
    " WHERE AssignedTo = " & AssignedTo

' Run the query.
qdfReassign.Execute
```

 NOTE   Be sure you put spaces before and after quotation marks, exactly as shown in this code. Otherwise, you may encounter an error when you try to run it.

Here's what this code does:

- The first line you added uses the CurrentDb function to store a reference to the current database.

- The second line uses the CreateQueryDef method of the database to open a new query object, storing it in the variable qdfReassign. The argument to the CreateQueryDef function allows you to specify a name for the query—using an empty string ("") as you have here creates a temporary query object. Because you're going to use the query in this procedure only, you don't need to give it a name.

- The next line sets the SQL property for the query object. Setting this property tells the query what data you want it to return—or, in the case of an action query, what changes you want it to make. For example, using the UPDATE statement tells Microsoft Access that you want it to change values in existing records. As you can see, this line of code concatenates several items together to produce the SQL statement. This code could be typed as one line, but you've broken it up using the underscore (_) character to make it easier to see in the Module window.

The string you create for the SQL property setting combines the SQL text itself with the values of two fields on the Reassigner form: the AssignedTo field and the NewAssignee field. When the code runs, Microsoft Access will combine all this text to produce a single string that defines the action query. For example, the complete string might look like this:

```
UPDATE Issues SET AssignedTo = 14 WHERE AssignedTo = 20
```

If you ran this particular query, Microsoft Access would find all records in the Issues table that were assigned to employee 20 and reassign them to employee 14.

- The final line you added uses the Execute method of the QueryDef object, which tells Microsoft Access to go ahead and run the query you've defined.

5 Click the Compile Loaded Modules button on the toolbar.

Compile Loaded Modules button

6 Click the Save button on the toolbar.

7 Close the Module window.

Save button

Try out the ReassignAll_Click procedure

Now you're ready to test the procedure. You just need to select two employees and click the button.

Form View button

1 Click the Form View button on the toolbar.

2 In the Show Issues Assigned To box, select Charles Willmes.

The two issues you reassigned previously show up in the list.

3 In the Reassign Issues To box, select Bonnie Christensen.

4 Click the Reassign All button, and then click OK when the procedure asks you to confirm the reassignment.

Your code runs, creating and running the action query for the employee values you selected. When it finishes, the list box displays Bonnie Christensen's issues—and as you can see, all four issues belong to her as they did at the beginning of the lesson, which is just what you want.

The Recordset and QueryDef objects you've learned to use in this lesson are perhaps the most common DAO objects for working directly with databases. However, they are just the tip of the iceberg. Fortunately, most of the techniques you've learned in this lesson will apply to any work you do with objects and collections. Just remember that by working directly with objects in your code, you can accomplish practically anything Microsoft Access does on its own—and even more.

Close the dialog box and exit Microsoft Access

1 Click the Close button.

2 On the File menu, click Exit.

Lesson Summary

To	Do this	Button
View the objects in an object library	In the Module window, click the Object Browser button. Select an object library or database, and then click object classes to view their members.	
Refer to an object in a collection	Follow the collection reference with the name or number of the object in parentheses, such as *Forms!Issues.Controls(0)* or *Forms!Issues.Controls("IssueID")*. Or, if the item is the default member of the collection, use the exclamation point operator, as in *Forms!Issues!IssueID*.	
Run a block of code for each item in a collection, such as every control on a form	Use a For Each...Next block, specifying a variable for storing each object as your code loops through the collection.	
Create a list box that allows multiple selections	Set the MultiSelect property of the list box to Simple or Extended. Get the position of each selection in the ItemsSelected collection, and then access the selected data using the ItemData method.	
Find a record in a table-type recordset	Use the Index method of the recordset to specify the field you want to search, and then use the Seek method to move to a record in the table.	
Change data in the current record of a recordset	Use the Edit method of the recordset, assign values to fields, and then use the Update method to save the changes.	
Group several changes to data so that they all occur at once	Open a transaction using the BeginTrans method, and then use the CommitTrans method to commit changes when you're finished. If you don't want to save changes, use the Rollback method to discard all changes made since the beginning of the transaction.	
Run an action query in code	Using the CreateQueryDef method, create a temporary query object in the database. Set its SQL property to the SQL statement you want to run, and then use the Execute method to run the query.	

For online information about	On the Help menu, click Microsoft Access Help Topics, click the Index tab, and then
Using the Object Browser	Search for "Object Browser"
Referring to objects and collections	Search for "referencing, objects"
Using DAO to work directly with databases	Search for "DAO"
Handling run-time errors	Search for "error handling"
Writing applications for multiple users on a network	Search for "multiuser environment"
Using Structured Query Language (SQL)	Search for "SQL statements"

For more information on	In *Building Applications with Microsoft Access,* see
Using the Object Browser, or referring to objects and collections	Chapter 5, "Working with Objects and Collections"
Using DAO to work directly with databases	Chapter 9, "Working with Sets of Records" and Chapter 17, "Accessing External Data"
Handling run-time errors	Chapter 8, "Handling Run-Time Errors"
Writing applications for multiple users on a network	Chapter 10, "Developing Multiuser Applications"
Using Structured Query Language (SQL)	Chapter 9, "Working with Sets of Records"

Preview of the Next Lesson

In this lesson, you learned general rules for referring to objects and collections, and you discovered a few new types of objects. You'll continue working with new objects throughout Part 4. In the next lesson, for example, you'll learn more about using report objects in your code. Although most of the code you've written so far in this book has applied to forms, you'll find that you can customize reports with code as well—providing more power and flexibility for your applications.

Customize Reports with Visual Basic

Estimated time
25 min.

In this lesson you will learn how to:

■ Respond to events that occur in reports.

■ Change the formatting of individual fields and records as a report prints.

■ Calculate totals while a report is running.

When you're learning a whole new subject, such as database programming, it's easy to lose the forest for the trees: picking up lots of details but forgetting the main purpose your applications will serve. And as your experience increases, there's still a tendency to spend lots of time adding frills to an application while losing track of its primary goals. Let's face it—for all the complexities involved in working with databases, the whole endeavor comes down to two basic activities: getting data into the database, and getting data back out.

So far, you've spent lots of energy on ways to get data into forms and work with it easily. In this lesson, you'll turn your attention to one of the primary ways to get data *out* of a Microsoft Access database: by printing it in reports. You'll team up the built-in reporting tools with your own Visual Basic procedures to customize and enhance an application's reports—and you'll learn techniques for taking control of exactly what prints on the page.

Start the lesson

1 Start Microsoft Access and open the 12 Issues database in the practice files folder.

As you saw in the previous lesson, the Issues application opens to a dialog box asking you to enter your name before it opens the Issues form.

2 In the combo box, select Bonnie Christensen.

3 Click the Show All Issues button.

The button's Click event procedure opens the Issues form.

Using Standard Reporting Features

Microsoft Access reports are extremely powerful tools for presenting information, regardless of whether you write any Visual Basic code for them. The Report Wizard can help you create many complex types of reports for grouping or summarizing information—or, by designing your own custom reports, you can accomplish most anything you'll need in your applications. Before you write any code, be sure to explore the powerful features built into reports, such as grouping and totaling, automatic growing and shrinking of sections, and flexible page numbering, just to name a few. The Issues report included in the practice database shows off some of these features.

Preview the Issues report

The custom menu bar for the Issues form includes the Preview Issues Report command on the File menu, which opens the Issues report automatically. As you'll see, the report prints all the open issues in the database, grouped by the employee they're assigned to.

1 On the File menu, click Preview Issues Report.

The Issues report appears in Print Preview.

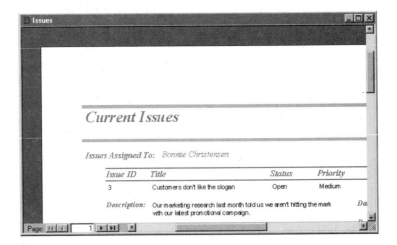

The Issues report is based on a query called IssuesForReport, which combines information from several tables. The report was initially created using the Report Wizard, and then rearranged and polished a bit in Report Design view.

2 Using the vertical scroll bar on the report window (not the Microsoft Access scroll bar), scroll down a bit to view additional issues on the page.

The report groups all the issues assigned to each employee—in this case, the first group of issues belongs to Bonnie Christensen. The report also displays the total number of issues for each group at the bottom of the employee's section.

The following illustration points out several features of the Issues report.

Issue records are grouped by employee, with headers repeated for each group of issues.

Microsoft Access automatically counts the number of issues in each group.

Each page shows the current date, page number, and total number of pages.

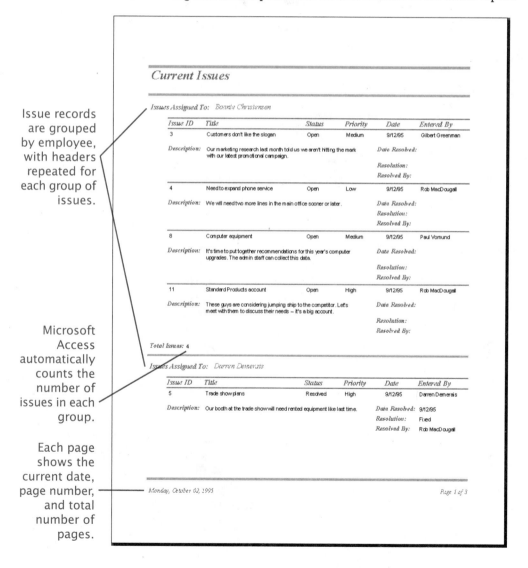

All the elements you see on the Issues report as it exists in the practice file—grouping of data, automatic totals, and a customized layout, for example—are standard features of reports that don't require any code. And this is just the beginning of what you can do in your reports.

In some cases, however, you won't be able to accomplish what you want using standard reporting features alone. For example, if you want to make changes to the formatting of certain fields depending on the data that appears in any given record, or if you want to change the layout of the report only in certain cases, no standard mechanism will get the job done—it will take some creative intervention on your part. In the following sections, you'll start adding features to this report that require a bit of Visual Basic code.

Responding to Report Events

When you want to accomplish something in your reports that isn't possible using standard reporting features, you'll be happy to know that you can control nearly everything about your reports by writing Visual Basic code. Programming reports is very similar to programming forms—reports have events you can respond to with Visual Basic event procedures. But the event model for reports is a bit trickier, because users don't actually interact with reports, as they do with forms. Instead, report events occur at certain points during the report printing process—the time between when you tell Microsoft Access to preview or print a report and when it arrives on the screen or at the printer—and you can write Visual Basic code to change the outcome of this process.

Here are the two types of report events you'll commonly respond to, along with typical reasons for using them:

General report events   There are several events that apply to a report as a whole. Some of these will be familiar to you from programming with forms, such as the Open event, which you can use to perform actions when the user first asks to preview or print the report. Two other useful report events are the NoData event, which allows you to intervene if the record source of the report turns out to have no records, and the Page event, which gives you a chance to run code once for each page—to draw a border around every page, for example.

Events for each report section   The most interesting events are those that occur one or more times for each section in the report, including the report header and footer, page header and footer, group headers and footers, and of course the Detail section, where individual records appear. The two most important section events are the Format event, which occurs just before Microsoft Access lays out each section of the report, and the Print event, which occurs after page layout is complete but before printing actually occurs. During these events, you have access to the data in the record being formatted or printed—and as you'll see, this gives you the opportunity to make changes based on what's about to print.

In this lesson, you'll write event procedures that respond to the Format and Print events, customizing the Issues report that's included in the practice database. Although you'll try only a few of the many techniques for controlling report output, you'll learn the fundamental concepts you need for customizing reports.

Customizing Reports by Setting Properties at Run Time

You can determine the look of the formatting on your reports to a great extent by setting properties for controls and sections. You might change the text of an important control on your report to a larger font size, or perhaps to a bold font style—and your change will be reflected throughout the report. But what if you want a control to print differently depending on the data contained in each record? For example, suppose you want the text of the Priority field on the Issues report to appear bold if the priority of the issue is high, while continuing to appear normally for other records. You need a way to change the font properties for the control while the report is printing.

This is where event procedures come in. By responding to the Print event for the report's Detail section, which occurs just before each record is printed, you can change the control to display the way you want it to. Your code will check whether the record that Microsoft Access is about to print is high priority, and set the FontWeight property of the Priority field accordingly.

Make the Priority field appear bold for high-priority records

When you work with an event procedure in a report, it's important to make sure you associate it with the appropriate section in the report. In this case, you'll select the Detail section of the Issues report, because you want your code to run for every detail record— every single issue printed in the report.

1   On the View menu, click Report Design.

The report switches into Design view.

In order to create an event procedure for the Detail section, you'll first view event properties for that section in the property sheet.

2   Double-click the Detail section bar.

Microsoft Access displays the property sheet for the Detail section.

Double-click the Detail section bar to display the section's properties.

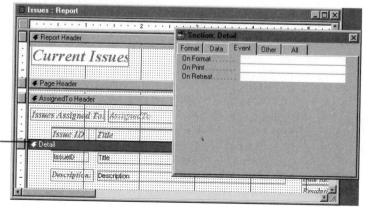

291

3 In the property sheet, click the Event tab, click the OnPrint property, and then click the Build button.

4 Double-click Code Builder.

Microsoft Access opens the Issues report's module and displays the Detail_Print event procedure.

5 Add the following code to the event procedure:

```
Private Sub Detail_Print(Cancel As Integer, PrintCount As Integer)
' Perform desired actions just before each issue record prints.

    Const conNormal = 400
    Const conHeavy = 900       ' Extra bold.

    ' If the priority of the issue is high, display the
    ' Priority field in bold.
    If Priority = "High" Then
        Priority.FontWeight = conHeavy
    Else
        Priority.FontWeight = conNormal
    End If

End Sub
```

Here's what this code does:

- At the beginning of the procedure, the two Const statements declare constants that sets the FontWeight property. When setting the font style to light, bold, or extra bold, you use a number, such as 400, 700, or 900—these constants will make your code easier to read by providing names for these numbers.

- The If...Then statement checks to see if the Priority field contains the string High, which determines whether you want to display the field in bold or normal style. As this procedure illustrates, each time the Detail_Print procedure runs, it will have access to the fields of the current record—in other words, the Priority field expression will return the value of the issue record that's just about to print.

- Depending on whether the priority is high, one of two statements sets the FontWeight property for the priority field to the appropriate constant value.

This code will run every time Microsoft Access prepares to print data for an issue in the report. If you print the complete report, which currently contains 11 issues, the procedure will run 11 times.

Preview the report

Let's preview the report again and see how it works now.

1 Switch to the Issues report window, still in Design view.

2   Click the Print Preview button on the toolbar.

Although it happens so quickly you'll doubt it happens at all, Microsoft Access runs your event procedure once for every single issue record on the page, allowing your code to set the Priority control's property separately for each one.

3   Scroll down in the window to display the fourth issue on the page.

The priority field for this issue—which contains the value High— stands out because it's displayed in bold.

Your event procedure changed the text to bold in this record.

Changing Report Layout Programmatically

The Print event procedure is a good place to perform most types of actions on a report section, because it occurs for every record in the section. Beware, however: when the Print event occurs, Microsoft Access has already laid out all the elements of the section to be printed, so it's too late to make any changes to the layout of the section. For example, if your code performs actions that affect the current section by changing how many records fit on a page, the Print event won't work. If you want to perform actions that affect the layout of a section, you should attach the code to the Format event instead.

In the Issues report, you probably noticed the three labels at the right side of each issue record. Although most issue records in the report don't have any values for these fields (because the issues themselves aren't resolved), these labels appear in every record of the Detail section. To cause them not to display except when the current issue is resolved, you can write an event procedure. And because the changes you'll make in your code *will* affect the layout of the section, you'll add this code to the Format event procedure of the Detail section, rather than to its Print event procedure.

Add code that hides the labels of unresolved fields

To show or hide controls, you set their Visible property. If you do this for the resolution fields in the Format event procedure, Microsoft Access will take into account whether the controls are to be shown when laying out the section.

293

1 On the toolbar, click the Close button.

The report returns to Design view.

2 With the right mouse button, click the Detail section bar, and then click Build Event on the shortcut menu.

You can use this method for opening the Format event procedure because it's the default event procedure for any report section.

3 Double-click Code Builder.

Microsoft Access opens the Issues report's module and displays the Detail_Format event procedure.

4 Add the following code to the event procedure:

```
Private Sub Detail_Format(Cancel As Integer, FormatCount As Integer)
' When formatting each issue record, display the labels for
' the resolution fields only if the issue is resolved.

    Dim blnResolved As Boolean

    ' Determine whether the DateResolved field has a value.
    blnResolved = Not IsNull(DateResolved)

    ' Set the Visible property for the three labels.
    DateResolvedLabel.Visible = blnResolved
    ResolutionLabel.Visible = blnResolved
    ResolvedByLabel.Visible = blnResolved

End Sub
```

Here's what this code does:

■ The procedure uses a Boolean variable, called blnResolved, to record whether or not the current issue record is resolved. The second statement sets the variable to True or False based on the expression *Not IsNull(DateResolved)*, which refers to the DateResolved field in the Detail section of the report. If the DateResolved field contains a date—if it doesn't contain a null value—blnResolved gets set to True.

■ The next three lines of code use the blnResolved value—which is True if the resolution fields should appear, False if they shouldn't—to set the Visible property for the three labels.

This procedure will run each time Microsoft Access starts to lay out a record on the page—at least once and potentially several times for each record in the report. Because most issues aren't resolved, it will make these labels invisible in most cases.

Set properties to shrink the Detail section as appropriate

By default, Microsoft Access leaves space for fields on a report—even if they're blank—so even when the resolution labels on the Issues report are invisible, there will be extra space for them in every record on the report. Fortunately, Microsoft Access provides the

CanShrink property to correct this situation automatically. By setting this property to True for the three text boxes and for the Detail section itself, you'll tell Microsoft Access to "shrink" these fields whenever they're empty—effectively making sure they don't take any space at all.

1 Switch back to the Issues report window.

2 If the Detail section isn't still selected, double-click its selection bar.

3 In the property sheet, click the Format tab, and then set the CanShrink property to Yes.

4 At the right side of the Detail section, select the three text boxes that display resolution information. (Click one of the text boxes, and then hold down the SHIFT key while clicking the other two. Be sure to select only the text box controls, not their labels.)

Select these three text boxes so you can set properties for all of them at once.

5 In the property sheet, set the CanShrink property to Yes.

Preview the report

It's time to see how the changes affect your report.

Print Preview button

1 Click the Print Preview button on the toolbar.

Again, Microsoft Access runs your code for every issue on the page—first the Detail_Format procedure runs several times as Microsoft Access lays out each record on the page, and then the Detail_Print procedure runs several times as it prints each record. Your newest event procedure makes the three labels invisible in most issue records, because only a few issues have been resolved.

You'll notice that the first page of the report now fits several more issues than before, because it no longer displays empty fields for issues that aren't resolved. By scrolling down in the report, you can verify that the three text boxes do still appear for any issue that is resolved.

2 Scroll down in the window to display the fifth record on the page—the first issue in the second group. (If necessary, scroll to the right a bit to display the resolution fields.)

The three resolution fields appear only once on the page, for the one issue that's currently resolved.

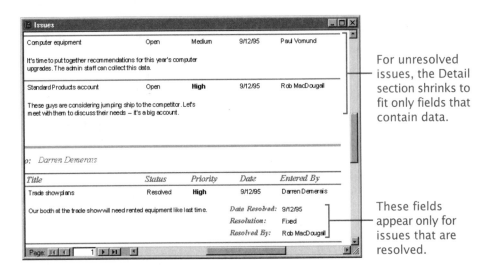

For unresolved issues, the Detail section shrinks to fit only fields that contain data.

These fields appear only for issues that are resolved.

You've now seen how to make two types of changes while Microsoft Access prepares your report for printing: changes both before and after the section is formatted. But your changes so far have been limited to setting properties for controls in the section. Although these common types of changes can be very powerful, it's only the beginning—you can also perform calculations, set control values, and even combine various event procedures throughout the report to achieve the results you want. In the next section, you'll use a simple example of these techniques to improve on the Issues report.

Calculating Totals While a Report Is Printing

One standard feature of reports is the ability to calculate totals—the sum or average of values, for example—for all the records in a section or in the entire report. The Report Wizard often sets up such totaling fields for you. You can also add them yourself by placing a text box in a group footer or report footer section and setting its ControlSource property to the appropriate expression. The Issues report has just such a control in the group footer section for each employee: the TotalIssues control calculates the "count" or number of issues assigned to that employee.

Although standard totals can perform a wide variety of operations for your reports, you may also want to perform your own calculations using Visual Basic. A common reason for doing this is to include totals for a group of records other than the standard grouping in a report. For example, in addition to the total for each group, you might want to display a running total on the current page of the report. To accomplish this, you would have to keep track of the running total in code while Microsoft Access prints the report.

At the appropriate points, you would put the running total into a text box control on the report.

Another similar reason for calculating totals yourself is to break down the values in a way that the default report grouping cannot. The Issues report, for example, groups issue records by the employee they're assigned to. But suppose you want to display the number of open issues or high-priority issues at the end of each employee's section—in other words, you want the report to summarize by saying, "This employee has four issues total, three of which are open and one of which is high priority." There's no simple way to ask for these values in an expression—you have to write Visual Basic code to count the issues yourself. In this section, you'll add code in event procedures that calculates these totals and displays them for each employee in two text boxes in the group footer.

Create text boxes to display section totals

To print the results of calculations you perform in a report's event procedures, you need to put unbound controls on the report to contain them. You'll create two text boxes for the group footer section of the Issues report, one to show the number of open issues each employee has, and another to show the number of high-priority issues.

1 On the toolbar, click the Close button.

The report returns to Design view.

2 If you can't see the AssignedTo Footer section of the report, scroll down in the window to display it.

In this group footer section, you'll notice the TotalIssues control, which demonstrates the standard method for showing section totals. The control source expression for the control, =Count([IssueID]), tells Microsoft Access to count the number of records in the section that contain an IssueID value.

Text Box tool

3 In the toolbox, click the Text Box tool.

4 Click the AssignedTo Footer section of the report, to the right of the TotalIssues field and near the center of the report.

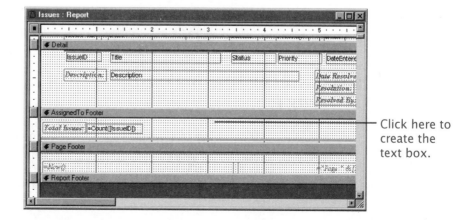

Click here to create the text box.

An unbound text box appears on the report. Its label shows a default name (something like Text55). To make it easier to refer to in code, you'll enter a new name for the control.

5 In the property sheet, click the Other tab, and then set the Name property to **OpenIssues**

You also need to change the label to the left of the text box.

6 Click the label for the new text box to select it.

7 Change the control's label: double-click the text in the label, and then type **Open Issues** to replace the existing text.

This finishes the OpenIssues text box, which you'll use to display the number of open issues for each employee's section of the report. Next, you'll create a second unbound text box to the right of the one you just finished.

8 In the toolbox, click the Text Box tool, and then click the AssignedTo Footer section between the OpenIssues text box and the right edge of the report.

Another unbound text box appears in the footer section.

9 In the property sheet, set the Name property to **HighPriority**

10 Change the control's label to **High Priority**

11 If necessary, drag the two text boxes to position them evenly across the AssignedTo Footer section of the report.

Add code that increments the OpenIssues and HighPriority fields

As an employee's issue records print, you want your code to count the number of open and high-priority issues. You could keep track of the count in either of two ways: by storing the totals in variables you declare, or by placing them in the two unbound text boxes themselves. Here you'll use the latter method (the simpler of the two). Each time the report prints an open or high-priority issue, you'll increment the value of one or both of the text boxes you created. You can do this in response to the Print event, which occurs just before each issue is printed.

Additionally, you'll need to reset the values of these fields each time you begin a new employee's section—otherwise, the code would create a cumulative total, adding the new issues onto those of the previous employees. To reset these fields to 0, you'll add code to the AssignedTo Header section's Print event procedure, which occurs just before each employee's section begins printing.

1   Click the AssignedTo Header section bar.

2   In the property sheet, click the Event tab, click the OnPrint property, and then click the Build button.

3   Double-click Code Builder.

The report's GroupHeader0_Print procedure appears in the Module window. Microsoft Access will run this procedure each time it's about to print the AssignedTo header for another employee.

4   Add the following code to the procedure:

```
' Reset the totals boxes in the footer for each employee.

    OpenIssues = 0
    HighPriority = 0
```

This code sets the values of both of the unbound text boxes you created to 0, because at the beginning of each section an employee has no issues. As Microsoft Access progresses through the report, of course, these numbers may change. That will be up to the Detail_Print event procedure, your next stop.

5   In the Object box, select Detail.

6   In the Proc box, select Print.

The Detail_Print event procedure already contains the code you added earlier in the lesson.

7   At the end of the existing code in the event procedure, just above the End Sub statement, enter the following code:

```
' Increment total fields if issue is open or high priority.
If PrintCount = 1 Then
    If Status = "Open" Then
        OpenIssues = OpenIssues + 1
    End If
    If Priority = "High" Then
        HighPriority = HighPriority + 1
    End If
End If
```

299

This code will keep track of the open and high priority issues while the report is printing. While the code is simple, it illustrates a couple of key concepts. Here's how it works:

■ The Print event usually occurs only once for each section printed in a report. In certain cases, however, it can occur more than once, such as when the Detail section spans two pages. For this reason, the Print event procedure has an argument called PrintCount, which can tell you whether the event is occurring for the first time. Because you wouldn't want to count any records twice, the code uses an If...Then statement, running the rest of the code in the procedure only if PrintCount is 1—in other words, only the first time the procedure runs for a given issue.

■ The rest of the code consists of two nearly identical If...Then blocks. The first block checks whether the current issue record is open—whether the Status field contains the value Open—and increments the value shown in the OpenIssues control by one if the issue is open. The second block does the same for high-priority issues, incrementing the value of the HighPriority control if the Priority field contains the value High.

As you see here, when you want to increment a value in Visual Basic, you follow the control or variable name with an equal sign, and then with the expression that calculates the new value. The first of these statements, for example, can be read as: "Set the value of the OpenIssues field to its existing value plus 1."

After this code runs for a given record, the OpenIssues field will contain the number of open issues printed so far, and the HighPriority field will contain the number of high-priority issues printed so far. By the time the group footer section prints, these fields will contain their final values, which are what will appear on the report.

Compile Loaded Modules button

8 Click the Compile Loaded Modules button on the toolbar.

9 Click the Save button on the toolbar.

10 Close the Module window.

Save button

Preview the report

You're ready to try the report and see how your totals work.

Print Preview button

1 Click the Print Preview button on the toolbar.

Now that you've added even more code, all sorts of things are happening when you preview or print the report! When Microsoft Access gets ready to print the header section for each employee that has open issues, the GroupHeader0_Print procedure runs, setting the unbound fields to 0. Then the Detail_Print procedure runs for every issue record. By the time the footer section for an employee prints, the text boxes should contain the correct values. Then, when Microsoft Access moves on to the next employee's section, your code again resets the text boxes to 0.

2 If necessary, scroll down in the window to display the footer section for Bonnie Christensen, and then the one for Darren Demarais.

As you can see, the text boxes you created now display the correct totals.

Your new fields display the totals for each group.

The examples you've used in this lesson demonstrate how you can access the data in individual records of a report. Your own needs in customizing reports will vary greatly, and you'll probably need to experiment quite a bit to get your reports right. You'll have a head start, however, if you remember the different places you can attach code to—the Format and Print events for each section—and the ways you can affect the report, such as setting report and control properties, and setting the values of unbound controls.

Advanced Control of Section Printing and Placement

The report changes you made using code in this lesson had a very practical effect on the way the Issues report prints. But even though your code set a few properties and values, it didn't significantly change the course of the report—it more or less assumed that the report would print along to completion, including every record and section in its turn. Because you may want to change which sections print and where, Microsoft Access provides run-time report properties and event procedure arguments that allow your code to affect the printing process.

The simplest technique for controlling whether a section prints is setting the Cancel argument for the Print event procedure. If you determine in your code that you don't want to print a given section at all, you can set the Cancel argument in the procedure to True, and Microsoft Access won't print the section. For example, in the Issues report, you might want to exclude issues that belong to the employee who's currently logged in. To do this, you'd write code to cancel printing of sections in which the AssignedTo field contains that employee's ID number.

301

Advanced Control of Section Printing and Placement, *continued*

For finer control over which sections print and where, you can use three run-time properties: MoveLayout, NextRecord, and PrintSection. All three of these properties are normally set to True for every section and record. By setting them to False in your code, you can change how the report prints.

MoveLayout tells Microsoft Access whether to move to the next position on the page after printing the current section. If you set this property to False, the following section will print in the same place on the page.

NextRecord tells Microsoft Access whether to move to the next record in the recordset. If you set this property to False, you can cause the current record to be repeated on the page. You might want to do this in a mailing labels report, for example, to print more than one of each label for each address.

PrintSection determines whether the current section prints on the page. You can set this property to False to leave a blank space on the page.

By experimenting with these properties in various combinations, you'll be able to control printing in endless ways. Beware, however: some combinations of these properties can produce strange results, and you may have trouble diagnosing problems that arise.

Close the report and exit Microsoft Access

1   Close the report window.

2   On the File menu, click Exit.

Lesson Summary

To	Do this
Perform actions before each record gets laid out on the page of a report	Write a Format event procedure for the Detail section of the report.
Perform actions before each record (or header or footer section) of a report prints	Write a Print event procedure for the Detail section (or other section) of the report.
Cause controls not to print if they don't have values	Set the CanShrink property of the controls, and the section they belong in, to True. If the controls have labels in the Detail section that you don't want to show, set the Visible property to False for records that don't have values.
Calculate section totals while a report prints and display them on the report	Create unbound text box controls to store and display the totals in the appropriate footer section on the report. Write one event procedure that resets the total values to 0 at the beginning of each section, and another that updates the value as each record or section prints.

For online information about	**On the Help menu, click Microsoft Access Help Topics, click the Index tab, and then**
Creating and customizing reports	Search for "reports"
Grouping data in reports	Search for "groups (reports)"
Responding to report events using event procedures	Search for "Format event" or "Print event"
Changing the layout of data and blank space on a report	Search for "CanShrink property" and "MoveLayout property"

For more information on	**In *Building Applications with Microsoft Access*, see**
Opening and filtering reports in your applications	Chapter 3, "Using Forms to Collect, Display, and Filter Information"
Using events in reports	Chapter 6, "Responding to Events"

Preview of the Next Lesson

The techniques you're learning in the final lessons of this book are more specialized, teaching you about new Microsoft Access objects, and pointing you in the direction of new areas of programming you may want to explore as you create more advanced applications on your own. In the final lesson of the book, you'll delve into yet another heap of concepts known as OLE Automation, which allows you to work directly with other Windows applications from within your Visual Basic code in Microsoft Access. In particular, you'll combine the capabilities of Microsoft Access with those of Microsoft Word, learning how to send commands from Microsoft Access to Word in Word's own programming language.

Share Data with Other Applications

Estimated time
25 min.

In this lesson you will learn how to:

■ Use OLE Automation objects.

■ Send commands and data to Microsoft Word.

■ Gather data from another application, such as Microsoft Excel.

When traveling far from home, communicating with strangers can be both challenging and rewarding. Although differing cultures and languages can present obstacles, it seems we humans can usually find a way to communicate our messages to one another—whether by body language, hand signals, or perhaps a broken approximation of a foreign tongue. And as anyone who has traveled much will attest, exposure to other cultures can be very broadening—we seem to absorb a bit of the experience and wisdom of others out of such encounters.

As a Microsoft Access programmer, working with other Windows applications is a little like communicating with people of different cultures—it's a challenge, but there's a lot to gain in sharing the capabilities of other systems. Fortunately, Windows provides a mechanism for talking between two different applications, such as Microsoft Access and Microsoft Excel, or Microsoft Access and Word. It's called *OLE Automation*. OLE Automation gives you a framework for using objects that belong to another application as if those objects were an extension of the application you're working within. But just as with human communication, you'll find that it helps to know a bit about the other party's language. With OLE Automation, you combine the programming language of the other application with the Visual Basic code you write in Microsoft Access.

In this lesson, you'll learn the general techniques of communicating using OLE Automation. Working with Microsoft Word, you'll find out how to combine the capabilities of two systems to accomplish more in your database applications.

NOTE You must have Microsoft Word for Windows 95 installed on your computer in order to complete the steps in this lesson.

Start the lesson

1   Start Microsoft Access and open the 12 Issues database in the practice files folder.

    As you saw in previous lessons, the Issues application opens to a dialog box asking you to enter your name before it opens the Issues form.

2   In the combo box, select Bonnie Christensen.

3   Click the Show All Issues button.

    The button's Click event procedure opens the Issues form.

Using OLE Automation Objects

Microsoft Access isn't a very good word processor. Sure, you could create a Microsoft Access report that would look a lot like a professional letter—but it would take a great deal of work, and would lack the flexibility you take for granted in any word processing application. By the same token, Microsoft Access isn't a statistical calculator, a project manager, or a presentation graphics program. But it's a great place to store your data!

One way to extend the capabilities of your Microsoft Access applications is by teaming them up with the capabilities of other applications. OLE Automation is the mechanism that Windows provides for doing this. If the databases you're creating need the capabilities of other Windows applications—and if those other applications support the OLE standard—you can use OLE Automation code to combine the power of Microsoft Access with the strengths of other systems.

In previous lessons, you've learned about several types of objects you can control in Microsoft Access, such as the Form, Report, Database, and Recordset objects. Other applications have objects as well, and through OLE Automation, your code running in Microsoft Access can work with them behind the scenes. Microsoft Excel, for example, has the Worksheet and Chart objects, which you could incorporate seamlessly into a Microsoft Access application using techniques similar to those you've learned for working with Microsoft Access objects. And many other Windows applications expose their objects for use through OLE Automation.

Although the possible ways you could combine applications are endless, here are some common ways to use OLE Automation with Microsoft Access:

Create or edit documents.   From your Visual Basic code in Microsoft Access, you can create or open a document in Microsoft Word or a worksheet in Microsoft Excel, for example, and control it using the other application's commands. Without any interaction by the user, you can send data from your database to the document or worksheet, and even use the other application's commands to print it. You'll use these techniques in this lesson to work with a document in Microsoft Word.

Edit linked or embedded objects. When you design forms and reports, you can include linked or embedded objects from another application. If you want to change linked or embedded objects from within your application's code, you can use OLE Automation to activate the other application and manipulate them. A common example of this is a chart created using Microsoft Graph: if you want to change the attributes of the chart from your code, you use OLE Automation to control Microsoft Graph.

You can also store another application's objects in a table using the OLE Object data type—for example, you could keep a database of Microsoft Word documents. Using OLE Automation, you can activate the other application and work with its objects from within your Microsoft Access procedures.

Gather data from another application. Although you'll usually store your application's data in Microsoft Access tables (or another format that Microsoft Access can link to), you might occasionally want to bring in data from another application's files. For example, you might want to incorporate a list of project milestones and dates stored in Microsoft Project. Using OLE Automation, you can use the properties and methods of Microsoft Project to access this information.

Provide data as an OLE Automation server. All the techniques discussed to this point involve writing code in Microsoft Access to control other applications—alternatively, you can write OLE Automation code in another application's programming language to work with data in Microsoft Access databases. With this strategy, Microsoft Access is referred to as a *server*, because it provides data and other capabilities at the request of another application. This strategy makes most sense if your application is primarily suited for another programming system. For example, if you create a financial system using VBA in Microsoft Excel, you might want to store some of the data in Microsoft Access tables, and perhaps even print Microsoft Access reports from the Microsoft Excel application.

Although you won't get a chance to try all these techniques in this lesson, you'll discover many OLE Automation concepts that apply to all of them.

Sending Commands to Microsoft Word

Suppose you want your application to create and print a memo, merge names into a mailing list, or print envelopes—tasks you want to perform in Microsoft Word. Some applications that support OLE Automation, such as Microsoft Excel, allow you to open a document object directly. With Microsoft Word, you can't do this—instead, you use a special object called *Word.Basic*, which represents the WordBasic programming language used by Microsoft Word. After you open a Word.Basic object, you can send commands to Word just as if you were programming in WordBasic itself. You can open documents, insert text, and control Microsoft Word in any way you please—all from within a procedure in your Microsoft Access application.

In this lesson, you'll write OLE Automation code to perform actions in Word: creating a memo and inserting text into it. The memo your application creates will be a reminder to employees who have open issues stored in the database—and your code will automatically determine which employees to include on the "To" line of the memo.

Open the Microsoft Word template that your application will use

Before you write the OLE Automation code in the Issues application, you'll first open a Microsoft Word document *template*, from which you'll create the memo. Using a template is a great way to get a head start on a document you send regularly, such as a form letter. If your template is nearly complete, all your code has to do is fill in any missing information, such as names or addresses stored in your database.

1 Start Microsoft Word for Windows 95. (Click the Windows Start menu, point to Programs, and then click Microsoft Word.)

2 On the File menu, click Open.

3 In the Files Of Type box, select Document Templates.

4 Move to the Access VBA Practice folder on your hard disk and open the 14 Memo template.

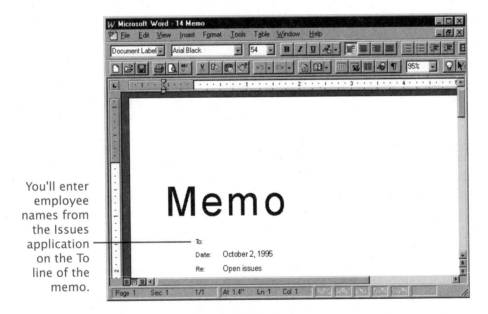

You'll enter employee names from the Issues application on the To line of the memo.

Add a bookmark to the template

When your code creates the memo, you'll want to insert employee names into it. The first step is to mark the spot that you'll enter text in the document, so your code can locate it easily. A simple way to do this is to use a *bookmark*, a named Word place marker, because you can jump to any bookmark in a document by using the WordBasic EditGoTo command.

1 Click the second line of the memo document to the right of the string *To:* to position the insertion point.

This is where you'll enter employee names from Microsoft Access.

2 On the Edit menu, click Bookmark.

Word displays the Bookmark dialog box.

3 Type **MemoToLine** and then click Add.

Although you can't actually see the bookmark in the document, it will provide a quick way to jump to this spot from code in Microsoft Access.

4 Close the 14 Memo document, clicking Yes when Microsoft Access asks if you want to save changes.

5 On the File menu, click Exit.

Word closes, and Microsoft Access returns to the front.

Open the CreateWordMemo function in the Miscellaneous module

The Records menu on the Issues form includes the command Create Word Memo, placed there so users can run the OLE Automation code you'll write. The menu item runs a function called CreateWordMemo, which already exists in the Miscellaneous module. You just need to open this function and then add the OLE Automation code to make it work.

Database Window button

1 Click the Database Window button on the toolbar.

2 Click the Modules tab, and then double-click the Miscellaneous module.

Microsoft Access displays the Declarations section of the Miscellaneous module.

3 Press the PAGE DOWN key twice.

The CreateWordMemo function appears.

The function already contains some important code—but it's also code you're familiar with from earlier lessons. Here's what it does:

- The Dim statement declares variables used to open a recordset.

- The next two lines of DAO code open a recordset based on a query called EmployeesWithOpenIssues. As its name declares, this query returns a record for each employee who has at least one issue open in the Issues table—exactly the list of people you want to send the memo to. The code assigns this recordset to the rstEmployees variable.

- The If...Then...End If block makes sure there is at least one employee in the recordset—otherwise, there would be no point in sending the memo. The condition that the If...Then statement tests refers to a property of the Recordset object that you haven't seen yet—the RecordCount property. This property returns the number of records in the recordset that Microsoft Access has read from disk so far. (Note that this isn't necessarily the total number of records in the recordset, unless you've already moved to the end of the recordset). If the RecordCount property returns 0, it means that the recordset is empty—in this case the code would display a message and exit the procedure.

Write OLE Automation code that creates a Word document and inserts text

It's time to get your feet wet. First, you'll add a line of code to declare a variable for your OLE Automation object. Then, you'll add a block of OLE Automation code that creates a WordBasic object using the CreateObject statement. Your OLE Automation code will "talk" to the WordBasic object, telling it to create the memo document and sending various other commands, and then inserting the employee names from the rstEmployees recordset into the document.

1   Add the following code underneath the existing Dim statement:

```
Dim objWord As Object
```

You'll use this object variable to store the Word.Basic object. When writing OLE Automation code, you'll often use the Object data type—the generic data type for storing objects that don't belong to Microsoft Access.

2   Add code at the end of the procedure, just above the End Function statement (if Microsoft Word or the Step by Step practice files are not in their default folders on your hard disk, be sure to substitute the correct path names in the code):

```
' Switch to Microsoft Word so it won't go away when you finish.
On Error Resume Next
AppActivate "Microsoft Word"

' If Word isn't running, start it.
If Err Then
    Shell "c:\MSOffice\WinWord\WinWord"
End If
On Error GoTo 0

' Create a WordBasic OLE Automation object.
Set objWord = CreateObject("Word.Basic")

' Maximize Word, open a document based on the memo template,
```

```
' and change to Page Layout view.
With objWord
    .AppMaximize "", 1
    .FileNew "c:\Access VBA Practice\14 Memo"
    .ViewPage

    ' Move to a bookmark in the memo, preparing to enter names.
    .EditGoTo "MemoToLine"
End With

' Loop through the recordset returned by the query, inserting
' the name of each employee into the document.
Do Until rstEmployees.EOF
    objWord.Insert rstEmployees!EmployeeName & "    "
    rstEmployees.MoveNext
Loop
```

Here's how this code does its work:

- The first block of code uses the AppActivate statement to switch to Microsoft Word if a copy of it is already running. Switching to Word from the start ensures that when the procedure finishes, the memo document it creates won't disappear. Although not the most common way to use OLE Automation—you don't usually want the other application to appear at all, but just to do its thing—this strategy allows users to do as they please with the memo in Word after you create it.

- The On Error Resume Next statement is included before the AppActivate statement to tell Microsoft Access to ignore any errors that may occur in trying to switch to Word. If Word isn't running, the AppActivate statement would cause a run-time error. This strategy allows code to continue, so that you can check whether or not an error occurred.

- To determine whether AppActivate caused an error, the If...Then statement checks the value of the Err object. If Err is 0 (or False), it means that the code successfully switched to Word. If Err is non-zero (or True), you assume that the code couldn't start Word, and the line of code underneath the If...Then statement runs. This line uses the Shell statement to start a copy of Microsoft Word. Like AppActivate, Shell ensures that Word—and the memo you create—will stick around after the procedure ends.

- On Error GoTo 0 tells Microsoft Access not to ignore subsequent errors in the procedure—it cancels out the earlier On Error Resume Next statement so as to avoid overlooking unexpected problems. (Note, however, that a more complete version of this procedure would also have its own error-handling code, because working with other applications can often cause errors. To keep things simpler, we've left it out.)

- The next line uses the CreateObject statement to create the WordBasic object (an OLE Automation object) and store it in the objWord variable. Since your code already made sure that Word is open and active, the WordBasic object will simply refer to the copy of Word that's already

311

running. If Word weren't running, this statement would cause a copy of Word to start up in the background—however, when your code finished, the copy of Word would automatically shut down.

Now that you have a WordBasic object, you can use it to send commands to Word—as you do in the next block of code.

■ The next block of code uses something new: a With...End With block. The With statement simply provides a shortcut in your code for performing several actions using the same object. Microsoft Access interprets this code as if you'd put the name of the object before each period in the subsequent lines. For example, the first line below the With statement is equivalent to *objWord.AppMaximize*, which tells Microsoft Access to pass on the AppMaximize command to WordBasic. Note that you can use a With...End With block in any object manipulation code—but it's especially useful for OLE Automation, because you often want to perform several commands at a time concerning one object.

■ Inside the With...End With block are four WordBasic commands:

AppMaximize maximizes the Word window.

FileNew tells Word to create a new document based on the memo template you opened earlier in the lesson.

ViewPage tells Word to switch to Page View.

EditGoTo moves the insertion point in the memo document down to the bookmark you created on the To line of the memo.

Note that you pass arguments to a WordBasic command the same way you pass them to a statement or method in Microsoft Access.

■ Now that the memo is ready and you're in the right spot, the code can go ahead and insert the names from the recordset. To insert every name in the recordset, this code introduces a new method for repeating code, a Do...Loop block. The Do statement is followed by an Until condition: as long as the condition returns False, the block of code runs. The Loop statement tells it to run again—assuming the condition still isn't True—and the loop continues until the condition returns True.

The condition for the Do Until statement refers to the EOF property (EOF stands for End Of File) of the Recordset object. The value of a recordset's EOF property is False so long as there is a "current" record in the recordset. If you move past the last record in the recordset (or if there aren't any records to begin with), the value of the EOF property will be True.

■ The next line uses the WordBasic Insert command to actually type a name into the Word document. You can follow the Insert command with any string expression that you want to put into the document—in this case, it's the value of the EmployeeName field in the recordset, followed by three spaces (to separate each name from the next).

■ The next statement uses the MoveNext method of the Recordset object to move to the next record in the rstEmployees recordset. Then it's time to loop: if there is another employee, the Insert code runs again; if not, the expression *Not rstEmployees.EOF* returns False, and the loop is complete. As is the memo!

Compile Loaded Modules button

3 Click the Compile Loaded Modules button on the toolbar.

4 Click the Save button on the toolbar.

Save button

Note that when your procedure finishes, the objWord variable goes away. If you hadn't used the AppActivate and Shell statements to ensure that a copy of Word was open and active, Word would go away as well—but as it stands, Word should stay open and display the memo for users to edit as they please.

Try out your OLE automation procedure

Let's create a memo! To run the event procedure, you can use the custom menu command on the Records menu of the Issues form's menu bar.

1 Switch to the Issues form.

2 On the Records menu, click Create Word Memo.

Your code runs—it opens a recordset, activates Word and opens a WordBasic object, creates the new memo, and then inserts names from the recordset. In fact, you can even see it happening. When it finishes, you're left in Microsoft Word looking at the completed memo.

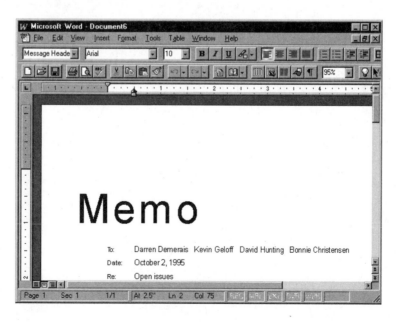

3 Close the memo document, clicking No when Word asks if you want to save changes.

4 Minimize Microsoft Word.

The Issues Tracking Application returns to the front.

Although this memo involves transferring only a small amount of data, you can easily imagine more powerful uses for this type of OLE Automation. With Word, for example, you could use the same techniques to do easy printing of envelopes, merge data into documents and save them, or even create and print an entire mailing to clients stored in your database. And if you don't want users to have to work in Word themselves, you can do all this work behind the scenes.

Getting Information from Another Application

So far, you've sent commands and data from Microsoft Access, but you haven't gotten anything back from Word. Using OLE Automation, you can also request information from an application's objects, such as the value of a function or property. This allows you to interact with its objects in more powerful ways. For example, suppose you want to run a Microsoft Excel financial function that doesn't exist in Microsoft Access. You can create an OLE Automation object, and then use it to run the Microsoft Excel function, assigning the answer to a variable in your Microsoft Access code.

Now, you'll add a final section to the CreateWordMemo procedure that will run a WordBasic function and use its return value. In this code, you'll announce that you're finished creating the memo and ask the user whether to print the document. Since the user is in Word at that point, it makes sense to have Word display the message. To do this, you can use the MsgBox function in Word, which is similar to the MsgBox function you're accustomed to using in Microsoft Access.

Display a message box in Word that responds to the user's choice

Before you add code to the end of the procedure, you'll need to add a few declarations at the beginning.

1   Switch to the Miscellaneous module, still showing the CreateWordMemo function.

2   Add code above the existing Dim statement:

```
Const conOKCancel = 33, conOK = -1
```

You'll use these two constants with the Word MsgBox function. The function in WordBasic works almost the same as the one in VBA does, but because the values for its arguments and return values are slightly different, you need to use your own constants.

3   Add code below the existing Dim statement:

```
Dim strMessage As String, intChoice As Integer
```

This line declares two variables you'll use with the Word function: strMessage to store the message you'll display, and intChoice to store the value of the choice the user makes in the message box.

4   Add code just before the End Function statement, beneath the Do...Loop block:

```
' Ask the user whether to print the document, displaying the
' message on top of the document in Word itself.
strMessage = "Memo complete. Send it to the printer?"
intChoice = objWord.MsgBox(strMessage, conAppName, conOKCancel)
If intChoice = conOK Then
    objWord.FilePrint
End If
```

This code looks very similar to what you've used in the past to display a message box.

■ The first statement assigns the text of your message to the strMessage variable.

■ The MsgBox line passes arguments to the Word MsgBox function, and then assigns the value that Word returns to the intChoice variable. Note that the variable you assign a value to and the return value from the other application must have compatible data types—because Word's MsgBox function returns an integer value, you declared intChoice with the Integer data type.

■ If the user clicks OK in the message box, the value of intChoice is the same as the constant value conOK, so the If...Then block runs. The statement sends one final command to Word, the command to print the current document.

Compile Loaded Modules button

5 Click the Compile Loaded Modules button on the toolbar.

6 Close the Module window, clicking Yes when Microsoft Access asks if you want to save changes.

The Issues form becomes active again.

Create the memo again

Let's try out the procedure with these changes.

1 On the Records menu, click Create Word Memo.

This time, when the memo finishes, a message box appears on top of the document.

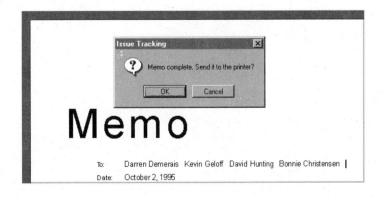

Even though Word is active, your code in Microsoft Access is still running in the background, waiting for Word to tell it your response. If you were to click OK, your code would tell Microsoft Word to print the document—but you don't need to test it unless you want to print the memo.

2 Click Cancel.

3 Close the memo document, clicking No when Word asks if you want to save changes.

4 Close Microsoft Word.

Using Microsoft Access Objects from Microsoft Excel

OLE Automation is a two-way street: just as the procedure you wrote in Microsoft Access controlled Word, you can write code in another application to control Microsoft Access. For example, if you write code in Microsoft Excel—which happens to use VBA, so the code is very similar to code in Microsoft Access—you can open and work directly with Microsoft Access and DAO objects from those applications.

Here's a function that works in Microsoft Excel. It creates a Microsoft Access OLE Automation object, then uses it to run a query and return the number of issues in the Issues table:

```
Function GetAccessIssueCount() As Integer

    Dim objAccess As Object, objIssuesDb As Object, objIssues As Object
    Dim strQuery As String

    ' Create an Access OLE Automation object.
    Set objAccess = CreateObject("Access.Application.7")

    ' Open an Access database, by way of the DBEngine object.
    Set objIssuesDb = objAccess.DBEngine.OpenDatabase("c:\Data\Issues")

    ' Open a recordset to count issues.
    strQuery = "SELECT COUNT(IssueID) AS NumIssues FROM Issues
    Set objIssues = objIssuesDb.OpenRecordset(strQuery)

    ' Assign the value from the query to the result of the function.
    GetAccessIssueCount = objIssues!NumIssues

End Function
```

After it opens a Microsoft Access OLE Automation object, the code can use any methods or properties of the Application object. And by way of the DBEngine property, it can also use any methods or properties of DAO as well. Each object in turn gives access to other objects—as you can see, the procedure stores the database

Using Microsoft Access Objects from Microsoft Excel, *continued*

object in a variable called objIssuesDb, and then uses this object to open a recordset based on an SQL query. Finally, it uses the recordset object—objIssues!NumIssues—to get the result of the query, and assigns the value as the return value of the function.

This example demonstrates how powerful OLE Automation can be between applications that support VBA, such as Microsoft Excel and Project. If you write code in these applications, you can control everything from their programming languages in nearly the same way you can from Microsoft Access.

Exit Microsoft Access

 On the File menu, click Exit.

Lesson Summary

To	Do this
Open an OLE Automation object to send commands to another application	Use the CreateObject statement, assigning the resulting object to an object variable. Then, use the object variable to issues statements in the other application's programming language.
Carry out multiple statements pertaining to the same object without retyping the object name	Use a With...End With block, specifying the object variable on the With line and starting each line of code in the block with a period.
Activate another Windows application	Use the Shell statement, or if the application is already running, use the AppActivate statement.
Loop through all the records in a recordset	Use the Do Until statement, specifying a condition that checks the EOF property of the recordset. Then, just before the Loop statement, use the MoveNext method to move to the next record in the recordset.

For online information about	On the Help menu, click Microsoft Access Help Topics, click the Index tab, and then
Working with OLE Automation objects	Search for "OLE Automation"
Editing linked or embedded OLE objects	Search for "Action property" and "Object property"
Repeating code with the Do...Loop statement and control-flow statements	Search for "loops"

For more information on	In *Building Applications with Microsoft Access,* see
Working with OLE Automation objects	Chapter 11, "Communicating with Other Applications"
Using the With statement, or referring to Microsoft Access objects	Chapter 5, "Working with Objects and Collections"
Using DAO objects, the MoveNext method, or the EOF property	Chapter 9, "Working with Sets of Records"

Where Do I Go Next?

Congratulations—you've covered a great deal of ground concerning Microsoft Access and VBA in these lessons. Microsoft Access application development is an enormous subject, and as you continue working with Microsoft Access, you'll find many new frontiers to explore. Here are a few places where you may want to start:

Building Applications with Microsoft Access   In addition to the material referred to at the end of each lesson, this Microsoft Access manual includes chapters on advanced topics not covered here, such as using DLLs, creating your own wizards, and developing applications for a client-server environment.

Orders and Solutions sample applications   Microsoft Access includes two sample applications that you can take a look at to gather ideas for your own projects. The Orders application is a custom order-entry system. The Solutions database is a learning tool that shows you examples of many form, report, and Visual Basic strategies and includes instructions on how to create each sample object yourself.

Microsoft Access Developer's Toolkit (ADT)   This add-on product allows you to distribute your applications to users who don't have Microsoft Access—and it includes additional reference information on Microsoft Access and DAO.

Your own applications   Your database needs are different from anyone else's—for this reason, you may well learn more by creating your own Microsoft Access applications than you'll ever pick up in a book. So jump right in! Just as you did in the first lessons of this book, start by automating tasks on forms in an existing database. After you're comfortable writing and debugging Visual Basic code, try creating a custom application of your own. Then, as you discover complex tasks that you want to accomplish in your procedures, try delving into new areas of the Microsoft Access and DAO object models.

Index

Special Characters

! (exclamation point operator), 267, 268
& (ampersand)
    as accelerator key indicator, 29, 35
    as concatenation operator, 52, 156
'(apostrophe), 38
= (equal sign), 36
_ (underscore), 113, 282

A

accelerator keys, 29, 30, 35
Access. *See* Microsoft Access
Access VBA Practice folder, xxiv, xxv
action queries, 280–83
Activate event, 73, 238
add-ins
    Convert Macros To Visual Basic, 21
    Database Splitter, 251–52
    Linked Table Manager, 252
    Microsoft Access Developer's Toolkit (ADT) for
        Windows 95, 254
AddNew method, 156, 180
AddRecord button
    adding accelerator key, 29, 30
    changing properties, 29
    creating using Command Button
        Wizard, 17–19
    modifying Visual Basic code, 28, 29, 30–31
    saving changes to code, 31–32
    testing, 19–20
    viewing Visual Basic code, 25–28
Advanced Filter/Sort command, 55
AfterUpdate event, 41–43, 64–65, 77, 78–79,
        134–36, 140–43, 181, 182, 214–15
AfterUpdate property, 42, 78, 182, 215
AllowAdditions property, 34
AllowDeletions property, 34, 211
AllowEdits property, 32, 33, 36, 41, 211
ampersand (&)
    as accelerator key indicator, 29, 35
    as concatenation operator, 52, 156
Answer Wizard, xxvii–xxviii

apostrophe ('), 38
AppActivate statement, 311
applications
    adding database objects to, 13–16
    bypassing startup options, 248
    changing icon, 248
    closing from switchboard form, 21, 246
    creating dialog boxes for, 173–89
    creating menus for, 223–31
    creating toolbars for, 231–39
    creating using Database Wizard, 4–13
    creating without wizards, 170–72
    customizing appearance, 247–48
    customizing startup, 242–50
    customizing title bar, 247
    defined, 7
    distributing to users, 250–54
    hiding status bar, 248
    on networks, 242, 251
    as object libraries, 263
    overview, 7
    protecting, 248, 250
    running without Microsoft Access, 254
    signing in, 260–61
    splitting into separate database files, 250–52
    switchboard forms for, 243–47
    uses for dialog boxes, 172
    workgroup, 260–83
ApplyFilter event, 56, 67, 68
AppMaximize command (WordBasic), 312
arguments
    adding to procedures, 103–4
    constants as, 27
    defined, 26–27
    Help with, 27–28

B

BackColor property, 75, 76
back-end databases, 251
Beep statement, 59
BeforeUpdate event, 77, 83–84, 86–89, 107–10,
        125–32, 212

319

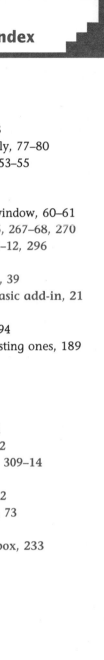

Index

database fields. *See also* controls
  adding to reports, 13–14
  incrementing values in reports, 298–300
  not printing when empty, 294–95
database forms. *See also* form modules
  adding command buttons to, 16–21, 187–88,
    202–4, 209–11
  adding general procedures to, 107–9
  adding option groups to, 62–68
  adding pop-up tips for controls, 239
  changing background color, 50, 74–76
  changing properties, 33, 40–41
  closing, 20, 206
  controlling access to, 201
  creating combo boxes on, 48–50
  creating menu bars for, 223–31
  creating separately for each table, 200–201
  entering values automatically, 77–80
  filtering records in, 56
  main, defined, 171
  making read-only by default, 32–34
  opening dialog boxes from, 187–88, 191
  overview of user actions, 72–73
  pop-up, 186, 201–9
  resizing, 174
  responding to errors, 148–51
  saving, 20
  setting focus, 30–31
  and subforms, 200
  synchronizing, 204, 205–6, 207
  unbound, defined, 173
  updating after data entry, 214–15
  using together, 200–217
  viewing records in, 12–13
database records
  creating button for finding, 178–82
  creating buttons for adding, 17–20, 209–11
  displaying in pop-up forms, 201–9
  filtering for reports, 190–96
  finding and changing in recordsets, 274–79
  finding using combo box, 48–55
  importing, 10–13
  related, 201–17

database records, *continued*
  requerying, 215
  using samples, 11
  viewing in forms, 12–13
database reports. *See also* mailing labels
  adding boldface, 291–92
  adding features using Visual Basic
    code, 290–302
  adding to switchboard form, 15, 16
  calculating totals while printing, 296–301
  creating, 13–15
  customizing, 291–93
  filtering data in, 190–96
  formatting, 291–92, 293–96
  naming, 14
  not printing empty fields, 294–95
  overview, 288
  previewing, 16, 288–90, 292–93, 295–96,
    300–301
  sections in, 290, 291–92, 294–95, 297–98,
    301–2
  setting properties at run time, 291–93
databases. *See also* applications
  creating using Database Wizard, 6–13
  importing data into, 10–13
  including sample records in, 11
  passwords for, 250
  splitting into separate files, 250–52
  types of, 5, 6
Database Splitter add-in, 251–52
database tables
  creating separate forms for each, 200–201
  multiple-table queries, 200
  refreshing links, 252
  relationships between, 170–71
  in Subscription database, 170–71
  viewing, 170–71
Database window
  hiding in applications, 247
  minimizing, 9
  overview, 8–9
  using switchboard form instead, 247
Database Wizard, 3, 5, 6, 8–9, 11

About the author

Evan Callahan owns Callahan Software
Solutions, a database consulting firm
specializing in Microsoft Access. He
worked for Microsoft Corporation from
1989 to 1995, where he created
documentation, online Help, and sample
applications for Access and Visual Basic.
He has delivered training in Access and
spoken at Microsoft Tech·Ed and other
conferences. He received a B.A. in
philosophy and comparative literature
from the University of Washington.

Evan was born and raised in Seattle,
Washington, where he lives with his dog,
Argus. In his spare time, he enjoys hiking
and cycling around the Pacific Northwest.

Evan welcomes comments and questions
about *Microsoft Access/Visual Basic Step
by Step* over the Internet. Send electronic
mail to ECallahan@msn.com.

WHO KNOWS MORE
ABOUT WINDOWS® 95
THAN
MICROSOFT PRESS?

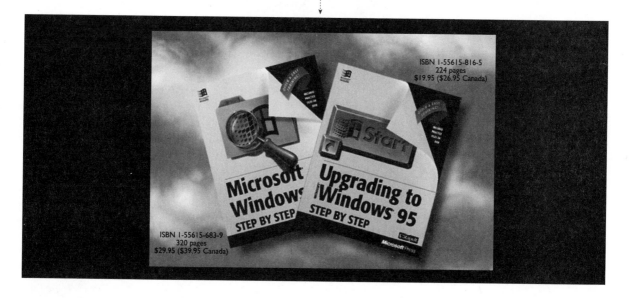

ISBN 1-55615-816-5
224 pages
$19.95 ($26.95 Canada)

ISBN 1-55615-683-9
320 pages
$29.95 ($39.95 Canada)

These books are essential if you are a newcomer to Microsoft® Windows® or an upgrader wanting to capitalize on your knowledge of Windows 3.1. Both are written in a straightforward, no-nonsense way, with well-illustrated step-by-step examples, and both include practice files on disk. Learn to use Microsoft's newest operating system quickly and easily with MICROSOFT WINDOWS 95 STEP BY STEP and UPGRADING TO MICROSOFT WINDOWS 95 STEP BY STEP, both from Microsoft Press.

The
Step by Step
Practice Files Disk

The enclosed 3.5-inch disk contains timesaving, ready-to-use practice files that complement the lessons in this book. To use the practice files, you'll need the Windows 95 operating system and Access version 7 for Windows 95.

Each *Step by Step* lesson uses practice files from the disk. Before you begin the *Step by Step* lessons, read the "Getting Ready" section of the book for easy instructions telling how to install the files on your computer's hard disk. As you work through each lesson, be sure to follow the instructions for renaming the practice files so that you can go through a lesson more than once if you need to.

Please take a few moments to read the License Agreement on the previous page before using the enclosed disk.